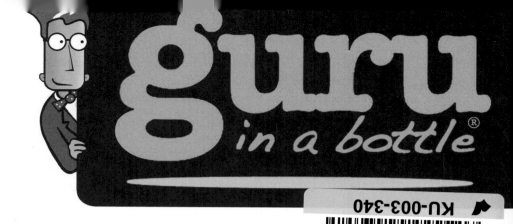

guru
in a bottle ®

High Impact Marketing that Gets Results

Ardi Kolah

KoganPage

First published in Great Britain and the United States in 2013 by Kogan Page Limited

120 Pentonville Road	1518 Walnut Street, Suite 1100	4737/23 Ansari Road
London N1 9JN	Philadelphia PA 19102	Daryaganj
United Kingdom	USA	New Delhi 110002
www.koganpage.com		India

© Ardi Kolah, 2013

The right of Ardi Kolah to be identified as the author of this work has been asserted by him in accordance with the Copyright, Designs and Patents Act 1988.

'Guru in a Bottle' is a registered trademark of Ardi Kolah. All rights reserved.

ISBN   978 0 7494 6452 3
E-ISBN   978 0 7494 6453 0

British Library Cataloguing-in-Publication Data

A CIP record for this book is available from the British Library.

Library of Congress Cataloging-in-Publication Data

Kolah, Ardi.
  High impact marketing that gets results / Ardi Kolah.
    p. cm.
    ISBN 978-0-7494-6452-3 – ISBN 978-0-7494-6453-0 (ebook)   1. Marketing.   2. Internet marketing.   3. Customer relations.   I. Title.
    HF5415.K5838 2013
    658.8–dc23
                                                                2012031192

Typeset by Graphicraft Limited, Hong Kong
Print production managed by Jellyfish
Printed and bound by CPI Group (UK) Ltd, Croydon, CR0 4YY

Contents

8 Using promotions 291

9 Top 10 common marketing mistakes to avoid 313

10 Top 10 ways to save money in marketing 319

About the author

Ardi Kolah, BA, LLM, FCIM, FCIPR, FRSA is one of the most influential voices in the global marketing and communications industry and is director of communications for a financial services Fortune 500 company in Europe.

He began his career as a TV and radio reporter/producer at the BBC, working in network news and current affairs and BBC World Service before embarking on a career within public relations, marketing and sponsorship, working with some of the world's most successful brands including Accenture, Logica plc, Disney, Ford of Europe, Speedo, Standard Chartered Bank, Shell, Procter & Gamble, Yahoo, Reebok, Pepsi, Reliance, Emirates, Great Wheel Corporation, MOBO, YouGov, QBE, Brit Insurance, WHO, Royal Navy and the Royal Air Force.

A prolific author, he's written some of the leading works on brand marketing, public relations, sponsorship and the legal aspects of marketing, with combined sales in excess of £2.5 million worldwide. He writes a regular blog for the UK's leading sales and marketing portal Brand Republic and has been a regular contributor to *Sponsorship News*, *Financial Times*, *Wall Street Journal*, *Bloomberg News*, CNN and BBC World Business Report and is on the editorial board of the *Journal of Brand Strategy*.

He holds several industry awards including the Hollis Award for 'Best Low Budget Sponsorship' for his work on the British Independent Film Awards and CIPR Excellence Award for Outstanding Individual in education and training.

He's a Fellow of the Chartered Institute of Marketing, the Chartered Institute of Public Relations, a member of the Public Relations Consultants Association, a Liveryman of the Worshipful Company of Marketors, an elected member of BAFTA and a member of the Society of Authors. In 2003 Ardi was independently ranked by the CIM as one of the top 50 gurus in the world – and he's been trying to live this down ever since!

He's a frequent speaker at conferences around the world and has been a judge on numerous industry panels including CIPR Excellence Awards, New Media Age Awards, National Business Awards and Scottish Newspaper of the Year Awards. A former Board Director of the CIPR and the European Sponsorship Association, he's been a visiting lecturer at the Judge Business School, Cambridge University, Oxford College of Marketing, Oxford, and Imperial College Business School.

He studied law at Kingston University London and then was awarded a scholarship to study for an international Master's degree in law at King's College London and University College London.

He lives in Wimbledon, south-west London, with his wife Fenella and their two children, Zara and Aviva.

About Guru in a Bottle®

Guru in a Bottle® is about taking technical, high-level subjects and making them clear, human and accessible.

Unlike Dummies®, which tends to treat the reader as a blank canvas for much of the content presented, the approach taken by Guru in a Bottle® is to guide the reader through technical subjects as their friend and personal guru. Buying a Guru in a Bottle® book gets the guru out of the bottle, empowering the business manager and student to tackle technical subjects and enhance their working and learning experience.

Ardi Kolah created the iconic character Guru in a Bottle® with cartoonist Steve Marchant and the unique approach has helped make the Guru in a Bottle® Series extremely popular throughout Europe, the United States and India.

Foreword

by Professor Malcolm McDonald

As author of 43 books on the subject of marketing, including one that has sold over a quarter of a million copies worldwide, I feel qualified to write a foreword to this excellent book.

It's refreshing to come across a book that's properly targeted and written in a delightfully understandable way. As it states, 'All the world's a stage, but most of us are desperately under-rehearsed', which is why this book is set to become such a classic and important work amongst younger marketers.

High Impact Marketing that Gets Results is full of wisdom combined with the very latest trends in marketing. For example, the brief history of marketing is outstanding, as is the section on how consumers make decisions. But there are lots of other gems to be found in these pages, such as how to write great marketing copy, e-marketing, direct marketing, PR and promotions. You'll find all these sections and more are right up to date.

The important difference between this and other marketing books is that all the material presented is set within the context of broader strategic marketing. And it's this which singles out this book from the madding crowd.

As a graduate in English language and literature from Oxford University, I hope you'll forgive my saying that the Guru in a Bottle® Series is where it's at. Of the thousands of marketers I know, I would always choose Ardi Kolah to be on my team. What's remarkable is that he's one of the few marketing practitioners in the world capable of capturing his vast experience and passing it on to others in an enjoyable and engaging way.

I highly commend all students and more seasoned marketers to learn the secrets of *High Impact Marketing that Gets Results* and to let the guru out of the bottle!

It's the real thing...

Introduction

Students of marketing theory and practice around the world are familiar with the following quote: 'Half the money I spend on advertising is wasted; the trouble is I don't know which half.' This was reported to have been said by the US retail and marketing guru John Wanamaker, who pioneered the concept of the department store in Philadelphia in 1874. As a pioneer of marketing, he doesn't fill you with confidence, does he?

Often the biggest sceptics of marketing are those who made their name being the titans in our industry, which sounds strangely paradoxical but true.

> *The sole purpose of marketing is to get more people to buy more of your product, more often, for more money. That's the only reason to spend a single nickel, pfennig, or peso. If your marketing isn't delivering consumers to the cash register with their wallets in their hands to buy your product, don't do it.*

So said Sergio Zyman, who was the chief marketing officer of Coca-Cola Worldwide and oversaw one of the biggest marketing budgets of all time, including the staggering amounts of money spent in sponsoring the Olympic Games.

Perhaps it's a bit unfair to label Sergio Zyman or even John Wanamaker as 'guru marketing sceptics' as both of them raise an important point about marketing. And it's this:

> *Great marketing isn't just about marketing output: it's about creating business outcomes.*

Incremental profit achieved through marketing activities is a 'golden goal' and return on investment is the measure of whether that goal has been achieved.

Of course it can be a long journey to achieve a measurable shift in the attitudes, values, beliefs and behaviours of desired customer and client segments that results in sales. And sometimes this can't be done in a single fiscal quarter, however big the marketing budget may be.

But unlike John Wanamaker, who didn't have access to the millions of pieces of data we have on just about everything we could wish to measure, marketers must work much harder to identify what part of the marketing programme is working and what part isn't and take appropriate action rather than leave this to luck and happenstance.

To achieve high impact marketing that gets results, we must become almost fanatical about walking in the footsteps of our customers and clients. Follow the approach advocated in this book and you'll be on your way to creating more sales for your business through better marketing of your business. And the guru won't just be out of the bottle. The guru will be you!

About this book

Chapter 1: Market and customer segmentation – how to carry out an effective segmentation of your markets and customers that will deliver clarity and purpose to your marketing efforts.

Chapter 2: Writing a marketing plan – how to put together an effective marketing plan and several tools to help you do just that.

Chapter 3: Understanding the marketing mix – an explanation of how best to deploy all the marketing tools that are available as well as guidance as to which ones are most effective depending on the circumstances.

Chapter 4: Brochures, press ads and print copy – a guide through the techniques of writing great copy and telling a compelling story.

Chapter 5: Signs, posters and ambient media – an exploration of those aspects of marketing that have the greatest decibel count.

Chapter 6: E-marketing, m-marketing and direct marketing – best practice digital marketing including the use of mobile as the most significant marketing platform in the 21st century.

Chapter 7: Public relations – how best to communicate with key audiences through a variety of 'transmit' and 'receive' channels as well as understanding the dynamics of the social web.

Chapter 8: Using promotions – the variety of promotional opportunities that exist and how to use them creatively.

Chapter 9: Top 10 common marketing mistakes to avoid – the key traps and pitfalls to avoid in managing a typical marketing campaign so that you can keep your job.

Chapter 10: Top 10 ways to save money in marketing – ways that will save your boss serious money from the marketing budget and keep a smile on his or her face!

"They're all the same... but different"

Market and customer segmentation

Introduction

When the business marketplace resembled a small jungle, those with goods and services chased those with money; and those with money chased those with goods and services until they caught each other. Sounds romantic, even quaint, doesn't it? Trouble is, that was ok when there wasn't much competition around: everyone knew each other by their first name and consumer choice options were limited, to say the least.

As Henry Ford famously said, 'Any customer can have a car painted any colour he wants, so long as it's black.' Not exactly in the vanguard of championing consumer choice, was he? Well, it doesn't work quite like that today compared with 1908. Very few buyers and sellers live and work in a world where everyone knows each other by their first name, unless of course they are polyglots and are just as at home in Cantonese as they are in Russian, Spanish and Hindi.

Instead, most of us belong to a community of marketing professionals who inhabit a global village where business is open 24 hours a day, seven days a week and never stops for breakfast, lunch or dinner. Sellers and buyers are everywhere and never log off. That means when you're asleep at night someone's out there trying to take your business by listening to what your customers and clients are talking about. And before you know it, you've sleep-walked into a nightmare scenario where you wake up one morning to find that little remains of the loyal customers and clients you once took for granted. They're not there anymore. And it may be too late to do anything about this.

All this frenetic sales and marketing activity happening around the clock has meant we have to rewire our understanding of 'markets' as it's not that obvious what business we're in anymore.

Markets continually rise and fall, converge, fragment, shape, reshape, dissolve, vaporize, transform and even re-emerge just when you thought they'd died. Who'd have thought BT in the UK would turn itself from a state monopoly known as the 'General Post Office' into a 21st century multimedia company, or for that matter 70s flared jeans would make an unexpected return to the catwalk in 2011? And of course, the most valuable markets in one year may well be different the following year, the year after that and the year after that one.

In the past, the markets were the constants: stable and predictable. Sellers jostled for the best positions within them. That was then. Competitive advantage is now much more about making smart choices about which market segments to compete in and which to avoid.

When traditional markets go into decline it's necessary to change, which some businesses find difficult and painful, particularly if they see change as an unnecessary distraction. But talk like that is dangerous. Very dangerous. The hard reality is that all businesses, irrespective of their chosen market segment, must embrace the need for change. The alternatives aren't worth thinking about.

Evidence from Judge Business School, Cambridge University, contained in a new book, *Jaagad Innovation: Think frugal, be flexible, generate break-through growth*, by Professor Jaideep Prabhu, shows that not embracing innovation leads to a company becoming less competitive and increasingly outmanoeuvred by its rivals that have stronger leadership, can match capabilities more accurately to customer needs and requirements and have shortened the product development pipeline from years to a matter of months.

Apple, Samsung, Google and Zara are in the vanguard of such brand innovators. Those that can achieve this feat of business gymnastics typically are the market leader in their category; more competitive and more profitable than the challenger brand that hasn't the same vision and purpose. But behind every great brand is a great marketing team.

In essence, marketing is the management process for understanding markets and customers; for quantifying the value required by the different customer and client segments in those market segments; for communicating this to everyone in the enterprise and for measuring the effectiveness of marketing outputs in terms of business and sales outcomes. In other words, finding out what the customer or client wants and delivering it.

And in the global village competition lurks in every corner and disruptive forces such as political, economic, social, technological, legal and environmental factors can kill even the best laid marketing plans.

There are some brand owners who believe that given the turbulence in world markets there's no point in undertaking a detailed marketing planning process as they can't see what's over the horizon. Such a view runs counter to the evidence that shows the difference between tactics and strategy is becoming more, not less, significant for business and marketing success.

Competing in fast-changing markets where borders have fallen and rules are broken on a daily basis can be very disorientating. However, the decisions you must take will determine who your customers and clients will be; what products and services you'll create; who you regard as your competitors and what the potential for commercial success looks like.

Today's successful business leaders share many common traits. For example, they have a strong sense of vision and purpose and this direction is articulated in well thought through marketing and communication plans that identify and develop those things that'll make the enterprise significantly more profitable.

The role of marketing planning

After more than half a century of marketing theory and practice, market and customer segmentation remains one of the most difficult and elusive of marketing skills, as it's both complex and multi-faceted.

The process of market and customer segmentation is a continuous dialogue with specific groups of customers and clients whose needs must be understood in detail. There are no short cuts: it's time-consuming but at the end of the day it'll be worth the effort.

A market segment is a grouping of customers and clients with similar buying needs, attitudes, values, beliefs and behaviours. Taken together, these provide a more accurate picture of whom we are trying to serve.

If we only looked at customer and client needs, we'd be severely limiting our options. For example, we all need food and if that was our only consideration there'd be only one segment in the food market: 'food'. Of course there're hundreds of segments because consumers don't just eat to live – they prepare food for a variety of reasons, from entertaining their guests to following a healthy diet.

It's true that no two customers and clients are identical. Nonetheless, except in very special circumstances, such as a specially commissioned designer dress or a hand-built sports car, it's not generally commercially viable to deliver exclusive products or services to individual customers and clients, unless they're prepared to pay a premium for that product or service. Instead, the majority of companies and organizations must work hard to find commonalities between customers and clients so that they can group them in a way that enables them to deal with such groups in a cost-effective and profitable manner.

Deciding which territories, which categories, which customers or clients you'll serve is likely to have much more impact on your performance than a slightly better product, service or price. Economically, markets appear to be good sources of revenue, yet the capital investment and operating costs may quickly spiral to make them less attractive. Choose the wrong customer or client segment, and you could find that you've made the biggest mistake of your business career.

It's tempting to want to serve everyone, to never say no to a customer, to be in ever more markets, to be a global player in the way McDonald's has become, selling convenience food around the world. But for the majority of businesses, this is rarely a smart choice. What's required is a deeper understanding of your existing markets, the relative value of different customer and client segments; understanding of how they will evolve, particularly in relation to adjacent categories or niches, and indeed broad awareness of the opportunities and competitive threats across the geographies and business sectors that you compete in (see Figure 1.1).

Stagecoach (UK)

In the UK, one of the largest bus operators that took such an approach is Stagecoach, which operates a fleet of over 7,000 buses carrying over 2m customers every day on its network, which stretches from Devon to the north of Inverness. The company developed a segmentation and positioning strategy using primary research that helped it identify three key market segments for its bus network: users, lapsed users and non-users.

An important and valuable desired segment for the company is the non-user segment. The company estimated that about 30 per cent of existing non-bus users in the UK have a propensity to switch the mode of transport they are regularly using, given the appropriate incentives. Stagecoach also felt it was important to address the perceived barriers associated with bus travel among this group.

Through profiling its customers using geo-demographic criteria, the company was able to identify micro-demographic segments within each of the local areas that it serves, to whom specific barriers to bus use are an

Figure 1.1 The market segmentation process

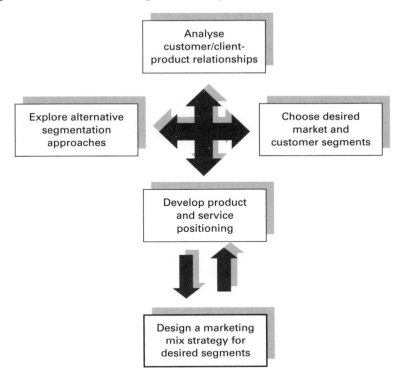

issue. This information has formed the basis of its segmentation strategy and how it subsequently tailored its communications with each of these prospect customer groups. Through further research linked to the journey experience of existing customers, Stagecoach was able to make the correlation between the journey experience and customer satisfaction, which are influenced by the following factors:

- reliability/punctuality;
- staff attitude;
- comfort during the journey;
- cleanliness of the vehicle;
- space for bags/pushchairs; and
- value for money.

Some of the key benefits of taking this approach to market and customer segmentation can be summarized as:

- enhanced understanding of the market dynamics and opportunities that run through to the end customer;

- enhanced understanding of competitor strengths (non-bus modes of transport) and the opportunities for competitor advantage;
- greater understanding of the needs, attitudes, values, beliefs and behaviours of desired customers;
- a better chance to see how to develop the capabilities of the business in order to match those needs;
- basis for reorganizing and restructuring the business focusing on the customer;
- improving the ability to manage the marketing and communication mix in a customer-focused way;
- enhancing the opportunity to add value, gain competitive advantage and build barriers to entry for rival transport operators (including other bus companies) and substitutes; and
- enhancing the opportunity to create, maintain and defend prices.

According to British sales and marketing guru Peter Fisk, for many companies looking to grow, often the easiest, fastest and lowest risk opportunities are to be found in adjacent niches. This may require product or service innovation or it may mean forming new strategic partnerships and alliances. He says:

> It might seem obvious but even when considering geographical markets people tend to look far before they look near. Before trying to conquer the United States or China, consider entering a market nearby, with a similar culture, language or climate. Managers tend to see opportunities with blinkered vision rather than looking around them to see what is nearby.

Broadly speaking, there are three types of adjacent markets:

1 *adjacent categories:* defined by business types (for example, beverages), product types (alcoholic drinks) or applications (social occasions);
2 *adjacent customers:* defined by segments (for example, teenage boys), geographies (Eastern Europe) or channels (Facebook); and
3 *adjacent capabilities:* defined by expertise and know-how of the enterprise (for example, technology), process (retailing) or assets (logistics and transportation).

There are many examples of successful organizations that have sustained growth over a long period of time by continually entering adjacent markets and then edging out further like the ripples made by a pebble dropped into a pond. One such organization is the Walt Disney Company.

Walt Disney Company

Since 1923, the company has been at the forefront of delivering some of the best family entertainment to be had anywhere in the world and has become a master at moving into adjacent markets when the opportunities are available. Its 140,000 employees are spread over four major business units: Disney Studio Entertainment, Disney Theme Parks and Resorts, Disney Consumer Products and Disney Media Networks (which includes Disney Internet Group).

Although each is an individual profit centre, they bring together a range of iconic and integrated brands and activities that are linked across the whole group to maximize exposure, engagement, impact and income. It's been so successful in its marketing of its four key businesses that it can now lay claim to 'owning' the following key brand equities that provide it with an incredibly powerful point of differentiation compared with other rival entertainment brands:

- fantasy;
- dreams;
- magic;
- creativity; and
- smile.

In 2005, the company became the first supplier of TV programmes to iTunes at US$1.99 an episode. In 2006, it was the first to stream full episodes for free onto the ABC website, upgrading the site's video player to something close to full HD standard. It also understood its audience and created ways in which they could vote online to shape the plots of their favourite TV shows.

In an age where other media companies have been concerned that free content would cannibalize TV audiences and reduce value for advertisers and sponsors, Disney was busy innovating in how to deliver higher impact with these audiences, working with advertisers through co-branded web versions of shows and other initiatives.

Market and customer segmentation is closely aligned with product differentiation. If you focus your marketing efforts at different market segments, you might adapt different variations of your offering to satisfy those segments. Equally, if you adapt different versions of your offering, this may appeal to different market and customer segments. For example, in fashion retailing, if you adapt your clothing range so that your skirts are more colourful, use lighter fabrics and have a very short hemline, this styling is likely to appeal more to younger women. Alternatively, if you decide to target older women, then you might need to change the styling of your skirts to suit them by using darker, heavier fabrics, with a longer hemline.

The former is product differentiation that focuses on the product offering and the latter is market segmentation – focusing on desired market segments. In the UK, high street retailer Marks & Spencer introduced the Per Una clothing range, which has been a huge success in generating a significant proportion of the total womenswear sales at M&S.

The difference between a product differentiation and market segmentation approach is illustrated in Figure 1.2.

Figure 1.2 The difference between product and market segmentation

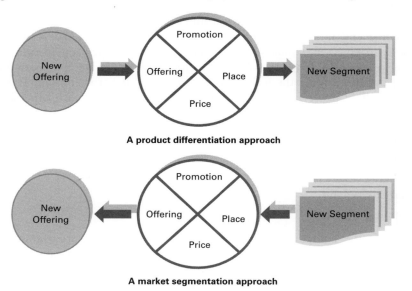

A product differentiation approach

A market segmentation approach

Market segmentation was first proposed as an alternative market development technique in markets where there are relatively few competitors selling an identical product – known as 'imperfectly competitive markets'. Where there are lots of competitors selling identical products, market segmentation and production differentiation produce similar results. This is because competitors imitate each other (copycat or 'karaoke' marketing).

As a result of a proliferation of tastes in today's markets, companies seek to design products and service offerings around customer demand (market segmentation) rather than around their own production needs (product differentiation) and market research is used to inform the process; see Chapter 2.

Determining the attractiveness of market segments

It's neither essential nor always desirable to serve every segment in the target market. The financial and managerial resources of the company need to be focused on those segments that provide the greatest opportunities for the enterprise to achieve its objectives. To make such an assessment, it's necessary to use external data.

The criteria for market and customer segmentation will be determined by carrying out the exercise but it's important to remember that the criteria should be independent of the company's position in these segments. As one of the criteria to be applied is likely to be the size of the segments, it's essential that you have access to up-to-date forecasts, usually three years ahead. 'The reason for such a lengthy period is that you're interested in sustainable competitive advantage,' explains Professor Malcolm McDonald of Cranfield School of Management in the UK. He also warns against allocating resources simply against segment attractiveness on its own as this needs to be balanced against the company's competitive position in each segment before any segment-specific strategies are developed.

Defining segment attractiveness factors

The criteria for comparing the attractiveness of segments must be specific to the market and mustn't be changed for different segments in the same market. As will be seen later, this will be a combination of a number of factors, which generally can be summarized under three headings: growth rate, accessible segment size and profit potential.

Growth rate

Typically, this will be the average annual forecast growth rate of revenue in that segment. For example, this means taking 2012 as the base line, the percentage growth of 2012 over 2011, plus percentage growth of 2013 over 2012, plus percentage growth of 2014 over 2013, and dividing the total by three: in other words, the number of years being looked at. Alternatively a compound average growth rate (CAGR) could be used. Clearly, in determining segment growth rates you will need to take account of the prevailing business environment.

Accessible segment size

An attractive segment isn't only large; it also has to be accessible. One method is to estimate the total revenue of the segment during the selected time span (say three years) minus revenue impossible to access, regardless of the investment made. Alternatively, a more useful approach is to calculate the total segment size. This is the most popular method used by marketers as it doesn't involve any managerial judgement that could distort the true picture.

Profit potential

This is much more difficult to deal with and will vary depending on the market and customer segment. For example, Michael Porter's Five Forces model could be used and adapted to estimate the profit potential of a segment. A sub-factor weighting (out of 100) needs to be given to each of Porter's profit potential sub-factors (see Table 1.1).

Table 1.1   Porter's Five Forces model

Profit potential sub-factors	Sub-factor weight (Total 100)	Segment rating 10 = Low 0 = High	Weighted factor score (weight × rating) ÷ 100
1. Intensity of competition	50		
2. Threat of substitutes	5		
3. Threat of new entrants	5		
4. Power of suppliers	10		
5. Power of customers	30		
	100		
Profit potential factor score			

Source: McDonald and Dunbar (2004)

A combination of Porter's Five Forces and market-specific factors could be used, but it's advisable to use no more than five or six factors for segment attractiveness in order to keep the exercise manageable. The specific criteria to be used will require management approval, but a selection of such factors can be seen in Figure 1.3.

Weighting segment attractiveness factors

For each of the factors for segment attractiveness, weight their relative importance to each other according to your own requirements by distributing 100 points between them. In the vast majority of cases, the overall objective of the company is usually represented in a profit figure and that profit is a function of:

Segment size × Margin × Growth

An example of weightings for growth rate, accessible segment size and profit potential can be seen in Table 1.2.

Table 1.2   Example weightings of segment size, margin and growth

Factors	Example weight
Growth rate	40
Accessible segment size	20
Profit potential	40
Total	100

Source: McDonald and Dunbar (2004)

In other cases, an even higher weighting for growth could be given, in which case the corresponding weightings for other factors will need to be reduced.

Figure 1.3 Segment attractiveness factors to choose from

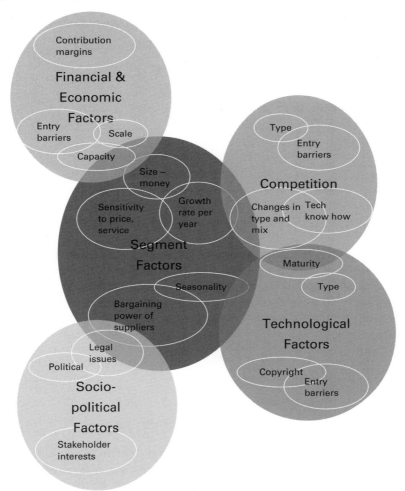

These factors could then be combined with market-specific factors, resulting in a more detailed set of attractiveness factors that have been weighted (see Table 1.3).

The simplest way of distributing weights to attractiveness factors is to first arrange the factors in descending order of importance, score the most important out of 100 and then score each of the others relative to this score. Reset them back to 100 by adding up all the individual scores, divide each individual score by this total and multiply the answer by 100. The weightings given to each factor is a matter of management judgement.

Table 1.3 Example weightings of segment attractiveness factors

Segment attractiveness factors	Example weight
Volume growth potential	25
Profit potential	25
Potential segment size (volume/value)	15
Vulnerability	15
Competitive intensity	10
Cyclicality	10
Total	100

Source: McDonald and Dunbar (2004)

Portfolio analysis

This initially came out of the work that the Boston Consulting Group began in the 1960s and it's had a profound effect on the way management thinks about their chosen markets and their activities within them.

The idea of a portfolio is for a company to meet its objectives by balancing sales growth, cash flow and risk. A portfolio plots markets, segments or products using at least a two-dimensional matrix. As individual segments grow or shrink, the overall nature of the company's portfolio will change. It's therefore necessary that the whole portfolio is reviewed regularly and active policies are pursued towards the move into new segments and away from less profitable segments.

The Boston Consulting Group (BCG) Matrix

The Boston Matrix is the most famous and simple portfolio planning matrix and is widely used for classifying and characterizing a company's activities in relation to the markets in which it operates. It can be used to represent strategic business units (SBUs) or product portfolios which are then located on the matrix for analytical purposes. Such a presentation enhances the ability of marketers to make judgements about how best to manage each product or service group and to identify gaps or areas that may prove problematic as markets grow, mature and decline (see Figure 1.4).

Market growth rates are depicted on the vertical axis and were originally rated between 0 and 30 per cent, with a growth rate of over 10 per cent being high and less than 10 per cent being low. In fact, what's considered a high or low growth rate will vary between industries and markets, so marketers will need to make their own assessment about where the breakpoints between high and low should fall.

Market share is depicted on the horizontal axis on a log scale and shows a product or SBU's share relative to that of the largest competitor in the

Figure 1.4 The Boston Consulting Group (BCG) Matrix

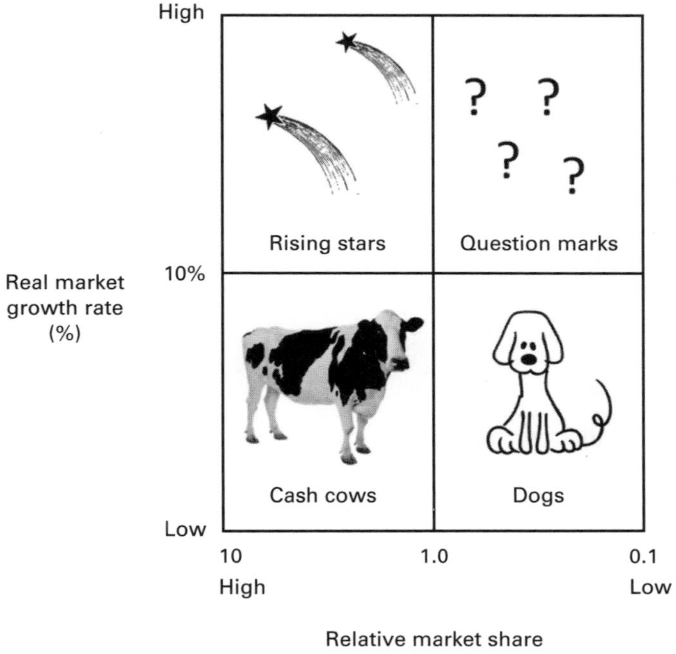

market. A relative market share of 1.0 means that its share is equal to that of its largest competitor; 10 will mean it is 10 times larger and 0.1 will mean that it has one-tenth the share of the largest supplier. The log scale is used so that equal distances on the axis represent the same percentage increases or reductions.

The rationale behind the matrix is that growth rates will significantly affect the attractiveness of a market to a company for investment purposes and relative market share is a good indicator of an enterprise's strength in that chosen market. Growth rates are also of interest because they relate to the stages of a product life cycle. High growth rates are associated with markets where the customer base is expanding rapidly and in which companies have to match or exceed the growth rate to maintain their market-share position. Low growth rates are associated with markets that are maturing and imply that a company doesn't have to compete with other suppliers for new customers entering a market in order to maintain its share of the market.

The BCG Matrix has four quadrants: Question Marks, Rising Stars, Cash Cows and Dogs.

Question Marks

High growth, low market share:

- Most businesses start as question marks (also known as problem child).
- They will absorb greater amounts of cash if market share remains unchanged (low).
- They have the potential to become a Rising Star and eventually a Cash Cow but can also become a Dog.
- They must be analysed carefully to determine whether they are worth the investment required to grow market share.

Rising Stars

High growth, high market share:

- This is a product or service that has attained market leadership in high growth markets.
- Priority in this segment is to invest to maintain leadership against challenges from the Question Marks of other organizations and so requires heavy investment.
- As the market's growth slows, Rising Stars will become Cash Cows if they have protected their leadership.

Cash Cows

Low growth, high market share:

- This segment is the bread and butter for the company and the Rising Stars of yesterday.
- They generate more cash than required.
- They extract profits by investing as little cash as possible.
- They are located in an industry or market that's mature and stable (neither growing nor declining).

Dogs

Low growth, low market share:

- This segment can end up being a black hole for cash.
- They don't have much potential to bring in cash to the same extent as the market leader.
- The number of dogs in a company must be minimized as they are at a declining stage.

An unbalanced portfolio can therefore have significant cash flow implications for a business either now or in the future.

An absence of Rising Stars could mean no Cash Cows in the future. The absence of Cash Cows will imply a need for external funding if it's to be in a cash-generating position in the future. Too many Question Marks may drain a business of cash if it has ambitions for leadership in each of the market segments in which they are launched. Dogs consume management time and a business must consider whether it's holding onto them for good reasons, since they are unlikely to be contributing much to the bottom line.

The implications of the matrix are that organizations need to invest heavily in those Question Marks and Rising Stars segments that are potential Cash Cows, and only moderately in Cash Cows and Dogs. It follows that each category of product or service will have different cash flow connotations and will require attention to different marketing priorities. In this way, a more rational basis for market and customer segmentation is possible.

Like all simplifications, there are a few drawbacks to using the BCG Matrix as a segmentation tool. For example, growth and market share aren't the only factors that make markets attractive. To overcome this difficulty and to provide a more flexible approach, General Electric (GE) and strategy consultants McKinsey jointly developed a multi-factor approach using the same fundamental ideas as the BCG Matrix. This alternative approach to portfolio analysis uses industry attractiveness and business strength as the two main axes and builds up these dimensions from a number of variables (see Figure 1.5).

Figure 1.5   General Electric/McKinsey Matrix

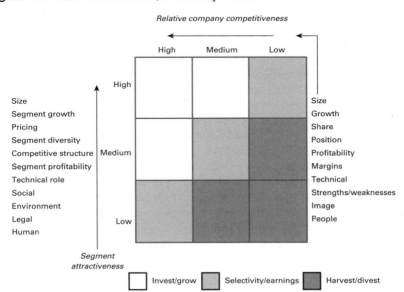

Using these variables (segment attractiveness and relative company competitiveness) and some scheme for weighting them according to their importance, segments are classified into one of nine cells in a 3 × 3 matrix. The same purpose is served as in the BCG Matrix – comparing investment opportunities among segments – but with the difference that multiple criteria are used. These criteria vary according to the circumstances but generally include some or all of those shown in Figure 1.5.

Market and customer segmentation in consumer markets

Back in 1963, the year that US President John F Kennedy was assassinated and Ronald Biggs and friends committed the Great Train Robbery in the UK, the average British household spent 13 per cent of its budget on rent or mortgage payments and utility bills. According to new research by Pricewaterhouse Coopers, the same costs were eating up 22 per cent of the average household budget in 2009.

By 2030, researchers at PwC predict that UK households will spend more than a quarter of their income on rent or mortgage payments, gas bills and water charges – more than double that spent in the 1960s. However, spending on food will continue to fall. The average British family paid out 6.9 per cent of its budget on a weekly food shop in 1963. By 2030 this is predicted to fall to 6 per cent as food prices continue to decline, despite recent rises.

PwC also forecast that the outlay on household costs will climb to 25.6 per cent of the average budget by 2030 as house prices rise faster than average incomes. Utility bills will also continue to increase as the cost of shifting to lower-carbon energy sources is passed onto customers.

British families are expected to spend far less on alcohol and cigarettes – only 2.5 per cent of their spending budget in 2030, down from 8.3 per cent in 1963. Spending on eating out and hotel stays isn't expected to change very much, which is good news if you run a business in the hospitality sector. It accounted for 9.7 per cent of budgets in 1963 but is predicted to rise to 10.7 per cent in 2030 (see Table 1.4).

According to Michael White, chairman and CEO of PepsiCo, around 97 per cent of growth in consumer markets in the next 25 years will come from emerging markets. These 'hotspots' represent markets where growth is high, prices are premium but competition is intense. Other consumer market segments can be seen in Table 1.5.

Figure 1.6 is a structure of the 'predetermined' approaches frequently used in B2C (business to consumer) market segmentation.

Market and customer segmentation is both an art and a science and is the bedrock of virtually every successful marketing programme. Depending on

Table 1.4 How UK families are predicted to spend the household budget in 2030

Area of household expenditure	Budget share in 1963 (%)	Budget share in 2009 (%)	Budget share in 2030 (%)
Food	24	9.6	5.9
Alcohol and tobacco	8.3	3.6	2.5
Clothing	10.4	5.4	3.4
Housing and utilities	13.4	22.1	25.6
Furnishings	7.6	5.0	5.5
Health	1.0	1.6	1.9
Transport	9.6	14.3	13.2
Communications	0.9	2.1	2.2
Recreation	7.8	11.3	12.6
Education	0.5	1.5	1.7
Restaurants and hotels	9.7	10.1	10.7
Miscellaneous services	6.4	12.2	14.8

Source: ONS data for 1963 and 2009, PwC baseline scenario for 2030

Table 1.5 Finding new B2C markets

Description of B2C emerging market	Features
Hot Spots	Where demand converges and all brands seek to play, for example, smart phones, integrated TV and computer sets.
Cool Places	Where style leaders go in search for the latest or newest in consumer products and services, for example, smart cars.
White Spaces	Where new opportunities emerge often through convergence of technologies and processes, for example, interactive TV shopping and cashless wallets.
Black Holes	Where traditional markets dry up and the leading players are blindsided and marginalized, for example, the film processing industry and video rental market.
Green Markets	Reflects the growing concern over the production of consumer goods and the impact these have on the environment.
Silver Markets	The 'baby boomers' are coming into their prime! From Bill Clinton to Paul McCartney, the jeans-wearing, rock music-loving shapers of the 1960s are now turning 60. They are wealthy, healthy, want to start new careers and travel the world. The last thing they want is quiet retirement – well, not yet!

Table 1.5   *continued*

Description of B2C emerging market	Features
Pink Markets	Gay markets aren't new but mainstream brands have been slow to address this large and wealthy market. Gays buy more premium technology products than anybody else. At the same time, there's a careful line to be drawn between serving and segregating audiences.
Red Markets	The former Eastern Bloc states of Europe are booming economies and many are now part of the EU. From Riga to Prague, Budapest to Warsaw, they seek the hottest fashions.
Blue Markets	While the East might be the new West, the South is the new North. From South Africa to Brazil, India to Dubai, southern domains are stepping up from the low-cost manufacturing economies into the sophisticated, knowledge-driven technological powers with high business and personal ambitions.
Grey Markets	The high-tech enthusiasts are early adopters of the latest gadgets such as the Apple Tablet.
Brown Markets	The fashion trend for 'retro' such as 'Adidas Classics' is enduring, and they tend to ride on a recurring fashion cycle. Such customer segments seek authenticity and originality – from the earliest models of digital watches to the original 1972 Nike Cortez running shoe, from antique furniture to items bought at auctions.
White Markets	The low-cost markets, from airlines like Ryanair and Virgin Blue to retailers like Aldi and TK Maxx – partly driven by the needs of the less wealthy, but also reflecting everyone's eye for a bargain given the depression in disposable incomes across the economy.
Gold Markets	The luxury goods market is perhaps the world's fastest growing market of all, worth a whopping $168 billion a year. The Candy Brothers latest über-luxury penthouse development in Hyde Park, London, is a good example of the strength of luxury even during challenging economic times for most of us! The appetite for luxury brands in Asia is booming as is the aspiration of mainstream markets throughout the western world.

Figure 1.6 Market segmentation in business to consumer (B2C) markets

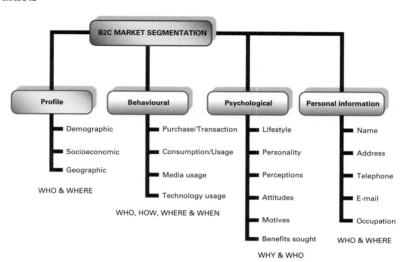

Source: Baines *et al* (2011)

the circumstances, it could be as simple as sorting buyers by zip/post codes or as complicated as layering behaviours, demographics and attitudes to produce deeper insights. A whole industry has been created specifically to empower marketers in carrying out market and customer segmentation.

These solutions tend to be customer relationship management (CRM) systems that can help automate the segmentation process, avoid duplicate customer records being held, tidy up inconsistent 'definitions' of segments and other related data sets, and break an over-reliance on attitudinal or demographic data to the exclusion of other data sets.

Alan Weber, principal of vendor of CRM solutions, Data to Strategy Group in the United States, explains:

> *House file segmentation fits into a strategy to grow the customer base, increase loyalty and grow share of customer. In some ways, it drives the strategy; in other ways, it reflects the strategy. For example, an organization with a goal of rapid growth would look more at lifetime value and future sales than an organization with a goal to maximize cash flow today.*

One of the issues facing many companies is that they look at the world from the 'inside out' rather than from the 'outside in'. In other words, they start with their own point of view (POV) first rather than that of the desired customer segment. The consequence of taking such an approach is that many organizations still predetermine how their market divides into segments based on, for example, criteria such as the products or services they offer, and organize the marketing effort principally around these dimensions rather than a market- and customer-based approach. Table 1.6 explores the segmenting criteria for goods and services in consumer markets.

Table 1.6 Segmenting criteria for goods and services in B2C markets

Base type	Segmentation criteria	Description
Profile	Demographics	Key variables are age, sex, occupation, level of education, religion, social class, and income. It's a bit of blunt instrument as it crudely suggests that all 30–35-year-olds, for example, will respond to the same product or service proposition.
	Life cycle	Based on the principle that people need different products and services at different stages in their lives, for example, childhood, adulthood, young couples, and retirement. This can at best be a general approach to each life stage as the permutations of variables are endless.
	Geographic	At one level, the needs and requirements of potential customers in one geographic area are often different from those in another area, due to climate, custom or traditions, etc. On the other hand, using a post code assumes that everyone in a predetermined area can be expected to react to a particular offer in exactly the same way.
	Geo-demographic	This type of segmentation is based on the relationship between where someone lives (type of housing and location) and their purchasing behaviours. It suffers from the same issues as demographics (above).
Psychological	Psychographic (lifestyles)	By analysing customers' attitudes, values, beliefs and behaviours we can get a deeper insight into individual lifestyles and patterns of behaviour that affect their preference and purchasing behaviours. This approach can also identify similar product and/or media usage patterns. On the other hand, psychographic segmentation can't on its own define the entirety of a winning customer proposition. However, by identifying internal drivers of customer behaviour that can be associated with specific segments, psychographics can help define the most appropriate promotional stance to take.

Table 1.6 *continued*

Base type	Segmentation criteria	Description
	Benefits sought	The motivations customers derive from their purchases provide an insight into the benefits they seek from product use, for example hair and beauty products and personal grooming products.
Behavioural	Purchase/ transaction	Data about customer purchases and transactions provide scope for analysing who buys what, when, and how often, how much they spend and through what transactional channel they purchase.
	Product usage	Segments can be derived on the basis of customer usage of product offering, brand or product category. This may be in the form of usage frequency, time of usage and usage situations.
	Media usage	What media channels are used, by whom, when, where and for how long provides useful insight into the reach potential of certain market segments through differing media channels and also insight into their media lifestyles.

One of the most interesting segments is 'life stage', which is based on the principle that people have varying amounts of disposable income and different needs at different stages in their lives (see Table 1.7).

Table 1.7 Life stage group segmentation

Life-stage group	Demographic description
Fledglings	15–34 years old, unmarried, no children, living with parents
Flown from the nest	15–34 years old, unmarried, don't live with relatives
Nest builders	15–34 years old, married, don't live with children
Mid-life independents	35–54 years old, unmarried, don't live with relatives
Unconstrained couples	35–54 years old, married don't live with children
Playschool parents	Live with children and youngest child is 0–4 years old
Primary school parents	Live with children and youngest child is 5–9 years old
Secondary school	Live with children and youngest child is 10–15 years old
Hotel parents	Live with children who are over 15 years old
Senior sole decision-makers	55 years old and over, live alone
Empty nesters	55 years old and over, married and don't live with children
Non-standard families	Unmarried, live with relatives, don't live with children and don't live with parents if 15–34 years old

Source: Kantar Media (WPP)

The research was carried out by Kantar Media, a WPP company in the UK. The researchers found that priorities for spending change at different points and these life stages don't occur at the same time. For example, adolescents need different products than a single 26-year-old, who in turn has different consumer needs than with a peer with young children.

In the UK, Tesco, Wal-Mart (which owns Asda) and Sainsbury's have all invested in the development of product lines targeted at singles with high disposable incomes and busy lifestyles, with their 'meal for one' ranges in contrast with the 'family value' and BOGOF (buy one, get one free) deals aimed at families.

As families grow and children leave the nest, so the needs of parents change and their disposable income is spent in different ways – in the UK, it's likely to be on university tuition fees and living expenses.

Research shows that holidays and choice of cars are heavily influenced by the life stage of desired customer segments. However, businesses also need to take account of our 'e-personalities' when attempting to target us as these affect the way we make decisions, according to recent research carried out by Dr Elias Aboujadoude at Stanford University's School of Medicine. The study, 'Virtually You', is one of the first psychiatric descriptions of how the internet is transforming us inside as well as out.

Dr Elias Aboujadoude fears that many people are developing 'e-personalities', alternative personae that exist not only online but also creeping into our offline lives with dangerous consequences:

> We binge-shop on Amazon and eBay because it's easy, we routinely lie about ourselves on Facebook and MySpace and get into nasty fights in chat rooms, where the insult is the default volume because we are anonymous. Online we behave like drunks. And not the fun kind but boastful, bullying and self-pitying drunks.

One conclusion to be reached from assessing these different approaches to segmentation is that although they may be administratively convenient, they don't on their own define segments but provide insights that are contributors to a successful segmentation project. Professor Malcolm McDonald of Cranfield School of Management explains:

> Customers segment themselves, they don't slot themselves into predetermined categories, and the propositions that appeal to them are those that satisfy their needs, by delivering the benefits they are looking for at a price they perceive as providing superior value for money.

Failure to conduct robust market and customer segmentation analysis can lead to critical consequences.

Air India

In May 2011, Air India was unable to pay its 40,000 employees as the cash-strapped airline sank into deeper financial trouble. The carrier, groaning under $8.9 billion of debt withheld salaries for about 33,000 pilots, cabin crew and ground staff as well as 7,000 casual workers. Bonuses weren't paid for the second consecutive month.

The airline was also forced to cancel some of its flights when oil companies refused to fill up its aircraft because of unpaid fuel bills. It was clear that the senior management team of the airline, once dubbed the 'Maharaja of the Skies', had failed to maintain market share in the face of fierce competition from no-frills rivals such as Jet and IndiGo.

Not diversifying its product offering in response to changes in the way its customers now choose to fly means that Air India now has less than 15 per cent of India's domestic air travel market and in 2010 announced losses of 34.5 billion rupees. It's not expected to make an operating profit until 2013 and a net profit by 2015.

In stark contrast to Air India, companies like Google, Apple, Nike and Zara have gained global market penetration by targeting niche customer segments of early adopters – those who are most likely to want to embrace newness. These are valuable customer segments and are seen by marketers as key to establishing a positive reputation for new products and services, given that these customers are also the most socially networked.

Finding the 'tipping point' has, for some, become the 'Holy Grail' of marketing and first gained intellectual currency through the research of US psychologist Dr Everett Rogers who conceived the theory of diffusion of innovation in 1962 and which is still relevant today.

Dr Everett Rogers called the seeding of the market amongst innovators in the first instance as the diffusion of innovation where communication is limited to members of a social system through certain channels. His insight was that people adopt innovations in an S-shaped curve: a few at first, then accelerating rapidly into the mainstream and then slowing down. He described adopters based on the innovativeness, in other words, how quickly they were open to embracing new ideas and products (see Figure 1.7):

- *Innovators:* the first 2.5 per cent of adopters are adventurous and well educated, have multiple sources of information and show a greater propensity to take risks. They appreciate technology for its own sake and are motivated by the idea of being a change agent, and are prepared to tolerate initial teething problems that may accompany new products or services.

- *Early adopters:* the next 13.5 per cent of adopters are social leaders. They are popular, social, personal, emotional and educated. They are visionaries in their market and are looking to adopt and use new technology to gain an edge amongst their peers. Highly influential, they are not price sensitive because they like to be seen as the 'first mover' but also demand personalized solutions and support.

- *Early majority:* the next 34 per cent of adopters have informal social contacts but are more motivated by evolutionary changes. They are more rational and cautious than early adopters, requiring reassurance

Figure 1.7 Theory of diffusion of innovations

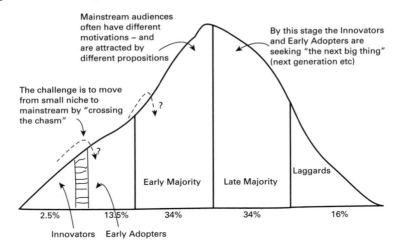

Source: Rogers (2003)

that they are backing a technology winner rather than the latest fad. They are believers in the wisdom of crowds and as a consequence are more susceptible to influence from within their own peer group.

- *Late majority:* the next 34 per cent of adopters are sceptical, traditional and often less wealthy and therefore often price sensitive and wanting off-the-shelf solutions. They are motivated by keeping up with the mainstream rather than getting an edge and often looking to advisers like price comparison sites to help them look for a bargain.

- *Laggards:* the final 16 per cent of adopters are natural born sceptics! Although it's a generalization, they tend to be less well educated or paid than other customer segments. They are happy with the status quo and have no interest in new technology. In fact they like to be thought of as not following the crowd!

While it may be fun to consider where you may fit in the above segments (are you really a laggard?) there are inherent contradictions that don't fit so neatly in the S-shaped curve. For example, why early adopters are attracted to a new innovation might be significantly different to what motivates the mainstream. Worse still, it might even put them off! Remember when you first heard New Order and none of your mates had? And then everyone was into them and you lost interest? And early adopters buy through different channels as if to emphasize their uniqueness, such as independent music stores and specialized websites! They also have different price points and respond to messages in a different way to the other customer segments. They may be fans of the controversial British artist Tracey Emin, but this could alienate other customer segments who aren't fans and don't want to emulate early adopters.

In his book, *Crossing the Chasm*, Geoffrey Moore described how visionaries and pragmatists have very different expectations and that a 'chasm' as big as the Grand Canyon can open up between the early and later adopters. He relates this phenomenon particularly to technology issues, illustrating it with the 'premature death' of many good ideas, but it can apply to any market.

Peter Fisk adds: 'If you want to reach a new audience, perhaps the smartest strategies are those that "piggy back" on a proven winner – ideally not one of your competitors, but from a related sector.'

Market and customer segmentation in business markets

In business-to-business (B2B) markets the aim of market segmentation is to arrive at clusters of like-minded companies so as to allow your marketing programme to focus on the subset of prospects that are 'most likely' to purchase your product or service.

There's a very strong pressure to use segmentation in B2B markets to win a competitive advantage as there is often little to differentiate one product from another. Segmentation therefore links strongly with a marketing strategy to achieve a sustainable differentiated position.

The benefits of market segmentation are not hard to grasp, as discussed above with respect to B2C markets. After all, the top 20 per cent of customers in a business may generate as much as 80 per cent of the company's profit, half of which is then lost serving the bottom 30 per cent of unprofitable customers. The challenge is arriving at the most effective groupings.

Segmentation can take the form of a demographic segmentation, sometimes referred to as 'firmographics' in B2B markets. This type of segmentation is based on geography of location, size of company and standard industrial classifications (SICs). However, firmographics doesn't offer a sustainable competitive advantage that competitors can't copy. It doesn't provide you with insights that aren't shared with your competitors.

A more challenging B2B market segmentation is one based on behaviour or needs: behavioural segmentation on what companies buy, what companies produce and how companies produce it. Needs-based segmentation is obviously one of the most difficult to assess: what do companies want and what drives companies in their actions?

Business to business segmentation isn't as well researched as its sister B2C segmentation and academic research in this area indicates that two key segmentation factors are organizational characteristics and buyer characteristics (see Table 1.8).

Table 1.8 Segmenting criteria in B2B markets

Base type	Segmentation base	Commentary
Organizational characteristics	Organizational size	This creates segments based on companies' relative size enabling identification of design, delivery, usage rates or size of order and other purchasing characteristics.
	Geographical location	This is becoming less of a meaningful way to segment B2B markets given the impact of the internet and the greater freedom this has created in serving organizations all over the world. Nevertheless, this approach provides the ability to segment business customers and clients in one geographical area.
	Industry and business type	In the UK, this is done along standard industry classifications (SICs).
Buyer characteristics	Decision-making structure	Within most organizations there is more than one entry point for making a sale. These can be segmented into influencers, specifiers and authorizers and in some cases you may need to have all three. Segmenting along the decision-making structure allows you to assess attitudes, policies and purchasing strategies of different organizations and create a cluster of these prospects along these lines.
	Choice criteria	Types of products/services bought and the specifications companies use when selecting and ordering products/services can form the basis for clustering customers and segmenting business markets.
	Purchase situation	Segmenting buyers on the way in which a prospective customer structures its procurement, the type of buying situations and whether buyers are in an early or late stage in the decision-making process.

Those companies looking to sell to other businesses will seek to establish and develop particular relationships that would normally be expected to start with these key factors, as well as to build up their market and customer intelligence. In addition, there are a number of criteria that can be used to cluster organizations and these include geographical location, industry type, value, number of employees, turnover/profit and other criteria (see Figure 1.8).

Figure 1.8 Market segmentation in business to business (B2B) markets

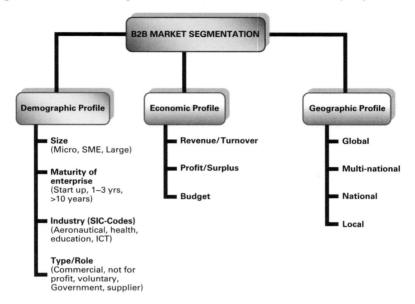

Source: Baines *et al* (2011)

According to US marketing guru Philip Kotler, for B2B segmentation to be successful, all segments must be:

● *distinctive* – each segment must be clearly different from other segments;

● *accessible* – buyers need to be reached through appropriate promotional programmes and distribution channels;

● *measurable* – the segments should be easy to identify and measure (which is a challenge); and

● *profitable* – the segment must be sufficiently large to provide a stream of future revenues and profits.

The approach to evaluation of these segments is exactly the same as described above (see Tables 1.1–1.3) for B2C markets, with the chief difference being that in B2C markets marketers tend to segment on the basis of psychographic and demographic variables whereas in B2B, marketers typically segment organizations on the basis of size and end use, and organizational buyers on the basis of decision style and other criteria.

Approach to international market and customer segmentation

Market and customer intelligence is the key ingredient in the development of a successful international marketing programme. Lack of familiarity with customers, competitors and the market environment in other countries, with the growing complexity and diversity of international markets, makes it increasingly critical to collect data on these desired markets. Where multiple countries are involved, the marketer also needs to have an appreciation of the different ways each market behaves in that territory.

Table 1.9 shows a standardized approach to the information required to effectively commence any meaningful international market and customer segmentation. As can be seen from the table, both internal (company-specific) and external (market) data are required. This can be sub-divided into primary and secondary data (see Figure 1.9).

Figure 1.9 Assessment of market potential in a foreign country

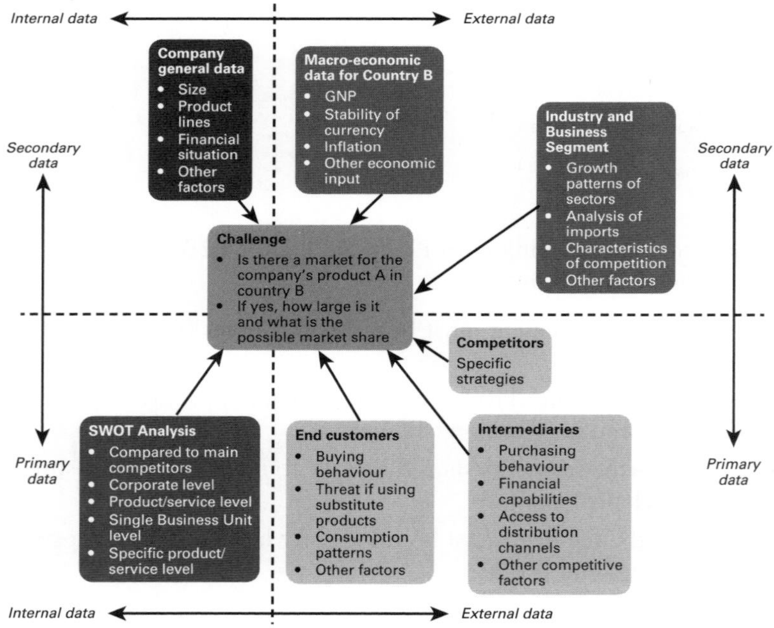

Source: Hollensen (2011)

Primary data can be defined as information that's collected first-hand, generated by original research that's been tailor-made for the purpose to answer specific research questions. The major advantage of primary data is that the information is specific (higher granularity of detail), relevant

Table 1.9 Global market and customer segmentation research

Global marketing decision phase	Data requirement for that decision
1. Deciding whether to grow the business internationally	Assessment of global market opportunities (global demand) for the company's products and services
	Management time and commitment to spread internationally
	Competitiveness of the company compared with incumbent rival companies and international competitors
	Legal barriers to entry
	Domestic versus international market opportunities
2. Deciding which markets to enter	Ranking of world markets according to market potential of countries/regions
	Local competition
	Political risks
	Trade and legal barriers
	Cultural
	Distance from your local market
3. Deciding how to enter foreign markets	Nature of the product or service being exported (complexity)
	Size of markets/segments
	Behaviour of potential intermediaries
	Behaviour of local competitors
	Transportation and logistics costs
	Government requirements
	Employment, fiscal , banking, insurance and regulatory controls
4. Designing the global marketing programme	Buyer behaviour
	Competitive practice
	Available distribution channels
	Media and promotional channels
5. Implementing and controlling the global marketing programme	Negotiation styles in different countries
	Sales by product or service lines, sales force customer type and country/region
	Contribution margins
	Marketing expenses per market

and timely. The downside is that primary data gathering can be expensive and time-consuming without any clear management outcomes for the investment made apart from helping to inform a 'go/no go' decision-making process.

Secondary data can be defined as information that's already been collected for other purposes and is more readily available. The major disadvantage is that the data are often more general with less granularity of detail. This needs to be balanced against lower costs and the amount of time required to get this data, which may make this a useful first step in the segmentation process.

The following fundamental sets of actions and questions will help you to qualify the nature of the market and customer segmentation that you'll be thinking of carrying out.

Action 1: In knowing who to contact, marketers need to be able to predict three basic behaviours:

● How likely are they to respond?
● If they respond, how much are they likely to spend?
● Are they likely to continue to respond in the future?

Action 2: To construct unique product or service offers for different segments requires marketers to have an understanding of the needs and behaviours of each segment. It leads to testing and defining reasons to test different offers with these segments:

● Is the average order substantially different among segments?
● Should buyers spending $50 each purchase receive a different offer than buyers spending $500 each purchase?
● Are different segments buying different things? Are the 'best buyers' simply buying expensive items and average buyers purchasing less expensive items or spending less?
● Are different segments purchasing more types of things while some buy only one or two things? In general, customers who buy a variety of items are more valuable.

Action 3: Knowing which customers have the potential to become more valuable helps to grow loyalty within the house file (database). Here are some of the things you should look for to spot a desired customer ready to move up to a more valuable segment:

● Does the customer look like a 'best customer' in demographic terms?
● If the customer is buying only one or a few items, could he or she be sold a greater variety of items?
● If you have only one contact name or no contact name (particularly in B2B markets), would reaching more people in the organization increase sales potential?

Action 4: The best timing of offers often varies substantially between segments. To know when to test these product or service offers, the marketer should understand:

- How seasonal is the market segment? Typically, seasonality takes on two components – 'best customers' tend to buy more regularly and often less seasonally than occasional customers or first-time buyers.
- How often do customers buy? The more often they buy, the more appropriate it is to contact them frequently and the less often they buy, the less appropriate it is.
- How soon do they buy again after the last purchase? For most consumable goods and services, customers are more likely to return sooner rather than later. A quick follow-up offer is generally effective.

Action 5: To devise a marketing strategy that will increase the number of 'best customers', the marketer needs to know:

- Are best customers moving up in the database or just dropping in from the outside?
- Is enough emphasis placed on keeping customers or are current customers being ignored while you chase prospects?
- What is the appropriate balance of marketing efforts between prospecting for new customers and clients and retaining existing customers and clients?

Action 6: To understand what triggers or tipping points are most effective, marketers need to look for specific customer or client behaviours that correlate with high or low spending. Typical differences include:

- The size of the average order – some customers make many small purchases and some make a few large purchases. In general, average order size is a more effective segmentation tool than total monetary value (overall spending). A recency-frequency-average order segmentation usually will be substantially more effective than a recency-frequency-monetary value segmentation.
- One-off purchased versus many items purchased – in general, the greater the variety of things customers buy, the greater the likelihood they are to return and repeat purchase. By contrast, a large customer who buys only one item has a high likelihood of defecting.
- Length of time on house file (database) – new customers often behave differently than customers who are set in a buying pattern. New customers often try many different things; they are ripe prospects for cross-selling.

References

Books

Aboujadoude, E (2011) *Virtually You*, WW Norton & Co
Arnould, E, Price, P and Zinkhan, G (2004) *Consumers*, McGraw-Hill
Baines, P; Fill, C and Page, P (2011) *Marketing*, 2nd edn, Oxford University Press
Cheverton, P (2005) *How Come You Can't Identify Your Key Customers?*, Kogan Page
Fisk, P (2008) *Business Genius*, Capstone
Hollensen, S (2011) *Global Marketing*, 5th edn, FT Prentice Hall
Kolah, A (2013) *The Art of Influencing and Selling*, Kogan Page
McDonald, M and Dunbar, I (2004) *Market Segmentation*, Elsevier
Moore, G (1999) *Crossing the Chasm*, HarperBusiness
Prabhu, J, Radjou, N and Ahjua, S (2012) *Jaagad Innovation: Think frugal, be flexible, generate breakthrough growth*, Wiley
Rogers, M E (2003) *Diffusion of Innovations*, 5th edn, Free Press

Websites

PricewaterhouseCoopers with respect to its research on UK household budgets: http://www.pwc.co.uk (accessed 23 June 2011)
Data to Strategy Group with respect to comments on segmentation and automation: http://www.d2sg.net (accessed 23 June 2011)
Kantar Media with respect to life cycle segmentation factors: http://www.kantarmedia.com (accessed 23 June 2011)

"Next, my plan for world domination..."

Writing a marketing plan

Introduction

There's a universal truth: that companies and enterprises succeed by getting, keeping and growing customers and clients. Customers and clients are the only reason why we build railroads, manufacture convenience foods, send satellites into space and make fire-retardant furniture.

But there's a trap – most managers are seduced into thinking that what worked yesterday will continue to satisfy consumers tomorrow. The trouble is, it probably won't and it takes courage to lift the scales from our eyes to see how we should change the way we serve customers and clients in the future. That's what great marketing – and great marketing planning – is all about. Yet most businesses are, well, crap at it. Now that may read like an extreme point of view but it's based on over 20 years' experience as well as observing why some companies and organizations succeed against almost impossible odds and why some succumb to intense competition, consigned forever to the pages of the business obituaries.

It's easy to see how decent companies with excellent products and services still end up screwing up their marketing. Science fiction novelist and scholar Isaac Asimov observed: 'No sensible decision can be made without taking into account not only the world as it is, but the world as it will be.' The issue for marketers is that the rate of change in global markets is so fast it's hard to make any kind of accurate prediction of what the future may look like.

Creating business success is extremely difficult today – probably more difficult than it's ever been. All the easy growth has now occurred. Every household in the industrialized world already has one, two or more PCs, a washing machine, a mobile phone or three, and access to the internet at broadband speeds rather than 56 k dial up. Once an economy matures, customers are no longer so hungry to buy, but businesses are even hungrier to sell.

As discussed in Chapter 1, global markets continually rise and fall, converge and fragment. They continually reshape. The most valuable markets in one year may be different by next year. In the past, the markets were the constants. They were stable and perhaps predictable, and businesses jostled for the best positions within them. 'Today, competitive advantage is more about making the smart choices of which markets to compete in and which to not,' explains British marketing guru Peter Fisk.

We've all benefited from unprecedented improvements in productivity over the last couple of decades, but the relentless quest for higher productivity has also put renewed pressure on profit margins. No matter how much streamlining we do today, we're just fighting to keep up. Everyone in your company or enterprise is already doing a job and a half, aren't they? The cost-cutting, downsizing and outsourcing you may have thought were reversible are in fact here to stay. And no business is immune from such change, irrespective of the sector you're in.

Globalization may have signalled the removal of physical borders but it also heralded the era of commoditization where products and services that were once sold at a premium now compete in a global marketplace on price. Outrageous but now a fact of life – so get used to it or do something about it – now.

Deciding which territories, categories, customers and clients you choose to serve is likely to have much more impact on your marketing performance than a slightly better product, service or price. Economically, some markets might seem good revenue sources, yet the capital investment and operating costs may quickly stack up, making them unattractive business opportunities, forcing you to take your marbles to a new playground in search of a new game. But that too is fraught with uncertainty.

As we've just noted, markets themselves are unstable and constantly morphing in shape and size, as well as composition. They are borderless and blur with others. Technologies converge rapidly, fusing fashion, media and entertainment whereby mobile phones become obsolete and have been replaced by powerful portable multi-functional devices that can fit in the palm of your hand with more computing power than Mission Control in *'out there' as it really exists. They're looking into a mirror reflecting their own internal obsessions back to themselves. A customer is someone who buys what we sell. When the organization looks at 'the customer' it's just looking at 'what we sell' from a slightly different perspective, a perspective designed to help it sell better. There's nothing wrong with this per se. In fact, there's a lot to be said for it. But it's a seller-centric projection. You can spend an entire lifetime peering into this mirror without ever seeing what lies beyond.*

One way of getting beyond this 'Alice Through the Looking Glass' condition is to recognize that every product or service that meets a need, that is sold for profit, also precipitates a new need: the need to make a decision. In the industrial age, meeting this meta-need – the need to make better decisions and to implement them better – wasn't the marketer's job. The job of the company or enterprise was to make a good product or deliver an excellent service. On the other side of the equation, the job of the 'consumer' was to make a decision – a choice. And the job of the marketer was to influence these consumer decisions so as to affect behaviour that would lead to a purchase.

As marketers we need to look at the world through a different lens – of the individual decision-making customer or client rather than looking in the mirror. Once we're able to do this it quickly becomes apparent that this meta-need – to make and implement better decisions – is bigger than all other needs because it embraces them all, subsuming them into the bigger task of achieving what the individual rather than the company or enterprise wants to achieve.

While 'core competence' thinking used to be the foundation of where to focus our marketing efforts it's now market opportunities that have grown in importance. Of course there's a balance between the two perspectives and the point here is where you start will define the frame of reference for everything else that follows. Getting to grips with this is critical.

Need for a systematic approach

Although all of what's been said may be easily grasped, strategic marketing planning still remains an elusive exercise for many marketers. As Figure 2.2 illustrates, part of the reason for this is that it involves bringing together all the elements of a business strategy so that marketing interlocks with this to form a coherent plan.

The commercial success of a company or enterprise can't just rely on brilliant marketing, and commercial success is also influenced by many other factors than just planning procedures. A myriad of contextual issues adds to the complexity of the marketing planning process. Some of these issues include organization size, degree of globalization, management style and culture, appetite for risk-taking and innovation, growth rate, profitability, structure of ownership, existing market share and market positioning relative to competitors. Irrespective of type or size of company or enterprise, some kind of structured approach is necessary for the marketing planning process to be successful.

A frequent complaint is marketing's preoccupation with short-term thinking and an almost total lack of strategic thinking that takes account of the long-term external and internal influences on the organization.

Another pitfall, according to Professor Malcolm McDonald, one of the foremost British academics in this area, is that many marketing plans consist largely of numbers that bear little relationship to current market position, key opportunities and threats, significant trends and issues and how sales targets will be achieved. In fact, they're as useful as a chocolate teapot.

Basing company or enterprise plans on a combination of forecasting and budgeting systems can only work if the future is going to be the same as the present or the past. As this is rarely the case, reliance on a forecasting and budgeting approach often leads to the following issues:

- lost opportunities for profit;
- meaningless numbers in long-term plans;
- unrealistic objectives;
- lack of actionable market information;
- inter-department dysfunction;
- management frustration;
- proliferation of products and markets;
- wasted promotional expenditure;
- confusion over pricing;
- growing vulnerability to changes in the business environment; and
- loss of control over the business.

'These problems are symptomatic of a much deeper problem emanating from a lack of marketing planning,' observes Professor Malcolm McDonald.

Research in this area has characterized certain conditions necessary for any marketing planning system to work:

- *Openness* – any closed-loop planning system, especially if based just on forecasting and budgeting, will kill any creative response and will eventually lead to failure. There needs to be some mechanism for preventing inertia setting into the bureaucratization of the system.
- *Integration* – marketing planning that isn't integrated with other functional areas of the business at general management level will be largely ineffective.
- *Coherence* – separation of operational and strategic marketing planning will lead to a divergence of the short-term thrust of the business at an operational level from the long-term objectives of the enterprise as a

Figure 2.3 Typical business and operational planning cycle

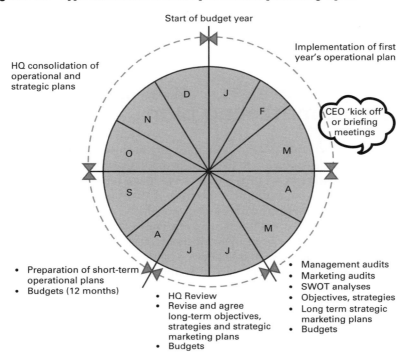

Source: Marketing Plans (2011), McDonald, M

It's prudent to repeat or improve upon the best-performing elements of the past marketing plans but cut back on any elements that didn't produce high returns. It's my experience that every plan contains some activities and spending that can be pruned, so be ruthless with the red pen!

Strategies for growth

It's probably stating the blindingly obvious but worth saying: an underlying assumption you need to make before getting stuck into crafting a marketing strategy and plan is that it's about growth. Otherwise there's not much point in investing in marketing, is there? So it pays to reflect on what this means in practical terms ahead of the marketing planning process.

Strategy is about making big choices, to align scarce resources and maximize success of the business in the short, medium and long term. It's about focusing on the most profitable markets of the future, ensuring that you secure competitive advantage in them and can reap the rewards from them.

Strategy is also about being clear and concise about what you do and what you don't do – irrespective of whether you're a commercial enterprise, a social enterprise, non-governmental organization (NGO), a local or central government department or municipal authority. The same principle applies in every case: you must define the boundaries and set priorities otherwise you're going to fail.

As already discussed, flexibility is important and strategy requires trade-offs to align the competing forces within a company or enterprise to ensure that value is created for all stakeholders.

Strategic marketing plan

Developing a marketing strategy is vital for any business. Without one, your efforts to attract customers are likely to be haphazard and inefficient. The focus of your marketing strategy should be to make sure that your products and services meet your customers' needs and that you develop long-term and profitable relationships with those customers.

To stay competitive, you'll need to keep your offerings constantly fresh and new. You'll need to keep up with the current trends in your market, any emerging technologies and changes or improvements to your existing products. You'll also need to create a flexible strategy that can respond to changes in customer perceptions and demand. It may also help you identify whole new market segments that you can successfully target. The purpose of your marketing strategy should be to identify and then communicate the benefits of what your business offers to your desired market and customer segments.

Once you've created and implemented your strategy, you should monitor its effectiveness and make any adjustments required to maintain its success.

Identifying your customer segments

Your existing and potential customers fall into particular groups or segments, characterized by their attitudes, values, beliefs, behaviour and needs. Identifying these groups and their needs through market research, and then addressing those needs more successfully than your competitors, should be one of the key elements of your marketing strategy.

As discussed in Chapter 1, undertaking customer research on loyalty, satisfaction and service can make a big difference to your business. You should focus your efforts on finding out as much as you can about existing and potential customers. If you can work out how they make their buying decisions you can adapt your sales and marketing methods and techniques to fit your customers' needs.

For business customers, you'll want to know how big their businesses are, what sectors they're in, and who would make the decision to buy your product or service. If you're seeking individual consumers, it may be useful to know such things as their gender, age, occupation, income, lifestyle, attitudes, values, beliefs and behaviours. You can then create a marketing strategy that makes the most of your strengths and matches them to the needs of the customers you want to serve. For example, if a particular group of customers is looking for quality first and foremost, then any marketing activity aimed at them should draw attention to the high quality of your products or service.

As discussed, it's essential that you get a handle on the desired customer segment for your product or service. Your marketing strategy will fail if you target the wrong audience or customer segment from the start, regardless of how good it is.

You need to establish whether your desired customer segments are groups or individual consumers (B2C) or other businesses (B2B). There are often two important differences between these customer segments: *individual customers* – sales to this group can be unpredictable, and customers usually have smaller budgets and specific buying preferences; and *businesses* – sales to this group are often more predictable and stable as there's usually a greater budget available to be used on various products.

It's possible to target both types of customer, though you need to be realistic about whether your product or service is relevant for them. For example, a cleaning service may apply to both consumer groups, whereas a new clothing brand will probably only interest individual purchasers.

Before looking at new markets, think about how you can get the most out of your existing customers – it's usually more economical and quicker than finding new customers. Perhaps you could sell more to your existing customers, or look at better ways to retain key customers.

Focus on the market

You need to analyse the different needs of different customer segments; focus on a market niche where you can be the best and dominate and then edge out from that niche like a pebble dropped into a pond, and aim to put most of your efforts into the 20 per cent of customers who provide 80 per cent of profits.

Don't forget the follow-up

Approach a third party for feedback about your strategy – they may be able to spot any gaps or weaknesses that you can't see.

Put your marketing strategy into effect with a marketing plan that sets out the aims, actions, dates, costs, resources and effective selling programmes. Measure the effectiveness of what you do and be prepared to change things that aren't working.

Understand your product or service

You can only identify your desired customer segments if you fully understand your product's benefits and features. You should consider the following points when assessing your product:

- The purpose of your product – is it to solve problems, satisfy basic needs, or is it a luxury item?
- The advantages your product has over other competitors' products.
- Customer problems, issues or challenges that your product or service can solve.

Product portfolio – product life cycle

Product life-cycle management is used for different phases of a product's life. It involves the conditions in which you sell your product – for example, advertising and PR – and how these change over time. To maximize the success of the product, these must be properly managed as the product itself develops. If you're aware of where your product is in its life cycle, you can market it in a way that will maximize its sales.

Having a steady flow of new products is critical to stay ahead of your competitors, particularly as a product moves into its growth stage. Profitability begins to rise and public awareness increases. There may be increased competition coming into your market, and as this competition becomes more established, your sales and prices may decrease. With the maturity of the product, costs are further lowered from production volumes and sales peaks. As the product's market saturates, your sales will either plateau or decline. In such a situation, generating profits will be more challenging.

It's a good idea to have new products or services to introduce as others decline. That way, there's always one part of your range showing a sales peak. Alternatively, you can make changes to the current product to create a new version.

Effective research into your markets and competitors will also help you manage your product's life cycle. If you're a smaller business with few resources, you don't have to necessarily be the first to market. In fact, being second can result in lowered costs and risks. However, rather than focus on innovation, you'll need to make differentiation your priority. Being different in a growing market can be successful because you can offer more than one product, but it's important to carefully manage your product portfolio to achieve profitability, a good return on investment and acceptable risk across multiple products.

SWOT analysis

Every business has strengths and weaknesses and your marketing strategy must take account of how they will affect your marketing. An honest and rigorous SWOT analysis, looking at your strengths, weaknesses, opportunities and threats is a good starting point for your marketing strategy document. Also, conducting some market research on your existing customers at this point will help you to build a more honest picture of your reputation in the marketplace.

Strengths could include:

- personal and flexible customer service;
- special features or benefits that your product offers; and
- specialist knowledge or skills.

Weaknesses could include:

- limited financial resources;
- lack of an established reputation; and
- inefficient accounting systems.

Opportunities could include:

- increased demand from a particular market and customer segments;
- using the internet to reach new market and customer segments; and
- new technologies that allow you to improve product quality and innovation.

Threats could include:

- the emergence of a new competitor;
- more sophisticated, attractive or lower-cost variants of your product or service;
- new legislation increasing your costs, such as compliance or capital adequacy regulations; and
- a downturn in the global economy, reducing overall consumer demand.

Having done your analysis, you can then measure the potential effects each element may have on your marketing strategy. For example, if new regulations will increase the cost of competing in a market where you're already weak, you might want to look for other opportunities. On the other hand, if you have established intellectual property (IP) rights then you could use the law as a weapon in protecting your market differentiation. (For a discussion on how to use law as a weapon for competitive advantage, see Guru in a Bottle® *Essential Law for Marketers*, 2nd edition.)

Developing your promotional strategy

When you've determined your desired customer segments, you should decide what message you're trying to get across to them in your marketing.

If you have more than one market segment, this message could be different depending on the potential customers or end users. It may also be necessary to focus your marketing in different ways – for example, based on product strategy, comparative competitive positioning and brand differentiation.

Brand awareness

To create a successful promotional strategy, you need to create brand awareness amongst your customers and prospects (B2C or B2B). Brand awareness relates to how well your specific product or service is recognized by current and potential customers. There're a number of marketing channels that can be used to create brand awareness within your desired customer segments:

- *advertising* – business directories, magazines, newspapers, billboards, radio or TV, video advertising, brochures, fliers, signs, posters and ambient media (see Chapters 4 and 5);
- *e-marketing and direct marketing* – through websites or mobile phone promotions, sales letters, e-mail, mail order catalogues, packaging designs or point of sale (POS) displays (see Chapter 6);
- *public relations* – news releases, background briefs, case studies, photography, product launches, events, speaking engagements, conferences, white papers (see Chapter 7);
- *sales-based methods* – coupons, competitions, discounts, gift vouchers, loyalty incentives for existing customers (see Chapter 8); and
- attending dealer or showroom events, exhibitions or trade shows to take advantage of any sales opportunities that may present themselves there or if your desired customer segments may also be attending.

Selling to existing customers

The Pareto principle – often referred to as the 80/20 rule – says that 80 per cent of your success in any given field is often due to 20 per cent of your effort. You can use the idea as a starting point to analyse how you can sell more to existing customers and this should be a core component of your marketing strategy. For example, if a small number of your products and services account for most of your profit, can you sell more of the less profitable products to your customers? Or if your higher-margin products or services are only being sold to a small percentage of your customers, how can you raise that percentage?

You may be able to increase awareness of your product or service by marketing it to your existing customers. If you understand your current customers – particularly those who deal with you often or spend highly – you should be able to develop ways to engage with them and increase your brand awareness.

You should also encourage existing customers to promote you to their partners and associates, friends and neighbours. In this regard, a marketing strategy that's designed to encourage greater use of word-of-mouth recommendations can be one of the most powerful ways of creating sustainable competitive advantage – and the best bit, it's free!

As already stated, it's often easier and more effective to sell more to existing customers than it is to acquire new ones. Once you understand why your existing customers buy from you, you can examine ways of getting them to buy more or more frequently.

Get customers to spend more

If your research shows customers buy at a particular time, then a key marketing strategy is to ensure you make contact with them just beforehand. For example, if you know that a business buys its stock from you at the end of each month, a courtesy phone call, e-mail or letter in the middle of the month can be effective. You can also add value to your products and services to ensure repeat business. Is there anything you can add to a service at little cost that's useful to your customers such as a free overall 'tune up' every time they send their car or computer in for repair?

Where appropriate, the marketing strategy should be to encourage customers to buy a premium product or service that better meets their needs and provides an improved return for you. This is known as 'trading up' or 'upselling'.

One of the masters of this technique is global PC manufacturer Dell, which built a phenomenally successful business by allowing consumers to select the components for their own PC – sort of 'made to order' online. Alongside your choice of processor, memory card and sound card would also be an option to select a 'superior' component at a slightly higher price, influencing the consumer into 'up-selling themselves' by spending a bit more in the expectation that they'd get a much better product. It was a brilliant marketing strategy that eventually turned Dell into one of the world's leading PC retailers.

You could also offer purchase incentives and price promotions on items that they usually buy from competitors, such as 'buy one get one free' (BOGOF) or 'buy for 10 months and get two free'. It's also useful to focus on selling complementary products; for example, hairdressing outlets sell hair care products for customers to use at home.

Timing and measuring your campaigns

Whatever promotional strategies you use, you should time your activities to reach your desired customer segments when they are at their most receptive. You should develop marketing strategies that combine both long- and short-term activities – for example, special offers, promotions and competitions (see Chapter 8).

Measuring the effectiveness of your marketing strategy is also important. This can include asking new customers how they heard about you, or using surveys before and after every marketing campaign. You could also monitor your website traffic and use individual promotional codes for specific sales or promotional offers.

All these and other measures, such as the value of the media coverage you generate in supporting commercial objectives, can help you determine what is and isn't working and show you where you can improve your campaigns.

Turning marketing strategies into action – the marketing plan

Once you've created your marketing strategy, you must then decide which marketing activity or activities will ensure your desired market and customer segments know about the products or services you deliver and why they meet their needs and requirements better than your competitors' products and services. There are many ways to achieve this, such as various forms of advertising, exhibitions, public relations initiatives, internet activity and an effective point of sale (POS) strategy if you rely on others to actually sell your products (see Chapters 3–8).

Try to limit your marketing activities to those methods you think will work best, to avoid spreading your precious marketing budget too thinly. Better to do a few things well than many things badly. Monitoring and evaluating the effectiveness of your marketing is an essential element of the marketing plan yet it often gets cursory attention. This control element not only helps you see how your marketing strategy is performing in practice, it also helps inform your future marketing strategy.

A couple of simple techniques are to regularly ask all new customers how they heard about your business and ask existing customers whether they would recommend you. The latter technique, often referred to as the 'Net Advocacy Score' is simple and effective. Respondents score points out of 10. On a cumulative basis, all points above seven count as 'advocacy' and all points under seven count as 'detractors'. The balance (taking one from the other) produces a net advocacy score.

Pitfalls to avoid are:

- making assumptions about what customers want – ask instead;
- ignoring the competition and ending up uncompetitive as a result;
- trying to compete on price alone rather than on value;
- relying on too few customers, which creates a risky basis for doing business;
- trying to grow too quickly so that cash flow problems sink the business; and
- becoming complacent about what you offer and failing to innovate not just in terms of products and services but also the business model.

Be sure to follow up all of your marketing and promotional strategies with a marketing plan. This sets out clear objectives and lists the actions you will take to achieve them.

Once you've decided on your marketing strategy, draw up a marketing plan that sets out how you intend to execute that strategy and evaluate its success. The plan should be constantly reviewed and, if necessary, updated so you can respond quickly to changes in customer needs and attitudes in your industry and in the broader economic climate.

How to write a 12-month tactical marketing plan

In essence, an effective marketing plan sets out clear objectives and lists the actions you'll take to achieve them. Perhaps most important of all, it turns the corporate strategy, business strategy, market strategy and marketing strategy into action.

The marketing plan is in many ways the sum of all of these parts and includes factors such as deciding which customers to target and how to reach them, how to win their business and keep them happy so they stay with you, as well as continually reviewing and improving everything you do to stay ahead of the competition.

The tactical marketing plan is the detailed scheduling and costing of the specific actions necessary for the achievement of the first year of the strategic marketing plan, whereas the latter is a plan that's usually for more than three years.

Research into the marketing planning practices of companies and enterprises shows that successful companies complete the strategic plan before the tactical plan. Unsuccessful organizations frequently don't bother with a strategic marketing plan at all, relying largely on sales forecasts and associated budgets.

Professor Malcolm McDonald observes:

The problem with this approach is that many managers sell the products and services they find easiest to sell to those customers who offer the least line of resistance. By developing short-term tactical marketing plans first and then extrapolating them, managers merely succeed in extrapolating their own shortcomings. Preoccupation with preparing a detailed marketing plan first is typical of those companies that confuse sales forecasting and budgeting with strategic marketing planning.

Contents of a tactical marketing plan

Cover page	Table of contents
Overview of the company or enterprise	Executive summary
Introduction	Business strategy
External and internal analysis	Marketing objectives
Marketing strategy	Marketing tactics
Implementation	Resources
Costs and revenues	Management and control

Overview of the company

You should write the plan with an audience in mind but where the company or enterprise is medium to large with several SBUs it may be useful to very briefly describe the business you're in and not assume that every person reading the marketing plan is an expert on your company or its market segment. You may wish to add existing market share, profitability, revenues and key profit ratios such as return on equity, and the number of geographical markets, number of employees and number of locations in which it operates from.

Executive summary and introduction

Your marketing plan should start with an executive summary that gives a quick overview of the main points of the plan.

Although the executive summary appears at the beginning of the marketing plan, you should write it last. Writing an executive summary is a good opportunity to check that your plan makes sense and that you haven't missed any important points.

In many respects, this is the hardest part of the marketing plan as it's the easiest bit to screw up. In essence, it's a one-page plan. It should convey essential information about your company's planned activities in a couple of hundred words or less. A good executive summary is worth its weight in gold as it's a powerful advertisement for your marketing, communicating the purpose and essential activities of your plan in such a compelling narrative that it's totally convincing.

If this isn't the first time the company has produced a marketing plan (which is likely to be the case) then spell out what's new and what's different from the previous marketing plan. Summarize the main points of the marketing plan and make clear whether the plan is efficiency- or effectiveness-oriented. If it's efficiency-oriented, explain that the plan introduces a number of specific improvements in how you market your products and services. If it's effectiveness-oriented, explain how the plan identifies a major opportunity, challenge or issue and adopts a new approach to deal with this.

Make sure you summarize the bottom-line results. This can be by product or service lines and what the costs are. Also show how these figures differ from the previous year's plan and keep the summary to one page in length if you possibly can.

Business strategy

It's a good idea to introduce the main body of the plan with a reminder of your overall business strategy, including:

- what your business or enterprise is about;
- your key business objectives; and
- your broad strategy for achieving those objectives.

where you have a competitive advantage or that you can conquer that niche. At the same time, you should assess whether you can expect high enough returns to make the segment worthwhile.

Often, the most promising segments are those where you have existing customers or clients. See what you can do to expand sales to these customers or clients. And if you're seeking new customers, you need to be sure that you have the resources to reach them effectively.

Once you've decided what your target market is, you also need to decide how you will position yourself in it. For example, you might offer a high quality product at a premium price or a flexible local service. Some companies or enterprises try to build a strong brand and image to help them stand out. Whatever your strategy, you need to differentiate yourself from the competition to encourage customers to choose your business first.

Don't get confused about strategy and objectives. The objective simply states something that your business hopes to accomplish in the next year. The strategy emphasizes the big-picture approach to accomplishing that objective, providing some pointers as to what the direction of travel looks like. An example of an objective would be: 'To become the leading underwriter in marine hull insurance by increasing gross written premiums by 5 percentage points'. The strategy to achieve this objective would be: 'To increase the profile of the underwriters with key brokers in order to write more business to increase market share by 5 percentage points'.

Ensure that the strategy chosen:

- reflects limitations in the resources available to achieve the marketing plan;
- affects not just perception and awareness but ultimately customer or client behaviour;
- is not 'me too' or a copycat of a competitor's strategy; and
- doesn't require you to know too much that you don't already know.

Marketing tactics

Once you've decided what your marketing objectives are and your strategy for meeting them, you need to plan how you'll turn the marketing strategy into reality. Many companies and enterprises find it helpful to think in terms of the four Ps:

Product – what your product offers that your customers value, and whether/how you should change your product to meet customer needs.

Pricing – for example, you might aim simply to match the competition, or charge a premium price for a quality product and service. You might have to choose either to make relatively few high-margin sales, or sell more but with lower unit profits. Remember that some customers may seek a low price to meet their budgets, while others may view a low price as an inference of quality.

Place – how and where you sell. This may include using different distribution channels. For example, you might sell over the internet or sell through retailers.

Promotion – how you reach your customers and potential customers. For example, you might use advertising, PR, direct mail and personal selling.

For a more comprehensive approach, you can extend this to seven Ps:

People – for example, you need to ensure that your employees have the right training.

Processes – the right processes will ensure that you offer a consistent service that suits your customers.

Physical evidence – the appearance of your employees and premises can affect how customers see your business. Even the quality of paperwork, such as invoices, makes a difference.

In this part of the plan, you need to explain the details of how you intend to use each component of the marketing mix. Devote a section to each component, which means that this part of the plan may end up being quite lengthy. The more of your thinking you get down on paper, the easier it will be to implement the marketing plan later, as well as rewriting it in future years.

Your marketing mix is the combination of marketing activities you use to influence the behaviour of desired customer segments so that they purchase your product or service. It's useful to think about the interactions or touch-points with your desired customer segments, not forgetting that excellence in marketing is about the 'receive mode' (listening) as well as the 'transmit mode' (talking).

Successful marketers don't go for the 'kitchen sink' approach and throw everything they can at attempting to engage with customers or clients – you just end up with information overload. Prioritize by selecting a few primary touch points – this concentrates the effort and resources you have at your disposal allowing you to create more leverage within the marketing mix (see Chapter 3).

Implementation

Your marketing plan must do more than just say what you want to happen. It must describe each step required to make sure that it *does* happen. The marketing plan should therefore include a schedule of key tasks. This sets out what will be done, and by when.

Refer to the schedule as often as possible to avoid losing sight of your objectives under the daily workload.

Resources

The marketing plan should also assess what resources you need to execute the plan. For example, you might need to think about what brochures you need, and whether they should be available for digital distribution by e-mail or from your website.

You might also need to look at how much time it takes to sell to customers and whether you have enough salespeople or whether you need to use other distribution channels.

Costs and revenues

The cost of everything in the plan needs to be included in a budget. If your finances are limited, your plan will need to take that into account.

Don't spread your marketing activities too thinly – as discussed earlier, it's far better to concentrate your resources to make the most of your budget. You may also want to link your marketing budget to your sales forecast. A sales forecast is an essential tool for managing a business of any size. It is a month-by-month prediction of the level of sales you expect to achieve. Most businesses draw up a sales forecast once a year and this is likely to be in a separate document.

Armed with this information you can rapidly identify problems and opportunities – and do something about them. For example, accurately forecasting your sales and building a sales plan can help you manage your production, staff and financing needs more effectively and possibly avoid unforeseen cash flow problems.

While it's always wise to expect the unexpected, a well-constructed sales plan, combined with accurate sales forecasting, can allow you to spend more time developing your business rather than responding to day-to-day developments in sales and marketing. You need to:

- Estimate future sales, in units and by value, for each product or service in the marketing plan.
- Justify these estimates and, if they're hard to justify, create a worst-case scenario too.
- Draw a timeline showing when your marketing incurs costs and when each component begins and ends.
- Compile a monthly marketing budget that lists all the estimated costs of your marketing activities month by month for the forthcoming year and breaks down sales by product or territory on a monthly basis.

Management and control

As well as setting out the schedule, the plan needs to say how it will be controlled. You need an individual who takes responsibility for getting things done.

A good schedule and budget should make it easy to monitor progress. When things fall behind schedule, or costs overrun, you need to be ready to do something about it and to adapt your plan accordingly.

From time to time, you need to stand back and ask whether the plan is working. What can you learn from your mistakes? How can you use what you know to make a better plan for the future?

Constructing a good marketing plan gives you focus, a sense of vision and purpose and dramatically increases your likelihood to succeed, as Professor Malcolm McDonald commented earlier in this chapter. But writing a good marketing plan takes time and many companies and enterprises don't have a lot of spare capacity to do this justice. As a sensible rule of thumb, spend an adequate amount of time on your marketing plan but not so much that you don't have a chance to stand back and see the wood from the trees – the world may have changed by the time you've finished writing it.

It's important for a marketing plan to:

- set clear, realistic and measurable targets – for example, increasing sales by 10 per cent;
- include deadlines for meeting targets;
- provide a budget for each marketing activity; and
- specify who's responsible for each activity.

Make sure you think through each of your objectives logically. For example, you might set a target for the number of new enquiries, but if you don't provide the resources and training to follow up these enquiries and turn them into sales, you'll have increased costs without any of the benefits.

Assess the business environment to identify the opportunities and threats that you face. Look for where you can capitalize on your strengths or where you need to overcome a weakness. All parts of your business must work together. For example, if you have limited cash flow you should avoid seeking large orders from customers who demand extended credit or that will involve you in heavy, up-front costs.

Remember to focus on your long-term strategy. Reducing customer service might boost short-term profits, but next year you might not have any customers left.

A plan will not happen by itself. You need to make someone responsible for monitoring progress and chasing up overdue activities. Reviewing progress will also help you learn from your mistakes so that you can improve your plans for the future.

Writing the marketing plan

- *Cover page* – have to have a nice cover to capture the reader's interest.
- *Table of contents* – a marketing plan can be comprehensive and complex but your reader can quickly find what they want.
- *Executive summary* – some word-processing packages allow you to generate this automatically, so assemble your entire plan and then edit the table of contents.

- *Overview of the company or enterprise* – this is good for those needing to be brought up to speed on who you are.
- *Market analysis* – how big the market is, what are the customer segments and quantify the opportunities.
- *Objectives* – what you want to accomplish; what the investment in marketing is actually going to deliver to the business or enterprise.
- *Customer analysis* – what are the attitudes, values, beliefs and behaviours of your desired customer segments? What are their challenges and problems, desires, wants and needs and how will you fix them?
- *Competitor analysis* – you are not alone. Take a look over your shoulder to check out what the competition is doing and, more important, what it's not doing.
- *Risk* – what's your appetite for taking calculated commercial risks and what's the upside in doing so? What contingencies can you put in place if things don't go according to plan (and they don't always)?
- *SWOT analysis* – strengths, weaknesses, opportunities and threats – needs to be crafted with a high degree of realism rather than pie in the sky thinking.
- *Present situation* – the situation analysis or 'state of the nation' is important as it's our starting point for answering: 'Where are we now, where do we want to get to and how are we going to get there?'
- *Products or services plans* – these are individual plans, a bit like a marketing plan within a marketing plan.
- *Marketing strategy* – there should be one overarching strategy and then sub-strategies supported by multiple tactics to achieve those strategies.
- *Sales strategy* – given the environment created by marketing, how you will make contact with your customers or clients.
- *Pricing* – the moment of truth: good to look at this from a variety of perspectives.
- *Distribution channels* – how best to get your products or services closer to your customers or clients.
- *Internet* – this marketing channel is on 24/7. How does this integrate with the rest of the marketing activities, both offline and online?
- *Strategic alliances* – other associates and partners who would benefit from working with you and why. Who and where are they? What business and financial synergies exist and can this take you a step closer in delivering the marketing required for the company or enterprise?
- *Marketing communications* – needs to be precise rather than random, as well as being joined up.
- *Advertising and public relations* – have you considered the cost-effectiveness of certain channels and the overall marketing mix?

- *Implementation plan* – all of the above sounds good, so how do you roll it out?
- *Team and milestones* – what gets measured gets done, but it will require a team effort.
- *Forecasts and budgets* – do the maths, prioritize your cash flow and get buy-in from the senior management team to move forward.
- *Appendix* – this is where you'll add the supporting research and data to back up your plan.

References

Books

Anderson, C, Flick, S and Reed, D (2008) *Sales and Marketing Policies, Procedures and Forms*, Bizmanualz
Fisk, P (2006) *Marketing Genius*, Capstone
Fisk, P (2008) *Business Genius*, Capstone
Fisk, P (2010) *People, Planet, Profit*, Kogan Page
McDonald, M (2002) *Marketing Plans*, Butterworth Heinemann
McDonald, M (2006) *How Come Your Marketing Plans Aren't Working?*, Kogan Page
McDonald, M and Morris, P (2000) *The Marketing Plan in Colour*, Butterworth Heinemann
McDonald, M, Kolah, A *et al* (2007) *Marketing in a Nutshell*, Butterworth Heinemann
Peppers, R and Rogers, M (2005) *Return on Customer*, Doubleday
Peppers, D and Rogers, M (1993) *The One to One future: Building relationships one customer at a time*, Doubleday

Websites

Marketing e-course on the learndirect business website:
http://www1.learndirect-business.com (accessed 31 July 2011)
Marketing Planning Tool on the CIM website:
http://www.cim.co.uk/marketingplanning tool (accessed 31 July 2011)
Download a marketing tactics guide from the CIM: http://www.cim.co.uk/filestore/resources/10minguides/marketingmix.pdf (accessed 31 July 2011)

The evolution of communication...

Understanding the marketing mix

Introduction

According to social anthropologists, the art and science of marketing can be traced back over thousands of years.

Simple trade era
This was when everything available was made or harvested by hand and was in limited supply. Here, the main activity was 'hunting and gathering' and survival. From a 'marketing' perspective, nothing really changed from

the time homo sapiens ventured out of their caves up until the early 19th century, known as the 'pre-industrial revolution phase'.

The earliest manifestation of 'marketing' was the branding of animals by farmers who needed to tell the difference between the beasts when they were grazing on adjoining lands. And the earliest example of a 'trademark' appeared in the Roman Empire where blacksmiths used distinctive marks to distinguish the swords they'd made for their customers.

Production era

It wasn't until the 1860s through to the 1920s that mass production techniques increased the availability of consumer goods and kick-started a renaissance in 'marketing' thinking. This was the era of 'if you build it, they'll come' marketing. Brand owners thrived because there were few alternatives available.

Sales era

There then followed the sales era (1920–1940s) after pent-up consumer demand had been satisfied after years of war-time austerity. It's at this point that marketing started to resemble something like a management discipline as consumers started to exercise buying power. No longer could brand owners easily sell everything they produced and competition for market share intensified.

In 1928, *The Law of Success* was published, in which US business guru Napoleon Hill argued that only through real and consistent belief can a business achieve its goals. Brand owners now had to work a lot harder than they'd done before to sell their products and services. Coupled with this, products were becoming commoditized and price had become a key factor in attracting consumers.

Marketing department era

The economic boom that followed post-World War II (1940s–1960s) pre-cipitated the emergence of the marketing department era. It was at this point that traditional manufacturers realized that the 'hard sell' approach wasn't going to work as well with the new generation of 'baby boom' consumers and a new strategy was desperately required. In addition, increasing afflu-ence levels amongst consumers meant they had more bargaining power at their disposal.

In response, brand owners started to consolidate marketing-related activities such as advertising and direct marketing, sales and price promo-tions, and public relations and sponsorship into a single department or unit. These new departments battled with the drive for commoditization in market segments that was squeezing profit margins for brand owners. At the same time brand owners faced new competitive threats from low-cost producers thousands of miles away that were disrupting traditional markets for goods and services.

Marketing company era

From the 1960s through to the early 1990s brand owners started to take seriously how they created products and services around the needs of customers and clients. In essence, they'd had to up their game. The customer was now king.

This new mantra marked a turning point in marketing thinking and a break with the past where marketing's purpose had been defined as that of a sales funnel. In addition, marketing now became the brand owner's 'nervous system' in the organization that was used to touch customers, clients, prospects, users and consumers. As a result, all employees were now expected to be involved in marketing and to feel connected with its customers and clients.

Relationship marketing era

The need for connection was overtaken by the need to build relationships, and in the mid-1990s brand owners switched their thinking to building long-term, mutually beneficial relationships with customers and clients.

In 1993, Don Peppers and Martha Rogers ushered in this new era with the publication of *The One to One Future: Building relationships one customer at a time.* Customer relationship management (CRM) and data-mining became the buzz-words for marketers. Getting all systems in sync to capture information about each individual customer's behaviour became the key pursuit of brand owners like Microsoft, Dell, Google, Facebook, Visa and other global brand owners.

Collaboration era

This is where we've ended up in 2012. The art and science of marketing is now about focusing on real-time connections and social exchanges, but the big difference is that it's consumer rather than brand owner-driven. Marketers live in a world where they must earn the permission and trust of consumers to do business with them. This is the decade of information exchange, collaboration and innovation that's determining commercial success and failure as well as laying the foundations for the next phase in marketing's evolution.

Marketing's new vocabulary

Whereas CRM was the buzz-word for marketers in the 1990s, it's become almost obsolete as the power for managing purchase interactions is now in the hands of consumers rather than the brand owners.

This has come about as a consequence of changes in the legal frame-work on the use of data, increased privacy protection for individuals and a greater access to information online that's turned the tables on brand owners by giving more legal rights to consumers. (For a discussion on the laws and regulations that impact this area of marketing practice in the UK and Europe, see Guru in a Bottle®, *Essential Law for Marketers*, 2nd edition.)

As a result of the shift in the balance of bargaining power, CRM is giving way to vendor relationship management (VRM); where the decision to engage is the legal right of the individual rather than the unfettered discretion of the marketer. The new relationship dynamics now require the marketer to seek legal and non-legal permission for customer and prospect communication, and this can't be taken for granted. In effect 'push' marketing has been displaced by 'pull' marketing.

Consumers simply don't buy the word of marketers any more. They search for verification on social networking sites such as foursquare and TripAdvisor where peer-to-peer communication is considered more trustworthy, reliable and accurate. James Surowiecki, in his seminal book, *The Wisdom of Crowds*, observed:

> *Groups are only smart where there is a balance between the information that everyone in the group shares and the information that each of the members of the group holds privately. It's the combination of all those pieces of independent information , some of them right, some of them wrong, that keeps the group wise.*

Brand owners like American Express have made the brand journey from its 'Don't leave home without it' positioning of its brand to its current messaging about the community of consumers, merchants and small business owners it seeks to serve.

The very things that made 'push' marketing effective in the past – tight, relatively centralized operational control over a well-defined set of channels and touch-points – holds it back in the new era of collaborative customer and client engagement.

The proliferation of media channels and products requires marketers to find new ways to get their brands included in the initial consideration set those customers and clients develop as they begin their purchase decision journey. The shift from monologue to dialogue, as American Express and other brand owners have made, requires a more systematic approach to marketing.

Brand owners must now not only align all the elements of the marketing mix, which includes strategy, spending, channel management and message, with the journey those customers and clients make but also integrate those elements across the whole organization.

When marketers understand this journey and direct their marketing budgets and messaging to the moments of maximum influence, they stand a much better chance of reaching consumers at the right time and place with the right message.

The customer and client journey

The decision to purchase a product or service is a rational as well as emotional decision for customers or clients. What's less well understood is that they also adopt new products and services at different speeds and time-scales; a key consideration for brand owners in attempting to understand the various customer and client journeys that lead to the decision-making point and eventually a sale. Their different attitudes, values, beliefs and behaviours will also have a bearing on this outcome.

Diffusion curve theory

Customer and clients can be segmented into one of five categories and the rate at which each adopts an innovation is referred to as the process of diffusion (see Figure 3.1).

Figure 3.1   The process of diffusion

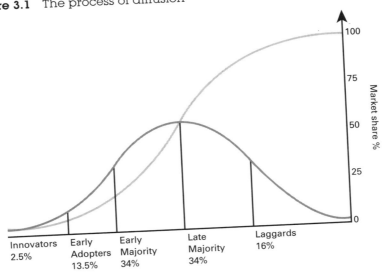

The rate of diffusion is a function of the rate at which sales occur and the pattern of diffusion is expressed in the shape of the curve and the size of the market. As can be seen from Figure 3.1, diffusion doesn't occur at a constant or predictable rate and it may be fast or slow. (For further discussion, see Chapter 1.)

Innovators

This segment makes up 2.5 per cent of the market and, although small, they are highly influential as they tend to kick-start the adoption process.

by the pace of change with the latest consumer technology. As this chapter illustrates, globalization, changes in consumer behaviour; and permission-based marketing are rewiring our understanding of marketing and the marketing mix in this decade. Every day, customers and clients form impressions of brand owners and brands from touch-points such as 48-sheet posters, websites, TV advertising, sponsorship, media coverage, in-store point of sale, product placement, competitions and promotions. However, unless customers are 'ready to buy', much of that brand exposure looks like it's wasted.

But what happens when something triggers a consumer's impulse to buy? Those accumulated impressions stored in the consumer's memory become crucial because they shape the initial consideration set: in effect, they help to funnel the purchasing decision-making process towards a limited number of preferred brand options. (For a detailed discussion on creating a realistic sales funnel, see Guru in a Bottle®, *Art of Influencing and Selling*.)

Research shows that consumers systematically narrow their initial consideration set as they weigh up their purchasing options. The post-sale phase becomes a critical point in building long-term relationships with customers and clients because they become a 'trial period' for the purchase and what happens next very often determines the strength of customer loyalty as well as the propensity to repeat purchase in the future.

This requires marketers to be less focused on 'pushing' messages and much more tuned in to influencing the process of customer and client brand consideration and purchasing behaviour in the future. As illustrated in Figure 3.2, this is a cyclical journey that can be broken down into four phases in the pre- and post-sales experience:

Figure 3.2   How consumers make decisions

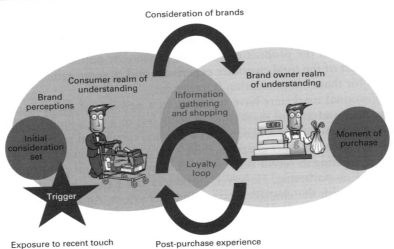

1 initial consideration;
2 active evaluation or the process of researching potential purchase options;
3 closure – when the consumer makes the purchase; and
4 post-purchase experience – when the consumer experiences those brands.

McKinsey marketing research study (2009)

A comprehensive research study involving 20,000 consumers across five different industries and three continents was carried out by global strategy management consultants McKinsey, examining the customer and client journey in some detail. The findings showed that purchasers tend to fall back on a limited set of brands when faced with a plethora of choices and communications.

Brand awareness is of course important: brands in the initial consideration set can be up to three times more likely to be purchased eventually than brands that aren't in that set. However, all is not lost for brands excluded from the first stage as the number of brands under consideration during the active-evaluation phase may actually expand rather than narrow as the consumer seeks information about a particular product or service category. Brands can 'interrupt' the consumer decision-making process by entering into the consideration set and even force the exit of rival brands from this consideration process.

The McKinsey research found that the number of brands added in later stages differs according to the market segment (see Table 3.1). The research showed that those consumers actively evaluating PCs, for example, added an average of one brand to their initial consideration set of 1.7 brands, while those in the market for a car added 2.2 brands to their initial consideration set of 3.8 car brands.

Table 3.1 Consumer decision survey across various market segments

Market segment	Share of purchases (%)			Average number of brands	
	Initial consideration	Active consideration	Loyalty loop	In initial consideration set	Added in active consideration
Automotive	63	30	7	3.8	2.2
PCs	49	24	27	1.7	1.0
Skin care	38	37	25	1.5	1.8
Telecom carriers	38	20	42	1.5	0.9
Motor insurance	13	9	78	3.2	1.4

Source: McKinsey (2008–9)

The research study indicates that a change in consumer behaviour can create an opportunity for marketers by adding touch-points within the decision-making process that can have the most impact.

In the past, as the consumer pondered brand options, marketers would turn up the dial in terms of 'push' marketing communications that included traditional advertising, direct marketing, PR, etc. However, such an approach isn't that effective where the consumer is now 'pulling' helpful information. For example, billboards alongside train tracks now struggle for attention in the rush hour when commuters are staring intently at their iPads, Kindles and smart phones before they reach their offices in the morning. (For a further discussion on market and customer segmentation, refer to Chapter 1.)

The McKinsey research showed that 75 per cent of the touch-points during the active-evaluation phase were consumer-initiated, such as reading blog reviews and getting word-of-mouth recommendations from family and friends as well as in-store interactions and recollections of past experiences. Over the past couple of years this trend has accelerated to the point where it's now part of the daily routine for millions of shoppers looking for the next bargain.

One reason is the dramatic fall in confidence in business, which some studies put as low as 14 per cent of those questioned. Not surprisingly, with this level of distrust individual consumers have left their inhibitions behind them and are now willing to share their thoughts on just about any experience they've had with a product or service – good or bad – on YouTube. The democratization of the internet has well and truly arrived.

Although traditional marketing remains important, marketers must also rethink their marketing strategy beyond 'push' media channels and influence the consumer decision-making process through more subtle means. For example, Japanese car manufacturers have for a long time focused on delivering excellent after-care service that's helped to create positive word-of-mouth and higher levels of initial consideration for their brands, such as Toyota and Lexus.

When consumers reach a decision at the moment of purchase, the marketer's work has just begun: the post-purchase experience shapes the consumer's opinion for every subsequent decision in the category, so the journey is an ongoing cycle. For example, in the McKinsey study, more than 60 per cent of consumers of facial skin care products went online to conduct further research after the purchase had been made.

Although the need to provide an after-sales experience that inspires loyalty and encourages repeat purchases isn't new, not all loyalty is equal in today's increasingly competitive, complex world. Of those consumers who profess brand loyalty, some are 'active advocates' and others are 'passive loyalists' who simply stick with the brand but don't bother to share the reason for their preference with others. It's the latter group that are most likely to switch brands should a better offer come along. The research found as much as a sixfold difference in the ratio of active to passive loyalists among major car brands, so car manufacturers have opportunities to interrupt the loyalty loop.

All marketers should make expanding the base of 'active advocates' a marketing priority and to achieve this they should focus their marketing efforts on the touch-points in the customer and client decision journey.

Aligning marketing with the consumer decision journey

Developing a deep knowledge of how consumers make decisions is an important first step. For most marketers, the difficult bit is focusing marketing and spending on the most influential touch-points.

In many cases the focus for the direction of marketing effort must change, for example away from brand advertising on the initial consideration phase to developing internet tools that help consumers gain a better understanding of the brand when they actively evaluate it. Other marketers may need to rewire their customer loyalty programmes by focusing on active rather than passive loyalists or by spending money on in-store point of sale activities or viral word-of-mouth marketing.

The increasing complexity of the consumer decision journey will force virtually all brand owners to adopt new ways of measuring consumer attitudes, brand performance and the effectiveness of marketing expenditures across the whole process (see later). Without such a realignment of marketing focus, marketers can face two risks: 1) a waste of marketing budget, and 2) using inappropriate marketing tools that aren't fit for purpose. At a time when revenue growth is critical and funding tight, traditional marketing communications will be less effective because consumers aren't getting the right information at the right time.

As we've already discussed, by trying to push products on customers and clients rather than providing them with the information, support and experience they want to reach decisions themselves, marketers could find themselves dangerously out of touch.

Strategies for addressing the realities of the customer journey

There are a number of strategies that marketers can adopt to respond to these challenges.

Prioritize objectives and marketing spend
In the past, most marketers consciously chose to focus on either end of the marketing funnel: building awareness or generating loyalty among current customers. The McKinsey research reveals a need to be much more specific about the touch-points used to influence consumers as they move through initial consideration to active evaluation and closure.

By looking just at the traditional marketing funnel's front or back end, brand owners could overlook opportunities not only to focus marketing spend on the most important points of the decision journey but also to target the right customers and clients.

In the skin care industry, for example, the McKinsey study found that some brands are much stronger in the initial-consideration phase than in active evaluation or closure. On this basis, some health and beauty brand owners need to shift focus from an overall brand positioning – already strong enough to ensure that they get considered – to efforts that will have a powerful influence on consumer behaviour or to focus on packaging and point of sale activities targeted at the moment of purchase.

More targeted and relevant marketing messages

A review of marketing messages that are delivered to customers at whatever part of the consumer journey is a useful exercise for any brand owner to undertake. An indistinctive message across all phases in the consumer journey is unlikely to be that effective and should perhaps be replaced by a series of targeted messages that address key buyer issues at specific points, such as at the initial consideration or active evaluation phases.

Take the automotive industry for example. A number of brands in it could grow if consumers took them into consideration. Hyundai, the South Korean car manufacturer, tackled precisely this problem a few years ago by adopting a marketing campaign built on protecting consumers financially by allowing them to return their vehicles if they lost their jobs. This provocative message, tied to something very real for Americans, became a major factor in helping Hyundai break into the initial consideration set of many new consumers.

Invest in turning consumers into 'active advocates'

To look beyond funnel-inspired 'push' marketing, brand owners must invest in marketing communications that let them interact with consumers as they make an informed consideration about brands. Simple, dynamic tools that help consumers decide which products make sense for them are now essential elements of the online marketing experience and brand owners shouldn't abdicate responsibility for doing this to intermediaries or price comparison websites that proliferate on the internet.

Many Fortune 500 CEOs often feel overwhelmed by the explosive growth of social media especially after witnessing the damage done by WikiLeaks. They fret about how social media tools, when placed in the wrong hands, can be used to spread false rumours, damage brands and ruin corporate and personal reputations within hours. However, none of these concerns provide a compelling reason for brand owners to completely refrain from being actively engaged in social media activities.

Table 3.2   The seven Ps of the marketing mix

Seven Ps of the marketing mix	Explanation
Product	The offering made by the brand owner and how it meets the customer or client's needs. In a physical product context, such as a consumer good, it also refers to the packaging and labelling of the product. Within services, the product can be intangible, such as an insurance policy or a mortgage, which is recorded in a legal document provided to the customer.
Place	This is not just where the product or service is to be delivered to the customer but also the means of distributing that product to the customer and end-user.
Price	This is the cost of acquiring the product payable by the consumer and also the cost plus profits of the brand owner (seller).
Promotion	This is generally thought of under the umbrella description 'marketing communications' and describes how the product's benefits and features are conveyed to the consumer through a variety of online and offline channels.
Physical evidence	This emphasizes the tangible components of services where the consumer can't 'walk round and kick the tyres'.
Process	This emphasizes the importance of service delivery as part of the customer experience, for example, post-purchase of the product or service.
People	This emphasizes the importance of customer service within the consumer decision journey and also includes personal selling.

or it may be an emotional benefit in terms of how the product or service can make the consumer feel. For example, a raincoat is a functional product but can also be a high ticket fashion item if it's a designer brand like Prada, conferring emotional benefits on the consumer.

Embodied product. This consists of the physical product or delivered service that provides the expected benefit and consists of many factors such as features, capabilities, durability, design, packaging and brand name. Typically, these products can be desirable, such as an expensive Swiss-made watch like Omega, a Nikon camera or a pair of Nike trainers.

Augmented product. This consists of the embodied product plus all those other factors that are necessary to support the purchase and post-purchase activities. For example, with a new IT system this could include delivery of

Figure 3.3   Three levels of a product

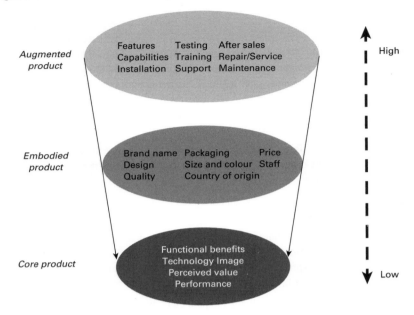

hardware products, installation, testing, training, regular software updates and IT support. When these product levels are brought together it's hoped that they will provide the consumer with a compelling reason to buy and to keep buying.

Each individual combination or bundle of benefits constitutes added value and serves to differentiate one sports car from another, one disposable camera from another. Marketing strategies need to be designed around the actual and augmented products.

The product life cycle (PLC). The basic concept of the product life cycle (PLC) can be seen in Figure 3.4, although it won't apply in every case to all products being brought to market. For example, a fashionable item of clothing can be adopted very quickly by the public, peak early in terms of sales and then decline just as fast.

The graph shows the various stages of the product life cycle, with the product development stage being the time taken to get the product to market. This is a critical point to manage, particularly in fast moving markets such as smart phones, laptops and computer games where changes within the technology can make a hot-selling product obsolete overnight.

The point at which sales start to drop off may be the time when the brand owner could consider a number of marketing strategies that could breathe new life into the product and continue to generate sales. These could include:

Figure 3.4 Typical product life cycle

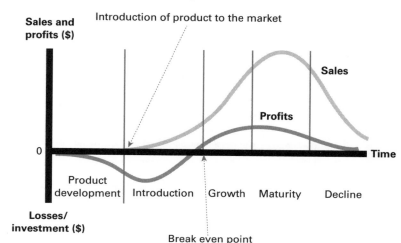

- product enhancements;
- new packaging;
- repositioning of the product with new customer segments;
- reaching new users via new distribution outlets; and
- promoting new uses of the product to meet a new customer want or requirement.

Table 3.3 provides an explanation of each phase in the product life cycle mapped against the marketing mix that has strategic sales and marketing implications for the brand owner.

Place

This part of the marketing mix refers to the ability of the brand owner to distribute the optimum amount of products and services at a time and location that will optimize sales within a market segment. This is particularly important within the retail sector, such as car sales and FMCG.

Zara and Samsung

For example, fashion high street manufacturer Inditex has seen its clothing sales leap by over 25 per cent because it adds new stock in its Zara retail stores twice a week, which helps to keep its stock up to date with the latest fashion trends. It achieves this fast flow replenishment by manufacturing over 40 per cent of its garments in Spain and Portugal which means it can deliver new products across Europe and the United States twice as fast as if it had to wait for delivery of stock that was manufactured in Asia where production costs are lower but delivery times are longer.

Table 3.3 Product life cycle and strategic marketing implications of each phase

Marketing Mix	Stage of the Product Life cycle (PLC)			
	Introduction	Growth	Maturity	Decline
Costs	Highest costs per customer	High costs per customer	Low costs per customer	Low costs per customer
Customers	'Innovators'	'Early adopters'	'Majority'	'Laggards'
Competitors	None or very few	Few	Maximum number of competitors	Declining number of competitors
Marketing strategy and objectives	High product awareness and trial – need to explain nature of innovation	Maximize market share before market segment attracts too many competitors	• Maximize profit while defending market share • Motivate customers to brand switching	• Reduce expenditure and cash cow the brand • Cost control is important
Product offering	Offer a basic product	Offer product extensions, services and warranty	• Product differentiation • Diversify brands and models	• Phase out weak items • Trying to create a re-launch of the product
Price	Premium price, but possibly not able to recoup investment at this point and so not profitable yet	Price to penetrate market segment – price may decline as competitors enter the market	Competitive pricing strategies where price is matched or is less than the competition – price under pressure from distributors	Price competition and price cutting may lead to losses
Place	Build exclusive or selective distribution pipeline for the new product	Build selective distribution	Build more intensive distribution	Become much more selective and phase out unprofitable outlets for the product
Promotion	• Build product awareness among early adopters and distributors • Use heavy sales promotion to entice trial	Build awareness and interest amongst large number of customer segments	• Stress brand differences and benefits • Increase promotion activities to encourage brand switching	Reduce to level required to retain only hard core customers; alternatively, re-launch product to new customer segments

In India, Samsung partnered with the Indian Farmers Fertiliser Cooperative to distribute its mobile handsets to rural customers who wouldn't step into a showroom to purchase a Samsung product. By adopting such a distribution strategy, Samsung achieved a massive uplift in sales of its handsets amongst this lucrative consumer group, achieving 90 per cent penetration in over 600,000 rural villages in India.

The experiences of Zara and Samsung are excellent examples of how the distribution activities of a brand owner can make a direct impact on the sales and marketing of its products and services.

Relying on intermediaries to distribute products, as the Samsung example illustrates, is an important part of the marketing mix as it often provides an essential link between producers and end consumers and, as can be seen in Table 3.4, this can achieve significant benefits for the brand owner.

Price

Pricing policy is one of the most important elements of the marketing mix. The other elements all lead to costs.

The only source of profit to the brand owner comes from sales, which in turn are dictated by pricing policy. In one sense, the outcome of excellent marketing is that a consumer buys the product or service being offered and this is profitable for the brand owner. At another level, the product is the tangible (physical) or intangible manifestation and fulfilment of the rational and emotional requirements of the consumer wrapped up in the body of a product or service that the consumer is prepared to pay for.

Although price is taken to be an established indicator of quality, such a concept is increasingly under pressure as brand owners in US and European markets feel the pressure from low-cost rivals in emerging economies. For example, Chinese consumer product companies HTC and Haier are giving Nokia and Whirlpool a run for their money by introducing feature-rich cell phones and kitchen appliances at low prices that greatly appeal to cost-conscious consumers. In other markets, such as India, where 300 million people earn less than US$1 a day, many brand owners have to contend with this frugal and demanding customer base where price is a critical part of the marketing mix.

Many of these consumers either go without or are very careful about what they buy. This forces brand owners to radically rethink price points and the offerings have to be extremely affordable, not just barely so. These consumers are also very value conscious. They may be low earners, but they also are high 'yearners'. Given their high aspirations, these consumers reject new offerings that don't deliver significantly higher value than existing offerings do. This puts a lot of pressure on brand owners to develop higher value offerings at a lower price.

By relying on a 'frugal' operating model, brand owners in emerging economies not only strive to reduce their own costs but also to pass value on to consumers, unlike the thinking of brand owners in developed economies

Table 3.4   Benefits of using intermediaries as a distribution channel

Type of channel intermediary	Description of function	Benefit	Description
Agent or broker	It acts as the principal intermediary between the brand owner and a buyer by bringing them together without taking ownership of the product or service. It has the legal authority (actual, usual and implied) to act on behalf of the manufacturer. For example, universities often use agents to recruit students from India and China.	Specialist service	It offers the brand owner an accessible way to reach a desired market or customer segment where the brand owner lacks physical presence in that market. In addition, where production of a product or component takes place a long distance from the brand owner, such as the maintenance and repairs of a ship, then an agent is essential.
Franchisee	It holds a contract to supply and market a product or service to the requirements of the franchise holder or brand owner. The franchise agreement will control the way in which all sales and marketing is to be carried out in accordance with a manual provided by the franchise holder or brand owner, as well as sourcing of products and how the product or service must be delivered. Cleaning companies such as Molly Maid, McDonald's and KFC are examples of successful franchise distribution businesses.	Cost-effective and profitable	This is a successful and scalable business model for the brand owner as the franchisee will pay for a franchise and in some cases this will be 'business in a box' where everything is made really easy for the franchisee to operate a business using the brand and trademark of the brand owner. The brand owner is left to focus on marketing the brand through advertising and other means and receives a licence payment on a regular basis for delivering the support to the franchisee.

Table 3.4 *continued*

Type of channel intermediary	Description of function	Benefit	Description
Official distributor	It acts as a dealer and distributes the product or service. It offers value through services associated with selling inventory, credit and after-sales service. This arrangement is often used in B2B markets and can also be found dealing directly with B2C segments such as car distributors.	Knowledge of the products and services	Might offer specialist services, such as after-sales, maintenance, installation or training services to increase the effective use of the product. These services are best offered and performed by those closest to the purchaser or user of the product.
Wholesaler	It stocks goods and precedes retail distribution. It takes possession of the goods and legal title passes to it in those products.	Improved efficiency	Brand owners often manufacture a small range of products in large quantities whereas consumers buy a wide range of products in small quantities. A wholesaler improves efficiencies in the delivery channel by breaking down large deliveries from the brand owner into single units and sorting these into a range of goods available for retailers.
Retailer	It sells directly to consumers and will often purchase directly from wholesalers and manufacturers, such as Zara and Wal-Mart.	Accessibility and time to market	Products are available immediately from the intermediary's stock, enabling ownership to pass to the consumer within the shortest space of time.

who won't think of doing the same, who typically focus their marketing efforts in wowing consumers with the latest product features and technologies. This isn't always the most successful marketing strategy to follow, particularly when marketing products and services in developing markets. Instead, successful brand owners often pursue functionally minimalist solutions that offer superior value to their customers – often transforming their lives in the process. In this context, price needs to reflect getting more value for less cost by offering consumers quality products and services at highly affordable prices.

As pricing is part of the marketing mix, pricing decisions must be integrated with the other elements given that pricing policy can be changed relatively rapidly. The danger of changing prices quickly in response to market conditions is that brand owners may be tempted to resort to pricing action as a 'quick fix' instead of making changes in other areas of the marketing mix. 'It's important that management realizes that constant fine-tuning of prices in overseas markets should be avoided and that many problems aren't best addressed by pricing action,' advises Professor Svend Hollensen, associate professor of international marketing at the University of Southern Denmark.

Research into how consumers will respond to a given price strategy shows that they're influenced by nine factors:

1 distinctiveness of the product or service;
2 greater perceived quality of the product or service;
3 less awareness of substitute products and services on the market;
4 difficulty in making comparisons in the quality of the product or service being offered;
5 price of product or service represents a small percentage of the total expenditure of the consumer's budget;
6 perceived benefit for the customer increases;
7 the product or service is used in association with a product or service previously bought, so that components and replacements are usually priced at a premium;
8 costs are shared with other consumers/third parties, which adds to the affordability of the purchase; and
9 the product or service can't be stored for later use.

Pricing policies. In addition to the pricing factors that influence the consumer's propensity to purchase, the brand owner also has to balance its needs with what the market will bear and must take account of its competitors' pricing policies as well. In reality, the brand owner's pricing policy is also a trade-off with factors associated with competition within its market segment and includes:

- How much competitors charge for similar products or services.
- Factors associated with cost of production of the product or service.
- The cost of individual components that make up the product or service.
- Factors associated with demand for the product or service.
- The quantities that the brand owner will sell of the product or service and at what price.
- Factors associated with value.
- Which components of the product/service consumers value and how much are they prepared to pay for them.

The pricing policy the brand owner will seek to adopt in the first instance may need to be reviewed at a later stage if sales don't meet expectations or targets.

The following are some of the typical pricing policies adopted by brand owners in business to consumer (B2C) and business to business (B2B) customer segments.

Pricing policies (B2C) *Market pricing.* If similar products exist in a market segment, then the brand owner may fix the price according to the prevailing market price.

List pricing. This is a relatively unsophisticated approach to pricing where a single price is set for a product or service. For example, a travel company may charge a list price for a two-week package holiday that includes air travel, hotel accommodation and half or full board plus transfers to and from the airport on both legs of the holiday.

Penetration pricing. This isn't the same as a loss leader pricing (below) but this pricing policy is used to stimulate market growth and market share by deliberately offering products at low prices. The approach requires mass markets, price sensitive customers and a reduction in unit costs through economies of scale. The basic assumption that lower prices will increase sales will fail if other competitors follow suit, for example in a petrol price war at the pumps.

In contrast, Japanese motorbike manufacturer Honda used penetration pricing intensively to gain a foothold in the US superbike market by under-cutting Harley Davidson and other more established US brands.

Loss leader pricing. This is a form of marketing that uses price to 'hook' consumers to enter the retail environment, typically a supermarket, with juicy offers on staple products like bread, milk, beer, baked beans, or toilet paper that consumers tend to buy as a repeat purchase and would be tempted with the opportunity to bag a bargain. The price is usually set at a lower level than the actual cost of production.

A brand owner will hope to recoup the loss by enticing the consumer to spend more money on other less price-sensitive items that it has increased in price. Alternatively, the brand owner may absorb the loss as a short-term promotional cost on the basis that it brings in more customers and boosts sales on more profitable product lines.

Promotional pricing. This is a popular way of creating a spike in sales where the brand owner may be linked to a specific time-bound event, such as sponsorship of a major sport or music event and during that period offers a special promotional price for its goods and services.

Alternatively, the special promotional period could be designed to capture interest and raise awareness without any other strings attached. Such a pricing approach often includes loss leaders, sales discounts, cash rebates, low interest financing (such as 0 per cent finance on a new car) and other price-based promotional incentives.

Segmentation pricing. Sometimes referred to as price discrimination – varying prices are set for different customer segments. For example, Unilever will offer the premium Ben & Jerry's ice-cream brand at a high price point within the retail area of a multiplex cinema and a low price point but higher volume ice-cream product in a supermarket.

Customer-centric pricing. This is a successful strategy where brand owners can leverage the interest of certain specific customer segments by bundling products that will appeal to them and offering them at a special price. This can work extremely well in clothing, fashion accessories, stationery and food and drink where multiple purchases can be very appealing as well as help to drive profits. It can also work well in professional services. (For further discussion on cross-selling and other techniques, see Guru in a Bottle®, *Art of Influencing and Selling.*)

Pricing policies (B2B). The major difference between B2B and B2C is that the business buyer and seller are both trying to make the best commercial decision for their respective organizations, where the outcome is a win-win for both parties.

Relationship pricing. This is pricing based on the customer or client's needs and where the seller is seeking a long-term relationship rather than simply making a quick turn on the transaction. This may involve offering favourable financial or credit terms, longer periods for payment, discounts and other incentives. The difficulty with such an approach is that it relies on a high degree of trust and commitment between the parties, which carries with it an opportunity cost for the seller should this not be reciprocated by the buyer.

Geographical pricing. This is pricing that takes account of prevailing market conditions in different countries where price points may be different. For example, prescription drugs are sold at various prices in different countries at levels set by governments rather than the brand owner.

Discount pricing. This is where a customer or client is prepared to commit to either buying a large volume of goods or services now or in the future, or paying for it within a specified time period. With such a commitment, the brand owner may decide to reduce the price.

Economic value to the customer (EVC) pricing. The brand owner prices the product or service for the customer or client on the basis of not just the acquisition cost but also the ongoing maintenance and other ancillary costs, usually benchmarked against other suppliers in the market.

Negotiated pricing. This tends to happen when the sale involves a large and complex project and the brand owner is involved in a form of 'consultative selling' to the client.

Transfer pricing. This tends to take place within very large organizations where there is a cross charge levied on a single business unit (SBU) for the use of intellectual property (IP) rights or other assets that it doesn't control but needs for the business.

Promotion

Most textbooks speak about the four elements of marketing communications: a sender, a message, a communication channel and a receiver (audience). This is flawed because it only describes the transmit mode of communication and, as discussed in Chapter 2, effective marketing is about transmit and receive modes and increasingly it's about the latter rather than the former. It also makes good business sense. Listening to customers and clients is likely to be a more profitable exercise.

The principal channels of marketing communication are a mixture of transmit and receive channels (see Figure 3.5). A successful marketing programme is a mix of one- and two-way communication channels (see Table 3.5).

Figure 3.5 Transmit and receive channels of communication

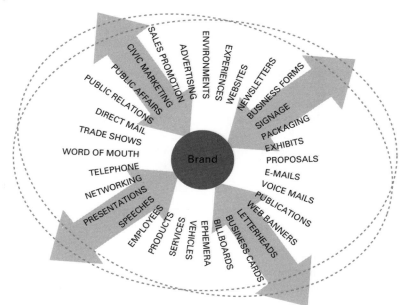

Table 3.5 Media channels segmented by one- and two-way communication

Channels used in the marketing mix		One-way communication	Two-way communication
Advertising	Newspapers	✓	
	Magazines	✓	
	Journals	✓	
	Directories	✓	
	TV	✓	
	Radio	✓	
	Cinema	✓	
	Outdoor	✓	✓
	Signs	✓	
	Ambient media	✓	
	Posters	✓	✓
	Web		✓
	Mobile		✓
	Product placement	✓	
Public Relations	Corporate image	✓	
	Media relations	✓	✓
	Public Affairs	✓	✓
	Annual Reports	✓	
	Events		✓
	Lobbying		✓
	Marketing		✓
	Community engagement		✓
	Corporate Social Responsibility		✓
	Corporate hospitality		✓
Direct Marketing	Direct mail	✓	✓
	Database marketing	✓	✓
	E-marketing	✓	✓
	M-marketing	✓	✓
	Telemarketing	✓	✓
	Viral marketing		✓
	Social networking		✓
Sales Promotion	Competitions		✓
	Prizes	✓	✓
	Incentives	✓	✓
	Rebates and price discounts	✓	✓
	Samples		✓

is an excellent way to complement print and broadcast media activities in the marketing mix. (For a more detailed discussion on the use of signs, posters and ambient media, see Chapter 5.)

Public relations. PR is one of the most cost-effective techniques in the marketing mix; the primary purpose is the management of the reputation of the brand owner, its products and services. Increasingly, the skill of PR is to manage communications on the web as well as offline channels and to engage customer and client segments in a two-way dialogue. (For a detailed discussion on best practice in this area, see Chapter 7.)

Sales promotion. Sales promotions are growing in importance; they offer a direct incentive to buy a product or service and can be targeted at consumers, distributors, agents and a sales force. Key forms of sales promotions include sampling, coupons, deals, premiums, competitions, sweepstakes and trade discounts. (For a detailed discussion on the regulations for using sales and prize promotions, refer to Guru in a Bottle®, *Essential Law for Marketers*, 2nd edition.)

In-store. The two main forms of in-store media are point of sales (POS) and packaging.

Retailers and manufacturers have a vested interest in getting consumers to purchase more products and both these methods are used to capture the attention of shoppers and stimulate further sales. Typical POS techniques include window displays, floor and wall racks, display merchandise, posters, information cards, counter displays and displays at the check-out. (For a detailed discussion on effective approaches to prospective customers and clients, refer to Guru in a Bottle®, *Art of Influencing and Selling.*)

Licensed merchandise. A rapidly growing area of promotional activity is licensed merchandise that allows fans and consumers to literally consume the brand through a variety of products and services. This is particularly a key part of the promotion in any major sponsorship arrangement. (For a detailed discussion on the use of intellectual property rights, refer to Guru in a Bottle®, *Essential Law for Marketers*, 2nd edition.)

Direct marketing. The primary purpose of direct marketing (DM) is to influence behaviour and drive a response from the recipient. This is a highly targeted and personalized communication technique that works well online and offline and, when done well, has a better response rate than other forms of communications in the marketing mix. The brand owner will use DM to create and sustain personal contact outside the intervention of an intermediary. (For a more detailed discussion on the use of DM, see Chapter 6.)

Personal selling. This involves interpersonal communication through which information is provided, positive feelings are developed and purchasing behaviour stimulated. Within a personal selling context, the sales professional is increasingly seen as an expert on the details of the sale, for example a qualified optometrist that sells high-end spectacle frames and glasses. This is one of the most powerful channels within the marketing mix as it can help to build trust and confidence extremely quickly as well as engender a high degree of loyalty over a long period of time. (For a detailed discussion on effective sales approaches to prospective customers and clients, refer to Guru in a Bottle®, *Art of Influencing and Selling*.)

Physical evidence

This part of the marketing mix emphasizes the importance of tangible components of services. For example, students applying from outside of the country in which they wish to study will request materials such as a prospectus and brochure of the academic or professional institution to help in deciding whether they wish to apply.

Process

This part of the marketing mix emphasizes the importance of the service delivery. For example, when processes are standardized, such as FedEx or Hertz, it's easier to manage customer expectations. The delivery of the product and service is deliberately standardized as that's what's expected from its desired customer and client base.

People

This part of the marketing mix emphasizes the importance of customer service personnel rather than just sales professionals. For example, this is particularly important within the travel sector, where the internet has allowed consumers to by-pass the traditional travel agent or 'bucket shop' in search of a cheap deal.

Travel agents now are highly specialized, demonstrate a deep understanding of a particular customer segment and have expertise in a range of travel, accommodation, leisure, sporting and culinary options for the discerning traveller. As Chris Goossens, global customer experience director with logistics and transport group TNT, explains:

As we saw the first signs of the recession, what we all agreed on was that in a growth scenario you focus both on retention and on bringing in new business, either through acquisition or through organic growth. But in times of a recession, what's absolutely paramount is to focus even more on your existing customers, to make sure they don't defect. So the recession actually confirmed and reinforced our commitment to customer experience as our differentiation strategy.

Budget considerations

The process for setting marketing budgets begins at the corporate level and generally filters down so that the marketing department then prioritizes spending at a campaign level. The corporate executives deliver the budget with the expectation of achieving revenue and profit goals for the enterprise.

Typically, the budgeting process is based on benchmarks such as the previous year's budget or a standard percentage of sales as a starting point. Financial projections are then run to determine how funds should be adjusted from previous benchmarks.

It's preferable to use last year's actual results as a basis for comparison. Some commentators argue that a prediction of future performance based on the assumption that the business will operate in the same way as it's done in the past is a reasonable approach to adopt, often referred to as the 'baseline forecast'. Very often, brand owners start with the presumption that budgets will be similar to the previous year; although this should be kept under continuous review to account for changing circumstances within the business.

A marketing budget that's derived from a promotional strategy must have adequate resources allocated to meet the performance objectives of the strategic marketing plan. (For guidance in writing a marketing plan, see Chapter 2.)

Typically, an estimate of market and profit performance is made for each year of a three-year strategic market planning horizon. There are three ways of building a marketing budget that's based on a specific strategic marketing plan:

1 *Top down budget.* A new marketing budget based on projected sales objectives is determined and is based on past marketing expenses as a percentage of sales.

2 *Customer mix budget.* The cost of customer acquisition and retention and the combination of new and retained customers are used to derive a new marketing budget.

3 *Bottom-up budget.* Each element of the marketing plan is budgeted for.

An example of a marketing budget based on the customer mix approach can be seen in Table 3.8.

Table 3.8 Marketing budget template

Marketing Expenditure	Q1			Q2			Q3			Q4			TOTAL		
	US$ Budgeted	US$ Actual	Chg	US$ Budgeted	US$ Actual	Chg	US$ Budgeted	US$ Actual	Chg	US$ Budgeted	US$ Actual	Chg	US$ Budgeted	US$ Actual	Chg
ADVERTISING															
Newspapers															
Magazines															
Journals															
Directories															
TV															
Radio															
Cinema															
Outdoor															
Signs															
Ambient media															
Posters															
Web															
Mobile															
Product placement															
ADVERTISING SUB-TOTAL															

PUBLIC RELATIONS												
Corporate image												
Media relations												
Public Affairs												
Annual Reports												
Events												
Lobbying												
Marketing												
Community engagement												
Corporate Social Responsibility												
Corporate hospitality												
PUBLIC RELATIONS SUB-TOTAL												

Table 3.8 continued

Marketing Expenditure	Q1 US$ Budgeted	Q1 US$ Actual	Q1 Chg	Q2 US$ Budgeted	Q2 US$ Actual	Q2 Chg	Q3 US$ Budgeted	Q3 US$ Actual	Q3 Chg	Q4 US$ Budgeted	Q4 US$ Actual	Q4 Chg	TOTAL US$ Budgeted	TOTAL US$ Actual	TOTAL Chg
DIRECT MARKETING															
Direct mail															
Database marketing															
E-marketing															
M-marketing															
Telemarketing															
Viral marketing															
Social networking															
DIRECT MARKETING SUB-TOTAL															

SALES PROMOTION															
Competitions															
Prizes															
Incentives															
Rebates and price discounts															
Samples															
Coupons															
Gifts															
Catalogues and brochures															
Licensing and merchandising															
SALES PROMOTION SUB-TOTAL															
PERSONAL SELLING															
Sales presentations															
Trade fairs and exhibitions															
Face to face															
PERSONAL SELLING SUB-TOTAL															

Table 3.8 *continued*

Marketing Expenditure	Q1			Q2			Q3			Q4			TOTAL		
	US$ Budgeted	US$ Actual	Chg	US$ Budgeted	US$ Actual	Chg	US$ Budgeted	US$ Actual	Chg	US$ Budgeted	US$ Actual	Chg	US$ Budgeted	US$ Actual	Chg
SALES FORCE															
Motivation programmes															
Recruitment															
Training															
Compensation															
Benefits															
Professional memberships															
Subscriptions															
Communications															
Sales tools/supplies															
SALES FORCE SUB-TOTAL															

MARKETING RESEARCH											
Computing											
Salary											
Benefits											
Supplies											
Communications											
Travel											
Tools (software)											
MARKETING RESEARCH SUB-TOTAL											
OTHER											
Item 1											
Item 2											
Item 3											
OTHER SUB-TOTAL											

Table 3.8 *continued*

Marketing Expenditure	Q1			Q2			Q3			Q4			TOTAL		
	US$ Budgeted	US$ Actual	Chg	US$ Budgeted	US$ Actual	Chg	US$ Budgeted	US$ Actual	Chg	US$ Budgeted	US$ Actual	Chg	US$ Budgeted	US$ Actual	Chg
CUSTOMER/CLIENT SEGMENT															
Segment A															
Segment B															
Segment C															
Segment D															
Segment E															
CUSTOMER SEGMENT SUB-TOTAL															
TOTAL MARKETING BUDGET															

Marketing measurement

Microsoft co-founder Bill Gates is often quoted as saying: 'If you can't measure it, you can't manage it' and of course he was absolutely right.

Key principles

When considering how to go about measuring the value of marketing communications, there are several key principles that are worth bearing in mind:

- Develop metrics and scorecards to measure what matters most to deliver business performance.
- Allocate marketing budgets and capital investments on the basis of what will deliver the best short- and long-term results.
- Seek to capture the value of brands, customer and client relationships and innovation.
- Marketing metrics should attempt to connect people and teams with activities and resources.
- Identify where and how to improve marketing performance as well as the quick wins and strategic marketing priorities.
- Attempt to capture the real value of marketing in boardroom reporting and the annual report.

All of the above are one way or another concerned with improvements to the bottom line. But there are also non-financial metrics that should be considered as part of the marketing measurement exercise and these include:

- Measuring the complete customer experience, not just customer satisfaction.
- Regularly gathering feedback from the front line of the organization on how the customer experience can be improved.
- Focusing on employee and customer satisfaction, not just the bottom line.
- Measuring the upstream indicators that drive results.

Successful brand owners may measure a host of things but fundamentally they focus on a few, and these tend to be the ones that are most closely aligned with their vision and purpose.

In addition to the financial metrics, many leading brand owners also factor in non-financial metrics into the mix. For example, O2 measures 'fandom' – fans of the brand, which is an extreme form of customer advocacy. In contrast, Burberry measures the 'Burberry experience' by using mystery shoppers across all its stores, and TNT Express measures the retention of its brand champions. However, none of these measures are meaningful unless they lead to successful financial outcomes such as incremental sales and sustainable profits.

A balanced scorecard approach will look at what the brand owner wants customers and clients to see, what employees must do to excel in that endeavour and how the organization can continue to learn and grow, as well as its financial performance.

A marketing balanced scorecard

On the basis of the above, a marketing balanced score may include the elements listed in Table 3.9.

Table 3.9 Marketing balanced scorecard

Marketing metric	Description
Marketing spend to marketing activities	How much is spent on marketing communications (above and below the line).
Marketing activities to purchase drivers	How marketing communications address the priorities of customer and client segments, for example, quality, functionality, price and image.
Marketing activities to customer attitudes	How marketing communications drive increased brand preference and perceived value.
Customer attitudes to purchase behaviour	How perceived value translates into price premium for the brand owner's products and multi-purchases.
Sales results to financial results	How sales and margins translate into operating profits and growth.
Financial results to shareholder value	How a brand owner's profits and growth translates into future cash flows and business confidence.

A successful marketing communications programme should therefore impact:

● *customer engagement:* customer awareness, customer preference, customer affinity;
● *market impact:* market share, customer retention, channel penetration;
● *marketing improvement:* product innovation, brand building, market development; and
● *financial performance:* sales revenue, profitability and growth.

The marketing evaluation framework

The evaluation framework (see Table 3.10) looks at three distinct performance areas for the marketing programme: brand value, commercial value and customer and client relationships. Each area has a broad definition of possible objectives and some suggested ways of measuring performance against them.

			Measure
		✓	Number of qualified sales leads gained via marketing-associated channels versus other marketing initiatives
Increase sales	Increase product or service sales, either for new product(s)/service(s) or to boost established product/service lines	✓	New brands: sales data, but with limited scope to differentiate between marketing-related sales and sales related to other marketing initiatives
		✓	Established brands: sales data compared to previous figures and trends, to establish impact
		✓	Stated purchasing among those exposed/not exposed to the marketing programme
		✓	Purchase panel information on those exposed versus those not exposed
		✓	Increased requests for product(s) received (especially if specifically coded against the marketing programme)
		✓	Increased footfall, especially of those customer segments presenting a marketing-related/coded leaflet/flier
		✓	Sales of product(s) based on a marketing-related offer
Increase market share	Increase/maintain market share	✓	Coupon redemption patterns – those distributed in marketing environment versus non-marketing environment
		✓	Market place analysis – growth, trends, dynamics, competitors
		✓	Market penetration – number of customers versus potential total

Table 3.10 *continued*

**Marketing measurement methodologies
Part 2: Commercial Objectives**

Commercial objective	Marketing objective	Research type: qualitative	Research type: quantitative	Other methods	Outline
				✓	Customer 'quality': level of customer scores against key 'quality' parameters (comparing those introduced via marketing to those introduced via other channels)
				✓	Stated share of wallet information (exposed versus not-exposed to the marketing programme)
			✓	✓	Market share data
				✓	Additional shelf space/other marketing exposure negotiated to display product(s) with marketing-related promotions
Sales promotion platform	Increase sales of related product(s) over the promotional period		✓	✓	Response to marketing-related sales promotion compared to other promotional platforms
					Stated preference for marketing-related promotions versus others
				✓	Response to marketing-related promotions versus others
Database building	Capture contact details and opt-ins for future marketing communications			✓	Number of records captured through marketing-related sources (such as web links, postcards, competitions, promotions and corporate hospitality) versus other sources
				✓	'Quality' of brand owner's database compared with other list sources measured by level of gone-aways/returned e-mails

Loyalty programme enhancement	Provide merchandise and activities to enhance customer loyalty programmes ✓	• Number of marketing-related rewards redeemed as a percentage of total redemptions, benchmarked against pre-marketing rewards ✓ • Stated interest in spending towards acquiring marketing-related rewards versus other rewards offered by the marketing programme • Redemption rates of similar items, for example, a marketing-related 'goodie' bag versus a similar non-marketing related 'goodie' bag ✓
Distribution and supply chain incentives	Incentivize desired behaviour up and down-stream, for example, improved credit terms and increased shelf space ✓	• Desired behaviour achieved post-marketing related engagement, based on benchmarks agreed with finance/sales/purchasing departments ✓ • Feedback on impact of the marketing engagement on influencing change of behaviour among supply chain elements
Direct sales opportunities	Secure a new sales channel directly associated with the marketing programme, such as exclusive new product(s) at a marketing event or selected retail outlets	• Sales revenue/profit generated by marketing-related sales channels ✓ • Sales revenue/profit generated by bespoke product(s) made for customer segments/marketing event (such as a sponsorship event) ✓
Innovation catalyst	Shorten new product development cycle and/or increase number of developments made	• Number of marketing-related product developments achieved ✓ • Relative speed or creativity of marketing-related NPD teams or previously accepted norms in achieving both incremental and breakthrough innovations ✓

Table 3.10 *continued*

**Marketing measurement methodologies
Part 2: Commercial Objectives**

Commercial objective	Marketing objective	Research type: qualitative	Research type: quantitative	Other methods	Outline
Tax benefits	Benefit from tax advantages where these exist			✓	• Savings accrued
Advertising alternative	Gain brand exposure more cost effectively than by purchasing advertising space				• Media cost comparison between cost of purchasing marketing rights (such as sponsorship) and estimated costs of advertising to gain equivalent level of brand exposure
			✓		• Level of brand awareness generated
			✓		• Level of brand awareness and awareness of associated brand attributes among key customer and client segments
					• Extent to which these were generated by individual marketing channels
Defensive marketing tactics	Prevent competitor brands from achieving same level of leverage, for example, product placement on a TV show or sponsorship of a sports event			✓	• Breadth of category and extent of exclusivity clause in marketing agreement, as evidenced by degree of absence of competitor brands
				✓	• Competitor response
				✓	• Market share of those brand(s) benefiting from such marketing activities compared with those brands that don't have such marketing support

			✓
Competitive differentiation (where relevant)	In a sponsorship programme, the alignment with a rights holder to secure a unique and defendable competitive advantage	• Revenues generated for products/services through the rights holder's network • Perceptions of products/services within the brand owner's competitive set between those customer/client segments exposed to the sponsorship versus those customers/client segments not exposed	✓
'Licence to operate'	Provide a corporate social responsibility (CSR) platform that meets local 'investment' requirements and as a result secures the brand owner a 'licence to operate'	• Number of key stakeholders engaged via the corporate social responsibility (CSR) programme	✓
New market entry	Invest in a marketing platform that portrays the right social, political, cultural and sporting approach to facilitate entry into a new market	• Number of new markets entered where the marketing programme is active	✓
Employee development	Use the marketing programme as a source of job-related training opportunities	• Level of skill among those utilizing marketing-related training versus employees using traditional training platforms to develop similar skill sets	✓

Table 3.10 *continued*

Marketing measurement methodologies
Part 3: Building Relationships

Relationship objective	Marketing objective	Research type: qualitative	Research type: quantitative	Other methods	Outline
Co-sponsor alliances (where appropriate)	In the context of sponsorship, create value through interaction with other sponsors involved with the same rights holder			✓ ✓	• Number of projects undertaken as a result of being a co-sponsor • Value of projects undertaken as a co-sponsor
Employee engagement	Improve productivity, reduce turnover, increase employee satisfaction, increase integration of the marketing communications team within the organization as a whole	✓ ✓	✓ ✓	✓ ✓	• Levels of marketing awareness and understanding of rationale for the marketing programme via internal questionnaire • Percentage take-up of marketing-related programmes • Detailed questioning on marketing communications and the role it plays in retention of customers/clients, driving preference, consideration and sales among different employee groups • Enhanced understanding of how the marketing programme affects different groups and of what could be done to increase the benefits accruable • Productivity, quality output levels between those motivated by the marketing and those not motivated by the marketing

Potential employee perceptions	Persuade pool of potential employees of brand owner's leadership as an employer		
	Regular tracking of key employee metrics comparing those highly engaged with the marketing programme versus those less/not engaged, including employee turnover	✓	
	Number of applicants responding to a job advertisement that includes marketing-related imagery/messages versus non-marketing-related advertisement	✓	✓
	Stated interest in being employed by the brand owner compared with competitors cross-referenced against awareness of the marketing programme		
	Number of positive mentions of marketing in relevant trade press, including marketing-related awards won	✓	✓
	Number of new hires surveyed who admit an attraction to the brand owner as a result of a specific marketing programme		
	Number of additional high-quality speculative approaches – especially those who mention the marketing and impact on recruitment agency costs	✓	

To use the framework effectively, you must first outline three to five (max) key objectives. You can then locate these within the framework and review the recommended measurement methodologies before deciding which of them are most appropriate for your specific requirements. The list of measurement methodologies isn't exhaustive but should cover most mainstream marketing objectives.

Some methodologies that can apply to a range of objectives may only feature once, in the interests of reducing repetition. It's therefore well worth reviewing all the suggested methodologies to see if there's a technique under an 'irrelevant' objective that might in fact be a relevant measurement methodology in a specific circumstance.

References

Books and articles

Baines, P, Fill, C and Page, K (2011) *Marketing*, Oxford University Press
Gladwell, M (2010) *The Tipping Point*, Little, Brown and Company
Kolah, A (2013) Guru in a Bottle, *Essential Law for Marketers*, 2nd edition, Kogan Page
Kolah, A (2013) Guru in a Bottle, *The Art of Influencing and Selling*, Kogan Page
Hollensen, S (2011) *Global Marketing*, FT Prentice Hall
Lenskold, J (2003) *Marketing ROI*, American Marketing Association
McKinsey Quarterly (2009) 'The consumer decision journey'
McKinsey Quarterly (2010) 'Beyond paid media'
Meerman Scott, D (2010) *The New Rules of Marketing & PR*, Wiley
Prabhu, J, Radjou, N and Ahuja, S (2012) *Jugaad Innovation*, Jossey-Bass
Smith, S and Milligan, A (2011) *Bold*, Kogan Page
Surowiecki, J (2007) *The Wisdom of Crowds*, Abacus

Websites

Affinnova is a new media tool used by Bayer, Chase, Kraft Foods, Mars, Johnson & Johnson, Nestle, Pepsico, P&G, Unilever and Wal-Mart: http://www.affinnova.com (accessed 29 April 2012)
Brand Republic: http://www.brandrepublic.com (accessed 29 April 2012)
Tremor is a word-of-mouth software developed by P&G that combines wide-ranging marketing expertise with key techniques from cognitive science: http://tremor.com (accessed 29 April 2012)
Vocalpoint is an online community of 600,000 socially engaged mothers who P&G uses as a sounding board for new product ideas: http://www.vocalpoint.com (accessed 29 April 2012)
World Advertising Research Council: http://www.warc.com (accessed 26 April 2012)

It's not just about words

Brochures, press ads and print copy

Introduction

Let's start by asking two simple questions: Do customers or clients desire a relationship with your organization? Who is it that they would have the relationship with – the organization, the brand, the product or the person?

According to UK marketing guru Peter Fisk, marketers need to focus on understanding what makes customers tick rather than becoming obsessed with trying to build a relationship with them. Tongue in cheek, he says:

> It would be foolish to kid ourselves that customers want relationships with a business in a way they would a friend or a lover. Not only this, but do companies really want relationships with customers, or to be honest, aren't they more interested in selling, and then being there for the repeat sell? Are they really after a relationship, or just sex?

After all, customers and clients are increasingly promiscuous when it comes to choosing who they want to do business with and can be influenced in changing supplier with increasing ease.

In the current economic environment, like it or not, price is a key driver, which tends to suggest that many commercial relationships entered into today are transactional rather than relational. And that's a big challenge for marketers. That may be a provocative viewpoint if you believe in forming a relationship with your customer or client, but Peter Fisk makes an important point.

What's the organization trying to achieve through its marketing and communications? What objectives can be satisfied through marketing that will impact the bottom line?

In Chapter 1 we discussed how to determine the attractiveness of particular market and customer segments, and in Chapter 2 we developed this thinking further with a discussion on the structure of the marketing strategy and plan. Ultimately, the tactics of marketing, such as brochures, press ads and print must fulfil strategic marketing objectives. Otherwise, they are unlikely to be successful and turn out to be a waste of time and money.

And yet many companies and organizations appear to be sleepwalking when it comes to doing some of the basics well. For example, have you ever stopped to think why airline in-flight magazines don't sell airline tickets? These in-flight glossy magazines generate their own income streams so as a marketing channel they are really brilliant as they are self-liquidating, putting them into a class of their own. In fact, they do a great job of selling everything under the sun – from cars to perfumery – but they don't sell more airline tickets. Doh!

Given that the airlines quite literally have a captive audience and for some trips this could be for a significant period of time, why haven't they woken up to the possibilities of marketing more flights to their existing customers rather than constantly chasing new ones to fill their seats? Sergio Zyman, the former chief marketing officer of Coca-Cola, adds:

> *Advertising as we know it is dead. Advertising isn't an art form. It's about selling more stuff more often to more people for more money. Success is the result of a scientific, disciplined process and absolutely every single dollar must generate a return. If you don't keep giving customers reasons to buy from you, they won't. Awareness is absolutely worthless unless it leads to sales.*

And that's coming from one of the most hardcore marketers who has been in control of one of the biggest budgets in advertising history.

Arguably, the 1960s were the golden age of Madison Avenue where the 60-second spot could sell breakfast cereal to a four-year-old and it could also sell that child the alphabet. After all, Jim Henson, one of the founders of the iconic TV show 'Sesame Street' was an ad man before he became a TV producer. Perhaps we are giving the game away when we tell you that lovable 'Big Bird' was really a variant of a seven-foot dragon created for Chinese convenience food brand La Choy, and the 'Cookie Monster' started life as the pitch-man for potato chips brand Frito-Lay.

Sesame Street was a rapid-fire stream of 60 second content that entertained, informed and engaged children up to the age of 10. But this 60-second approach was turned on its head by psychologists who found that three- and four-year-olds were able to follow more complicated plots because of the power of storytelling. US psychologist Jerome Bruner, one of the early pioneers of modern child psychology, observed:

> *They are not able to bring theories that organize things in terms of cause and effect and relationships, so they turn things into stories, and when they try to make sense of their life they use the storied version of their experience as the basis for further reflection. If they don't catch something in a narrative structure, it doesn't get remembered very well, and it doesn't seem to be accessible for further kinds of mulling over.*

Smash

In the early 1970s, packaged goods manufacturers were the biggest spenders on advertising in the UK and tended to make dreary advertising based on pseudo-scientific market research. However, a few ad land creative types such as John Webster of hot-shop Boase Massimi Pollitt (BMP) quickly realized that housewives were getting bored stiff with ads featuring other housewives.

John Webster wrote a script about a group of tin-headed Martians on board their spacecraft. 'On you last trip did you discover what earth people eat?' asked their leader. 'They eat many of these,' responded one of his lieutenants, holding up a potato between his robotic pincers. 'They peel them with their metal knives. They boil them for 20 of their minutes, then they smash them to pieces!' he explained. 'They clearly are a most primitive people!' observed the leader while his crew descended into hysterics.

John Webster hired the American Bob Brooks to direct the commercial. He recalls:

> *I arrived on set and saw these little tin robots and I worked out that I wanted to shoot them like real actors. I wanted them to talk and react to one another like humans would. So I decided to imagine that they were real people just wearing tin heads.*

A four-foot high stage had been built so that a team of puppeteers could sit below manipulating the Martians. Bob Brooks, however, refused to acknowledge the existence of the men sitting below. 'We started to shoot the commercial and there was this one f**** robot who kept doing the wrong thing. So I went and started shouting at the damn thing knowing full well that the guy underneath would be getting the message.' The Smash Martians were filmed as if they were human, shot in full focus and at interesting angles. The TV commercial's most popular moment occurred by mistake in the closing minutes of filming. 'On the final take, as they were all supposed to be laughing, one of these f**** Martians fell over sideways. It was an accident but when it came to the edit, I realized it looked pretty funny. As if he was falling over laughing. So I left it in.'

The behaviour of the Martians proved infectious with audiences. Brand owner Cadbury's had only planned the commercial as a one-off but ended up running the 'For Mash, Get Smash' campaign for over a decade. In 2005, a national poll in the UK to celebrate 50 years of commercial TV advertising saw Smash voted the most popular advertising campaign of all time. And advertising has never looked back since.

This chapter explores the power of storytelling and its significance in brochures, press ads and print. We've deliberately avoided getting bogged down in finding formulaic recipes because great marketing is about being different rather than 'marketing by numbers'. If you don't believe us, ask Bob Brooks.

Evidenced-based marketing

What differentiates 'bog standard' marketing and high impact marketing? How can you tell the difference?

It takes a special marketing person to be able to create a point of differentiation within market segments where there's a high degree of homogenization, such as shoes, cars, whisky, electronic and mobile devices, white and brown goods. In fact, it's a major challenge for practically all marketers and particularly those who work in service industries such as banks, insurance, or law firms. Or for that matter in engineering, a utility company, a government department, a charity or NGO. Getting sufficient cut-through and making sure that your messages reach the intended audience and customer segment aren't that straightforward, as we discuss later.

A key strategy that's highly effective is to play the role of detective and search high and low for evidence. Think Universal's 'Crime Scene Investigation' (CSI) show on TV. Without doubt, an evidence-based approach, coupled with a high degree of creative thinking is a powerful combination in helping to create high impact marketing and will separate your brochures, press ads and print copy from those of your competitors.

In other words, leaving aside the creative quotient for the moment, if the marketing you're producing has some form of quantitative value to it – it includes measurable stuff like statistics, values, numbers, percentages, ratios and other metrics – then it'll have impact compared with marketing that's simply a stream of subjective opinion that's got no substance to it.

If this is something that doesn't come naturally to you, then don't panic. British marketing consultant Tony Varey (2010) has written one of the best guides to the use of business maths in marketing, which could make a real difference in helping you think differently about how you use numbers in your marketing and advertising copy. He observes:

Numbers are used primarily to give perspective and thereby help in decision taking. So, most numbers express something 'relative' – how one thing compares with another. Maths taught at school was complicated, mainly theoretical and there seemed to be a lot of it. Maths used in marketing is simple by comparison, is 100 per cent 'applied' and actually there's not a lot of it. Business maths is usually about using numbers to measure and thereby understand the situation or environment you're operating in; past events and performance and their significance for the future and as an input for decision taking.

So wherever possible, think what numbers can be used to verify or underline the carefully crafted purple prose of your marketing literature.

It's not what you offer but what you deliver

Another major flaw in most marketing is this. Marketers love to talk about features and benefits because all the marketing books they've read have said you shouldn't talk about how the solution works, particularly in the IT sector, but focus on the business benefits. Ok, that's not a bad idea. But it's flawed.

This form of marketing bangs on endlessly about the features and benefits the product or service offers to the customer or client. And very soon all of this marketing stuff starts to look, sound and read the same. It even happens when the product isn't on the market and is colloquially known as 'vapourware'.

We said it wasn't completely a bad idea because this approach may work for a short while and at least it's a step in the right direction, away from extolling the virtues of some deeply complex technology where only a handful of customers will know what you're banging on about. But it won't differentiate you, your product or service. That's done by talking about what you deliver, not what you offer. It never ceases to amaze when senior managers often claim that what they do is too complicated or complex to explain in simple terms.

Despite all the expertise, experience and know-how used to solve some difficult problems, the real magic could be missing from the marketing output. And it's delivery. Ultimately, all successful organizations are about delivery. Get that right and there's no looking back, is there?

The power of photography

Using words on their own and nothing else can work in certain circumstances. At the BBC there was a saying: 'The pictures are always better on radio.'

Words are very powerful in creating pictures in the mind of the audience and of course the spoken word remains one of the most powerful forms of expression of thoughts and ideas. But within the context of brochures, press ads and print copy, sound isn't available unless this material sits on the web. So to have impact, words need pictures. As US photo journalist Vicki Goldberg observes:

> *Photographs have a swifter and more succinct impact than words, an impact that's instantaneous, visceral and intense. They share the power of images in general, which have always played havoc with the human mind and heart and they have the added force of evident accuracy.*

Basic principles of writing great marketing copy

Consider your objectives carefully

The first thing to do is *stop*. Before rushing into thinking about creative, photographs, fonts, layout, position of the corporate logo and so on you need to think about the following questions:

- Who is the audience for the brochure, press ad or print copy?
- What are the key messages we want to transmit to them? Do we want to reassure them?
- What outcomes are we looking to achieve from investing in this marketing activity – from a behaviour perspective?
- Do we want them to pick up the phone; make an appointment for a free demonstration; e-mail us; visit our website; enter a prize draw; complete an online questionnaire; get a free trial; attend a free seminar; meet us at a conference, seminar or exhibition; request further information; claim a free gift; get a discount; tell their friends and colleagues about our products and services?
- How will we measure the success of the brochure, press ad or print copy? Is there a dedicated freephone telephone number, freepost response mechanism, a website address?

This may sound pretty much like common sense but so much marketing simply doesn't cut it because either it's over-convoluted or the person devising the campaign hadn't thought to design it from the perspective of the person at the receiving end of the campaign.

Diffusion of innovation curve

There's a fair bit of evidence to suggest that marketing has an impact on our desired customer segments in terms of adoption of new products and services – otherwise what's the point of marketing communications?

Figure 4.1 Diffusion of innovation curve

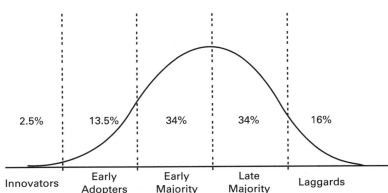

The research to date shows that these customers can be segmented in terms of type of adopter over the time it takes to adopt a product or service. Understanding this will help to sharpen up the focus for the brochure, press ad or print copy. The diffusion of innovation curve (see Figure 4.1) shows the typical percentage of potential adopters of a new product or service over time. Discovering a typology for those who are prepared to buy and try new products, such as 'early adopters' and 'innovators', can really help in the promotion of new products and services.

'If we can target our early advertising and sales effort at winning over the trendsetters and opinion leaders in the market, then we can proactively increase our chances of also convincing the more conservative and sceptical customers to adopt our product,' explains Professor Malcolm McDonald of Cranfield University in the UK. To be successful in these endeavours it's important to communicate to both existing and potential customers and clients.

A key principle in deciding whether to use a brochure, press ad or print copy is establishing the most cost-effective solution for achieving the desired marketing objectives. It's a fact that most marketers budget more for print advertising than any other form of marketing communications, unless they work within a major corporate where sponsorship and TV advertising tend to grab the lion's share of the marketing communications budget. For most local and regional advertising, print probably delivers the most efficient and flexible advertising medium.

Print advertising can be easily integrated with other forms of marketing communications such as e-marketing, m-marketing (see Chapter 6) and personal selling (see Guru in a Bottle®, *Art of Influencing and Selling*).

Print advertising shouldn't be used as a blunt instrument. It needs to be finely tuned because the role of print advertising will change over time and over the life cycle of the product. For example, the process of persuasion can't actually begin until there's some level of awareness about the product or service amongst the desired customer segments. Return to Figure 4.1, and it's clear that once the first 2.5 per cent of innovators have adopted the product, the early adopters are likely to try it, and once the 15 per cent point is reached, the rest of the customer segments are likely to follow. There's no guarantee this will happen in every case, but this model is pretty reliable for most situations where you're trying to advertise a product or service.

This pattern demonstrates the need for different kinds of advertising (brochure, press ad or print copy) for each customer segment and therefore different sets of advertising objectives and strategies for each stage in the life cycle of a product. Professor Malcolm McDonald argues:

> *A common misconception is that advertising objectives should be set in terms of sales increases. As advertising is one of a host of determinants of sales levels, which also include product quality, price and customer service levels, sales increases can't be a direct objective of advertising.*

However, the link between advertising and sales uplift is becoming increasingly strong, typically with new web-based businesses such as price comparison sites that depend on advertising for their lifeblood. Although much of this may be online, many are now turning to more traditional media channels, which may be less cluttered.

Having established and agreed the advertising objectives (above), all the other steps in the process of assembling a brochure, press ad or print copy will flow naturally from them. Table 4.1 provides a useful checklist for the production of a brochure, press ad or print copy.

Getting up close and personal

No one likes to be sold to or to think they are part of a 'target' group of customers, do they? So why do marketers love to talk about existing and potential customers and clients in this way?

You'll notice that we never refer to 'target' customers or clients but rather 'desired' customers and clients. That's much more powerful as immediately it forces us to consider how to appeal to them, or in other words how to capture and hold their attention. And you can only really achieve this if you visualize speaking to an individual rather than an amorphous group of customers and prospects. If you don't your writing is likely to suffer and in an effort to appeal to just about everyone under the sun you'll end up writing stuff that's bland and lacks impact.

The legendary ad man David Ogilvy once said: 'Don't address your readers as if they're gathered together in a stadium.' Indeed.

Adopt George Orwell's rules in the use of English

In his essay, *Politics and the English Language*, the English author and BBC broadcaster George Orwell offered the following six elementary rules for writers:

Table 4.1 Checklist of questions for a brochure, press ad or print copy

Questions to ask yourself	Considerations that apply
Who is this intended for?	• Who are the desired audience? • What do they already know, feel, believe about us and our product/service? • What do they know, feel, believe about the competition? • What sort of people are they? How do we describe/identify them?
What is the purpose of this?	• What response do you want to evoke from the desired audiences? • Are these specific marketing objectives? • What do we want to say to them to make them feel, believe, know, understand about buying our product/service? • What are we offering? • What don't we want to convey? • What are the priorities of importance for our objectives? • What are the agreed objectives within the company and the advertising agency (if print advertising is done externally)?
How is this to work?	• How are our objectives to be embodied in an appealing way? • What is the creative strategy or platform? • What evidence do we have that this is acceptable and appropriate to our audience?
Where should the copy appear?	• With respect to a press ad or print copy, how cost-effective is it?
When should it appear?	• What's the media schedule and how does this link to the business cycle/product cycle? • Are there any other constraints? • Does it need to fit in with other promotional activities? • Are there any particular events happening around the time that can be leveraged?
How do we measure outcomes?	• What results do we expect? • What measures are relevant? • Do we need to do any pre-, during and post-campaign measurement? • How are we going to judge the relative success of our marketing activities?
How much budget should we allocate?	• What's the cost internally and externally for executing a brochure, press ad or print copy? • Are there any external costs, such as a copywriter, designer, layout, print and fulfilment costs that need to be factored in?
Roles and responsibilities	• Who is to do what and by when? • Who is responsible for project management? • Who is responsible for final sign off? • Who is accountable for the whole project?

1 Never use a metaphor, simile or other figure of speech that you are used to seeing in print.

2 Never use a long word where a short one will do.

3 If it's possible to cut out a word, always cut it out.

4 Never use a passive voice when you can use the active.

5 Never use a foreign phrase, a scientific word, or a jargon word if you can think of an everyday English equivalent.

6 Break any of these rules sooner than say anything barbarous.

In his first 'rule' George Orwell is really talking about avoiding clichés: if you're used to seeing a particular metaphor in print, the chances are so has your reader, so avoid it. His last 'rule' means that you should focus above all on the impact your words have on the reader and the 'sound' your writing makes. It's not something marketers have a natural tendency to do and having a background in journalism will help.

British copywriter Andy Maslen makes the following amusing observation: 'What do copywriters and liberal judges have in common? They both like shorter sentences!' There's a whole science on how long a sentence should be, and the received wisdom tends to indicate no more than 16 to 20 words in length is ideal (well, what we've just written is longer than that, so have we failed?)

Putting an arbitrary limit on the number of words that can be used in a sentence is a bit like going into several restaurants but only being able to order food from the same menu. That would make dining out monotonous and boring. A better test is to read the sentence out loud to see if it works. If you find yourself gasping for breath halfway through a rather long paragraph then it's probably too long and needs to be broken up. Microsoft Word® has an in-built readability monitor that you can turn on if you click the 'spelling and grammar' icon and then click on 'options'. You may find this helpful in seeing patterns within your writing, and tightening up the purple prose is certainly a worthwhile exercise.

'Being a good copywriter is about more than using punctuation correctly: it's about selecting and using every word wisely and well,' reflects Andy Maslen.

Tone of voice

It's easy to forget that when you're speaking face to face with someone, how you feel about what you're saying and who you're speaking to will affect your tone of voice. For example, whether you're happy, frustrated, pensive, excited, engaged or bored will affect your tone of voice. It may be a conscious decision to control your tone of voice in certain situations but it's more likely that you don't think about it and subconsciously your brain is making the necessary adjustments as your vocal chords do the work.

Injecting tone of voice in the written word is a different ball game. You have to actively build this into your writing. It's one of the most important qualities of the written word and it's about the music of language. The Guru in a Bottle® Series has been deliberately written in a tone of voice that's friendly, uses colloquial English and as far as possible we wanted to make reading these books easy and enjoyable. And of course we'd love to hear from you at Kogan Page.

As a rule of thumb, given that great marketing is about building a dialogue rather than a monologue, you should write as you speak and choose plain, simple language rather than jargon and complexity. And if you must use jargon, explain the term at the outset rather than assume everyone reading your purple prose will get it first time. The chances are they won't.

Aim for conversational, natural language that would sound ok if you were to read it out loud. As Andy Maslen says:

> *The easiest way to judge the tone of voice of your copywriting is to read it aloud.*
>
> *Would you be happy reading your text to a customer down the phone, or to their face?*
>
> *If 'yes', good – you have a great tone of voice for selling.*
>
> *If 'no', bad news.*
>
> *Why are you embarrassed by what you've written?*
>
> *Must try harder.*

He provides some excellent guidance in this department and illustrates his point with reference to five moods (see Table 4.2).'

It's important to note that there's no absolute right or wrong, but at all times remember who you're speaking to. That should be your guide as to the type of feeling you want the words to convey to your audience. And don't be afraid to be challenging or creative – after all, marketing is about getting noticed rather than being ignored.

Table 4.2 The use of mood affecting tone of voice in the written word

Mood	Use	Feeling	Example
Indicative	Statements of fact	Neutral	'We are holding the seminar next Tuesday.'
Interrogative	Questions	Open/interested	'Are you coming to our seminar next Tuesday?'
Conditional	Bargaining	Looking for a win/win	'If you come to our seminar next Tuesday you'll receive a free pen.'
Imperative	Instructing/ ordering	Bossy/ authoritative	'Attend our seminar next Tuesday.'
Subjunctive	Hypothesis	Exploring possibilities	'If I were to offer you a discount, would you attend our seminar?'

Source: Maslen, 2011

Walking through the font door

At first glance, does it really matter whether you type in Times New Roman or Calibri? Surely it's about what you say that counts rather than the font used? But once you walk through the font door, there's no turning back. The choice of font is more important than you think and it's a powerful tool for getting your message across in a typographic way.

A font is a particular design's attributes for the letters, numbers and symbols used in printing. It refers to one particular size and style of typeface design, such as 12-point, bold, Calibri. Typeface, on the other hand, refers only to the distinctive design of the letter, such as Ariel or Verdana. The right font for the brochure, press ad and print copy makes your text easy to read and is in harmony with the rest of the written and visual material. The choice of available typefaces is endless and if you use Microsoft Word® there's a vast array of fonts available at your disposal.

Where you're looking for a clean, no-fuss font then a sans serif typeface will do the job. These typefaces don't have any decorative serifs such as flourishes at the end of the main lines in a character. The most popular body copy fonts without serifs are Helvetica, Arial, Univers and Avant Garde. The most popular body copy fonts with serifs are Garamond, Melior, Century, Times New Roman and Caledonia. A comparison of serif and sans serif fonts most commonly used in marketing is shown in Table 4.3.

In the opinion of some marketers, Helvetica and Century tend to be the most readable of typefaces. Capitalization of words should be avoided as the human eye reads non-capitalized words 13 per cent faster than upper-case letters and is the reason road signs tend to be in lower case. In terms of legibility, black 14-point Helvetica on white is probably the most readable font specification for the body copy of a press ad or print copy. Mixing two typefaces in brochures, press ads and print copy is very common, for example Helvetica (headline) with Times New Roman (body copy).

It's probably a good idea not to get too carried away experimenting with different fonts and font sizes as the human eye tends to read type quite conservatively. The spacing of characters and lines, the balance and flow of

Table 4.3 Popular fonts used in brochures, press ads and print copy

Serif fonts	Sans serif fonts
Bodoni	Arial
Century	**Bauhaus**
Clarendon	Calibri
Courier	GillSans
Garamond	Helvetica
Lucida	Verdana
Times New Roman	Univers

you may want to include in the brochure. You need to think very carefully about what you want to leave out as well as the response you want from recipients – for example, an e-mail enquiry; a phone call; a request for a visit; a request for a sample; visit to the website; to take a test drive; or to place an order or make a purchase in-store.

If the brochure is for a product, then typically it will include:

- the product's physical dimensions;
- weight;
- materials;
- colour;
- performance;
- benefits;
- options;
- price;
- packaging;
- delivery;
- environmental impact;
- materials it's made from;
- how it's tested;
- who else uses it;
- what other customers or clients say about the product;
- any service arrangements; and
- photographs and illustrations.

If the brochure is for a service, then typically it will include:

- details of the organization providing the service;
- qualifications and experience;
- what the issue, cause, problem or challenge the service being delivered is addressing;
- details of the service being delivered;
- price;
- who the service is designed for;
- how the service makes a difference; and
- photographs and illustrations.

It's now much easier to tailor-make brochures for the recipient by including their name and other details into the body of the copy if it's produced as a PDF soft copy and e-mailed to them directly.

It's also possible to create rich-media online brochures that contain video, audio, photographs, etc, but the decision to go down this route will depend on whether the desired customer segment is likely to be influenced by this one way or the other. It could look like overkill and end up being a waste of time and resources.

Structure of the brochure

This is important and there are no hard and fast rules except to put yourself in the shoes of the recipient and ensure that your perspective is outside looking in, not inside looking out. (For further discussion on this perspective, see Guru in a Bottle®, *Art of Influencing and Selling*.)

You may want to consider using lists and bullet points, which can save space. Also remember that white space in the brochure is there for a purpose – it allows the recipient to take in the information without overloading them and gives them a chance to digest all of it. It's not a waste of space.

If the intention is to create a corporate brochure then the same principles apply. Think very carefully whether a corporate brochure is in fact necessary at all. A corporate brochure could be the Annual Review of the organization in terms of what it's done over the preceding 12 months, or it could be introducing a strategic business unit (SBU) to a desired market or customer segment. It's vital to understand the purpose of the corporate brochure and the environment in which it's to be delivered if it's going to be a useful investment of time and resources.

Also remember that the corporate brochure is your 'public face'; if it looks cheap and nasty, what does that say about you as a brand?

You may want to consider investing time in ensuring the website is up to date, as this is likely to be easier to maintain than producing a corporate brochure, not to mention potentially more cost-effective.

Corporate speak

So much of this stuff is not only boring but reads like internal memos full of jargon and corporate speak. Getting the tone of voice right is also critical. The best way to achieve this is to think about the language that the intended recipient uses and adopt that approach.

You are much more likely to succeed in engaging with the reader if you adopt this approach as there won't be barriers for them to leap over to make sense of what you want to say.

Use of photographs and images

The important point to make here is that it's very common to use library pictures in brochures – but it's sometimes a false economy. The reason is very simple: library pictures tend to be used by many other organizations, including your competitors.

Given that a brochure is about you, your product or service, as far as possible it should be unique, distinctive, memorable, engaging and represent your brand and not confuse it with someone else's brand. Using library pictures destroys these values (unless it's not obvious it's a library picture).

For the vast majority of marketing communications required today, it's preferable to use a photographer to take pictures of customers and clients who are the best ambassadors for the product or service you're selling. This may sound expensive, but it usually generates enough fresh material that can be used for over a year or more – although avoid taking pictures of clients that may be here today and gone tomorrow, because you'll not be able to use their images in new marketing, moving forward. (For an explanation of the use of photographs and copyright issues, refer to Guru in a Bottle®, *Essential Law for Marketers*, 2nd edition.)

Table 4.4 is a helpful tool that will enable you to assemble your thoughts about the production of a marketing brochure.

Table 4.4 Marketing materials questionnaire

Questions	Information required
Requirements for the brochure?	• If it is a new brochure, do you have a sample of a similar brochure? • If it is an update of an existing brochure, do you have a copy of the previous brochure? • When was the previous brochure printed and how much stock is left? • Details of the sponsor of the new brochure (the person who has requested it and/or the budget holder). • Other useful contacts for the brochure. • What is the title of the brochure? • When is this brochure required? • What is the budget allocation for this brochure? Does this factor in postage costs? • How many pages and to what quality is the brochure to be produced? • What is the print run of the brochure? • Is the brochure to be produced in-house or outsourced?
Who are the desired customer or client segments for the brochure?	• Who are the primary audience for the brochure? • Who are the secondary audience for the brochure? • Is there a database of contact names/addresses to be sent this brochure? • What are the existing relationships with this audience? • What are the characteristics of this audience? • Importance to the SBU/division? • Past, present or future importance? • Importance to the organization?

Table 4.4 *continued*

Questions	Information required
Rationale behind the brochure?	• Why is a brochure required; for example, call to action, desired response, desired behaviours?
	• Have other communication channels and alternatives been considered? For example, direct approach (phone/letter/e-mail), PR, advertising, direct marketing, web-based communication, CD-ROM, conference, event, open day, seminar, networking lunch/dinner, other activities?
	• If all other activities have been dismissed in favour of producing a brochure, explain why.
	• If this is an update of an existing brochure, how did you evaluate the success of the previous brochure (explain)?
	• What criteria will you use to evaluate the success of the new brochure? This should be in terms of outcomes not outputs, such as enquiries to be made about the service/product.
	• What other marketing activities will be used around this brochure, for example, visits, presentations?
	• What has changed in terms of material for the new brochure?
	• Are there photographs, images, diagrams, illustrations that are relevant for this brochure?
	• What photographs, images, diagrams and illustrations will be required?
Contents of the brochure?	• Which customers/clients should be approached for comments, case studies, testimonials for this brochure (provide contact details)?
	• What are the four key messages (max) you want to deliver (specify)?
	• What special capabilities/benefits do you have/plan to have that your competitors can't match (specify)?
	• Why can't your competitors match these capabilities/benefits?
	• What actions will you take to put these capabilities/benefits into place?
	• How do you know what your customers/clients will want from you/what you can deliver?
	• What customer research have you done (specify)?
	• Which 5–10 customers/clients (specify) represent your most likely source of expanded business after 2012?
	• What actions do you plan to take to get closer to these customers/clients during 2012 (specify)?
	• Which new customers/clients are at the top of your priority list (specify)?
	• What criteria have you used to select these new customers (specify)?
	• What makes you think you can get their business (specify on a segment or individual basis)?
	• What are the political, economic, social, technological, legal and environmental (PESTLE) barriers to achieving new customers/clients and growing existing customers/clients?

Table 4.4 *continued*

Questions	Information required
Organizational issues?	• Which other SBU/departments/individuals within the organization could help you in achieving your goals (name)?
	• Which SBU/departments/individuals within the organization could present a competitive barrier to you in achieving your goals (name)?
	• How do you plan to get the buy-in of others (specify)?
	• What are the staffing implications (if any) of what you propose in your brochure?
	• What metrics are you using to price the service/product you are promoting in the brochure?
	• How much surplus do you expect to generate as a result of sales based on what is contained in the brochure?
Geographical territories?	On a scale of 1–5, where 1 = most important and 5 = least important, list the following territories:
	• UK
	• South and South East Asia
	• Africa
	• North America
	• Central and South America
	• Eastern Europe
	• Middle East
	• East Asia
	• Rest of Western Europe
	• Australasia
	• Other (specify)
Other relevant information?	Any other observations that are relevant (specify)?
Action plan	Action 1
	Action 2
	Action 3
	Action 4
	Action 5
	Action 5
	Action 6
	Action 7
	Action 8
	Action 9
	Action 10

The mechanics of a press ad

There's no 'painting by numbers' approach you can follow that will guarantee success in producing a press ad that will generate millions of new customers or sales. As discussed in the introduction to this chapter, having clear objectives is essential.

There tends to be a certain number of 'features' of a press ad:

- visual image that conveys what you are trying to communicate in a powerful way;
- headline;
- subsidiary headline;
- brand name (product or service);
- a key message (one is more than enough);
- benefits (these must be from the perspective of the reader, not your own, such as making more sales);
- relevant technical information (that can influence a purchase decision);
- price of the product (where this is relevant); and
- a call to action (such as an invitation to get a discount on the price of the product, visit the company's website, call a freephone telephone number).

It's important that the press ad works on several levels: both rational and emotional reasons for selecting the product or service must come through loud and clear.

You may want to consider building in a compelling reason for response, such as a sale or other time-dependent period where this can have an impact on purchase behaviour. You should also make it easy for your customers or clients to do business with you – so a freephone number, website address or even a coupon (if the press ad is also a promotion) can work really well. (For further information about the use of promotions, see Chapter 8.)

You may also want to think about putting your customer or client centre stage in the press ad. Although this is a powerful way of attracting other like-minded customers or clients, you should be careful that the person featured is comfortable with your doing this; that their organization is supportive and that they are the best choice of customer or client and are likely to be around for a long time to come.

Remember that the press ad is about projecting your reputation too – so the choice of a customer or client needs to be made with extreme care.

The same principle applies when looking at incorporating 'testimonials' by customers or clients, which is another very popular mechanic of a press ad. Too many are worthless because they don't say anything other than platitudes such as 'the best product I've ever bought' without explaining in a succinct way how it made a difference for them. Testimonials need to add value to the story you are telling about your product or service.

Taking your message to the street

Signs, posters and ambient media

Introduction

Out of home (OOH) advertising such as signs, posters and ambient media are often referred to as 'above-the-line' advertising and tend to command a bigger slice of the marketing budget.

In the past, it was common practice for advertising agencies to charge a commission on the media spend for booking such space on behalf of the client. This contrasted with 'below-the-line' advertising, such as those activities described in Chapter 4, where the agency would charge a flat fee.

Today, it's rare to talk in terms of above- or below-the-line as these distinctions belong to an era before the worldwide web and where such activities tended to be compartmentalized rather than integrated. Now signs, posters and ambient media are part of the marketing and communication mix and, in order to work, need to be integrated with other forms of promotional activities. As standalone activities, signs, posters and ambient media are unlikely to be effective and may deflect valuable resources for little return on investment, irrespective of what an agency may tell you about the effectiveness of outdoor advertising achieving cut-through with customers and prospects.

As we've discussed in this book, the concept of 'mass media' is long dead and buried. With the ability to target not just groups of consumers but individuals through the mobile platform with quick response (QR) codes, signs, posters and ambient media have been infiltrated in a way that has made them much more targeted rather than blunt instruments. Such OOH marketing techniques have the power to change people's minds as well as go out and get them to buy, which is why some of the biggest brand owners in the world, such as P&G, Unilever and Coca-Cola have become masters in this universe, closely followed by Hollywood film studios that achieve significant box office receipts as a result of using signs, posters and ambient media to drive ticket and DVD sales.

Research by the Outdoor Media Centre (OMC) in the UK, which represents the interests of media owners and buyers, shows that signs, posters and ambient media can add incremental reach to other marketing activities (see Table 5.1) by creating deeper penetration, frequency, presence, proximity and continuity to a media campaign.

According to Sergio Zyman, former chief marketing officer at Coca-Cola, the advertising industry literally fell in love with itself about a decade ago and nothing was more important than winning creative awards at flash advertising industry get-togethers. These creatives had lost touch with reality, argues Sergio Zyman:

Simply put, the goal of advertising is to sell more stuff to more people more often for more money. Everything you do communicates something about your brand to your customers and prospects. It all influences the way people view your company and your products and it all influences whether anyone will buy what you're selling.

Table 5.1   Incremental reach of signs, posters and ambient media techniques in a media campaign

Media campaign	Incremental reach achieved through signs, posters and ambient media
Television	+15%
Press	+25%
Radio	+35%
Online	+45%

Source: Outdoor Media Centre (2012)

So although signs, posters and ambient media can deliver awareness, if this isn't coupled with a clear message as to what you're doing, why you're doing it and why customers should buy your product, then it's potentially a waste of money.

'Jerry Seinfeld once described to me the metrics of a joke,' recalls Sergio Zyman. 'It has to have a setup, a delivery and a punch line. And marketing does too.' The old wisdom that 'grab their hearts and their wallets will follow' is long dead. Customers and prospects need reasons to buy. For example, although advertising and sponsorship are a key part of Adidas's marketing strategy, these have never been done at the expense of Adidas products and staying true to the original vision and purpose of its founder Adolph Dassler. The performance of Adidas products remains as important as the performance of the brand's advertising and marketing.

Other brand owners seem to be going the other way. For example, posters for Swedish vodka brand Absolut blurred the line between art and advertising and Benetton famously shocked audiences with highly controversial images. Although both have won advertising industry plaudits, it's far from clear whether such tactics drove incremental sales of their respective products.

Signs, posters and ambient media have become a part of people's everyday experience for centuries and, in the UK, posters and billboards have been a communication medium for almost 150 years. Whether as a political medium, an art form or for commercial brand communications, signs and posters have become part of the urban landscape. And this has happened despite the growth of newsprint in the late 19th and early 20th centuries, the arrival of commercial TV and radio in the 1950s and the growth of online advertising in the last decade.

In the UK, the previous patchwork quilt of small media owners offering a bewildering array of options has been streamlined in terms of media ownership, making media buying across a number of sites that much easier. The turning point came relatively recently in 2007, when CBS Outdoor began the installation of the first large-scale digital poster advertising network in the UK on the London Underground and was followed in quick succession by JC Decaux's launch of an airport-based digital network, and the roll-out of digital roadside panels by Clear Channel and J C Decaux. Alongside this rationalization has been investment in signage, poster site and ambient media inventories. New formats continue to be launched and there's now an increasing array of options in terms of poster sites in shopping malls and public amenities such as airports and metro systems.

According to research by Kinetic Worldwide, in the UK there are about 20,000 digital poster screens in traditional OOH environments and a further 50,000 screens in other places, designed in a myriad of shapes and sizes and installed at around 20,000 locations. According to research by Posterscope APAC, over the past five years OOH advertising spend in Asia-Pacific has grown at twice the rate of other media and new technologies and formats have helped to drive the growth of signs, posters and ambient media. For example, within this region, OOH advertising accounts for approximately

6.8 per cent of the total communication spend of major brands. Between 2005 and 2010, OOH advertising grew at a compound annual growth rate (CAGR) of over 15 per cent, nearly twice the rate of all other media in the Asia-Pacific region combined, even taking account of the fast growth in digital media.

Different Asian markets are at different levels of development. Some, like Singapore, Hong Kong, Korea and Japan, are highly developed markets whereas Malaysia, the Philippines, Thailand and Indonesia are developing markets. In India, the biggest driver of change has been the rapid deployment of better techniques and technology in OOH. Even up to the late 1990s, billboards were still hand-painted – whether they were for Bollywood films or brand ads. It meant that OOH advertising couldn't be used for global brands and creative execution was constrained by the ability of the poster artist. That all changed with the introduction of printing on vinyl, which helped to widen creative options and brought about standardization of output, which in turn attracted many new categories and brands to OOH advertising. Lately, the spectacular growth in large format LED and digital OOH advertising options has transformed many of Asia's city landscapes.

Tim Bleakley, CEO at Ocean Outdoor, believes the integration of digital technology will mark a strategic shift in status and capability of poster advertising:

Because OOH is now in the digital space, it offers advertisers an ever-changing, ever-evolving and ever-moving opportunity in the way that our static billboards aren't designed to. You might change the lighting on a static billboard, you might change it to scrolling, but fundamentally it's a billboard. There's always going to be a place for traditional billboards that can broadcast for brands and I think actually the solidity of the traditional side of the medium is even more important in this world where everything's moving all the time. But I think the addition of digital is enabling OOH to do more dynamic targeting using new technology. It allows it to compete on an equal footing with what, in effect, are the two mainstream mediums of today: TV and online.

Best practice in creating signage

In the battle of the brands on any high street, signage comes into its own. The thinking behind signage is very interesting. Hundreds of years ago when there was a higher degree of illiteracy than there is today, signage was one way for the consumer to purchase goods or products that (literally) wouldn't kill them! Signage has always been linked to trust and quality – something that many modern marketers have forgotten in the rush to make everything neon and flashing, which may not always be appropriate given the urban environment.

As we've discussed in other parts of this book, as consumers we tend to screen-out rather than screen-in brand messages given that we are surrounded by them from the minute we wake up to the minute we go to sleep. Signs are important if you want to be found by passing trade but tend to be treated like the Cinderella of OOH advertising. Very often it will be a local print shop that will offer some kind of signage service.

In the UK, the Department for Communities and Local Government has produced a guide to outdoor advertisements and signs which contains practical guidance in this area. Outside of the UK, you'll need to check with the local relevant planning authority in the first instance to ensure you are compliant prior to incurring costs on creating signage that you could be forced to take down or face other penalties if this doesn't comply with the relevant planning laws applicable in that jurisdiction.

The control of the use of signs and OOH advertising falls under the jurisdiction of the local planning authorities who are responsible for day-to-day operation of the advertising and signage system under the Town and Country Planning (Control of Advertisements) Act 1990 and the Town and Country Planning (Control of Advertisements) Regulations 2007 in the UK. (For more information on the legal restrictions placed on advertising and marketing activities, refer to Guru in a Bottle®, *Essential Law for Marketers*, 2nd edition.)

Signage is a pretty wide term and includes the following variants:

- posters and notices;
- placards and boards;
- fascia signs and projecting signs;
- models and devices;
- advance signs and canopy signs;
- estate agents' boards;
- captive balloon advertising (not balloons in flight);
- flag advertisements;
- price markers and price displays;
- traffic signs; and
- town and village name signs.

General principles

In the UK, there are five 'standard conditions' that apply to the erection of signs and other types of OOH advertising and these are likely to be similar in other jurisdictions. The signage and OOH advertising must:

1 be kept clean and tidy;
2 be kept in a safe condition;

3 have the relevant permission of the owner of the site on which it is displayed (this would include the Highways Authority if the sign is to be erected on highway land);

4 not obscure or hinder the interpretation of official road, rail, waterway or aircraft signs or interfere with these types of transport; and

5 be capable of being carefully removed when required to do so by the relevant planning authority.

In addition, if your company is a tenant in commercial premises then it's highly likely that there will be legal restrictions (known as 'restrictive covenants') on the use of signs and other OOH advertising under the terms of the lease agreement. In such cases, qualified legal advice will be necessary before any attempt is made to erect any sign.

Under local planning regulations some signs are deemed to have consent and may not need to be specifically applied for. This may apply to a brass plate outside a doctor's surgery, a notice board displaying the names of individuals in a partnership, or the name of a company operating from the premises. In all such cases, these are permissible for the purpose of advertising that a person, partnership or company is carrying on a profession, business or trade at that premises.

There are also detailed regulations that permit internal or 'halo' illuminated advertisements in restaurants and cafes, office buildings, supermarkets, vehicle showrooms, banks and other premises, and there are rules on dimensions and other technical specifications to be observed.

Best practice in creating posters

Outdoor posters are arguably the oldest advertising medium in the world and today it includes a wide variety of forms including traditional six- and 48-sheet roadside posters, sites in railway stations and shopping malls, airports and subways, as well as digital installations in many environments.

As discussed earlier, OOH poster advertising is the fastest growing traditional advertising medium in the world, and it's been a beneficiary rather than a victim of the digital age. In the UK, the OOH poster advertising industry is worth US$1 billion a year in revenues.

The industry trade body that represents 95 per cent of the interests of media owners and media planners is the Outdoor Media Centre (OMC). Far from wanting to be seen as a thorn in the side of government, regulators and local planning authorities, the OMC wants to be seen as a responsible partner that upholds both the spirit and letter of the law and is in the vanguard of raising the standards of OOH advertising to new levels that complement rather than destroy the environment as well as comply with regulations set by the Committee of Advertising Practice. (For more information on the CAP Code, refer to Guru in a Bottle®, *Essential Law for Marketers,* 2nd edition.)

Advertisers in the following sectors invest heavily in OOH advertising:

clothing and accessories	drink
finance	government campaigns
retail	travel
cosmetics and toiletries	entertainment and media
food	motors
	telecoms.

Planning gain

Many advertisers in the UK are prepared to engage in what's known as 'planning gain' to get their applications for planning consent for posters approved by the relevant planning authority. For example, it's common practice for advertisers to agree to fund the provision of bus shelters, toilets and other public amenities in exchange for advertising rights, saving hard-pressed local authorities considerable amounts of taxpayers' money. In this way, cities acquire shelters worth tens of millions of pounds but also, under the terms of the contract, these are installed, maintained, regularly cleaned and, if vandalized, promptly repaired.

There are other benefits that flow from this type of OOH poster advertising:

- bus shelters provide comfort and protection for the users of public transport;
- the advertisements inject colour and interest into the urban space;
- the extra illumination provides a sense of safety to the streets; and
- stylish design creates a modern urban environment and protects the urban heritage.

According to OMC, its members have agreed contracts with local authorities to provide:

- in excess of 50,000 bus shelters nationally;
- income from publicly owned land and facilities to help subsidize local services;
- maintenance of street furniture such as benches, kiosks, bins and public toilets; and
- subsidized local transport services.

For example, Transport for London (TfL) receives hundreds of millions of pounds that help to enhance public transport in the capital.

Formats for posters

There are four principal formats for OOH poster advertising:

1 *Roadside.* This can range from 96-sheet ads that are 40 feet wide by 10 feet high to bus shelters and phone boxes.

2 *Transport.* This can range from the traditional poster sites at airports, bus stations, railway stations, in trains and tube cars to a wide range of other media including taxi and bus sides ('L' and 'T' variations) and large goods vehicles.

3 *Retail.* This can range from OOH poster advertising sites near to large supermarkets and shopping centres, cinemas and gyms through to advertising on giant screens within a multiple shopping complex.

4 *Non-traditional and ambient.* The possibilities are only limited by lack of imagination! It's now commonplace to see moving A3-format posters aligning the walls of escalators at metro stations all over the world through to screens displaying short advertisements in washrooms at bars and clubs.

Latest research by OMC on effectiveness of OOH poster advertising (2012)

According to research conducted by OMC and its members, OOH poster advertising is highly effective within the marketing mix:

- On average, 97 per cent of UK adults will have seen OOH poster advertising within the last seven days.
- The strength of OOH poster advertising is to keep a brand message in front of millions of consumers every day.
- A wide range of formats and environments means a wide range of audiences to target: housewives, students, drivers, airline travellers, commuters, nurses; bar goers, cinema aficionados and shoppers;
- OOH poster advertising is a highly visual medium and can place a compelling image in front of consumers that can influence their behaviour – that image carries through to point of sale and triggers pack shot recognition by the consumer.
- OOH poster advertising is the medium that places an ad closest to the point of sale – more than 90 per cent of shoppers had seen some form of OOH advertising in the half hour before shopping.
- Research shows that OOH poster advertising works well with all other media in an integrated campaign and can add cover and frequency to every TV, press or online campaign.
- Research also shows that, more than any other medium, OOH poster advertising can stimulate an impulse buy, prompt a spontaneous

purchase or remind the consumer of a planned one – particularly if linked to a mobile device.

- In terms of reach, OOH poster advertising connects with an audience that's predominantly young, likely to be studying or in full-time employment and who are mobile, shop spontaneously and can be influenced by strategically placed messages.
- Special builds and 3D creativity on OOH poster advertising bring a campaign to life; econometric research by Brand Science suggests that OOH poster advertising should be given between 16 and 22 per cent share of FMCG advertising and marketing budget because of the effectiveness of reaching customer segments.

Launch of Magnum premium ice cream in the UK (2010)

Back in 1987, Unilever brand Magnum was the first hand-held ice cream to be marketed as a premium adult offering. Today, Magnum is one of the world's leading ice-cream brands, annually selling over 1 billion units worldwide.

The challenge facing the brand in 2010 was delivering market share growth in a competitive retail environment. Retail own labels had stepped up their promotional strategies, focusing on price point as a key differentiator and stealing share from Magnum and its variants. 'We had to convince our customers that Magnum was quality that was worth paying the extra for. Magnum Gold was crucial in providing a key differentiation against own label and we hoped that the novelty of the first golden ice cream would generate news and talkability to drive excitement and frequency in the ice-cream category,' explains Magnum PR brand manager Samantha Smith.

Inspired by the creative idea of an 'Ocean's 11' style heist with Benicio del Toro, Magnum Gold was launched like a blockbuster film – a first for an ice-cream category. The strategy was to drive high awareness and talkability with a heavy burst of activity at the start of the ice-cream season. High traffic spots and films were chosen for a short burst, high frequency approach to drive awareness quickly on TV. The UK spots were tailored to drive viewers to the website by adding 'story continues?' at the end of the ad.

The OOH poster advertising was used to drive 'fame' like a film launch and Magnum booked high impact outdoor sites during the Easter weekend. The focus was London with additional sites in key cities across the UK. In London, Magnum took over the IMAX cinema site for two weeks. Other channels such as digital and PR were also used.

The OOH poster advertising strategy delivered a huge sales uplift, creating a 28 per cent increase in sales of Magnum Gold as well as driving higher sales of profitable impulse products that resulted in £2 million in additional turnover to the category, driving up Magnum 14 places in the Grocer Top 100 UK brands. A Tesco buyer described the campaign as the 'best ice-cream activation for years'.

Use of digital OOH poster advertising

The use of digital has transformed OOH poster advertising by allowing advertising copy to be changed electronically; it is revolutionizing the medium. The shift for the OOH poster advertising industry is equivalent to the switch from black and white to colour TV, but perhaps more profound for advertisers.

Static paper and paste sites are being replaced by digital screens that are networked together, linked to the internet and capable of showing animated images or full motion video. Digital screens are opening up the opportunity to run more creative and noticeable advertising. Technology that can link a poster to a mobile phone and can recognize passers-by is currently under development. The potential to carry advertising, content, promotions and social media activity from the internet into public spaces and back again via poster-to-mobile campaigns is already recognized by many advertising agency planners.

The implications of the creation of national networks of digital posters is dawning on media traders who can see the potential value of using dealing models more akin to online or broadcast media, in the world of poster media. But hand-in-hand with apparent opportunities come major challenges and questions, for example:

- Where is it appropriate and cost-effective to deploy such technologies?
- Which technologies will prove durable and which ones will consumers respond best to?
- To what extent can and should OOH poster advertising become digitized?
- Is smartphone advertising a threat or a huge opportunity?
- What are the implications for a medium that could be segmented into digital and non-digital sectors and how will traditional static sites work with digital ones?

Latest research in OOH poster advertising (2012)

According to Kinetic Worldwide there's an opportunity to transform the status and role of OOH poster advertising.

In the context of the changing relationship between consumers, mobile technology, digitized media and the desire amongst advertisers for reach and engagement, digital technology could in the long term create two complementary OOH poster advertising propositions: highly targeted and engaging advertising via digital, and broadcast reach via static posters. With these external and internal forces at work, the OOH poster industry is now embarking on a process of change perhaps more radical and far-reaching than any period in its long history.

According to predictions made by Kinetic Worldwide, OOH poster advertising in the UK will rapidly switch from static standard sites (Table 5.2) to digital sites over the next decade (Table 5.3).

Table 5.2 Number of standardized sites in the UK

Format	2011	2015	Percentage change vs 2010	2020	Percentage change vs 2010
Roadside 96 sheets	2715	2200	(–19)	2000	(–26.3)
Roadside 48 sheets	20771	21500	3.5	21800	5.0
Premium/iconic	1598	1650	3.3	1800	12.6
Roadside/bus shelter 6 sheets	71411	72000	0.8	65000	(–9.0)
Retail mall	4079	4100	0.5	3900	(–4.4)
Retail other (inc POS)	1273588	1300000	2.1	1330000	4.4
Airport	2673	2500	(–6.5)	2350	(–12.1)
London Underground	118546	118000	(–0.5)	117700	(–0.7)
Rail	10035	10220	1.8	10630	5.9
Other transport	2400	2400	0.0	2400	0.0
Taxis	6500	6750	3.8	7500	15.4
Bus	18810	19100	1.5	19500	3.7
TOTAL	**1533126**	**1560420**	**1.8**	**1584580**	**3.4**

Source: Kinetic Worldwide (2012)

Table 5.3 Number of digital sites in the UK

Format	2011	2015	Percentage (%) change vs 2010	2020	Percentage (%) change vs 2010
Roadside 96 sheets	–	–	–	–	–
Roadside 48 sheets	31	60	93.5	400	1190.3
Premium/iconic	31	75	141.9	100	222.6
Roadside/bus shelter 6 sheets	–	200	–	7000	–
Retail mall	1359	1800	32.5	2000	47.2
Retail other (inc POS)	14561	16000	9.9	18000	23.6
Airport	971	1050	8.1	1180	21.5
London Underground	1407	1407	0.0	1600	13.7
Rail	238	350	47.1	380	59.7
Other transport	30	60	100.0	60	100.0
Taxis	1250	2250	80.0	6000	380
Bus	–	20	–	750	–
Other environments	52725	60000	13.8	70000	32.8
TOTAL	**72603**	**83272**	**14.7**	**107470**	**48.0**

Source: Kinetic Worldwide (2012)

As can be seen from these tables, there's rapid growth predicted in format and geographical spread of digital poster sites in the UK; some of this has been precipitated by the London 2012 Olympic Games. Notably, by 2020 it's predicted that up to 400 48-sheet sites could switch to digital or be installed in new locations, with potentially 7,000 roadside bus shelter sites adopting digital screen technologies.

Kinetic Worldwide expects the vast majority of capital expenditure on inventory will be in digital formats over the coming decade, with significant rationalization of traditional static billboards in the 96-sheet format and a reduction in static sites in enclosed environments as they are replaced by digital screens. In many locations and environments the total number of static sites is predicted to either grow marginally or remain stable. Taken together, the analysis suggests that rather than replace static inventory, digital screens will grow the total OOH poster advertising universe.

In terms of geographical spread, analysis of potential site locations and destinations capable of sustaining digital posters suggests at least 30 UK cities will see digital sites installed in key locations up to 2020. Major urban conurbations such as London, Birmingham, Leeds and Glasgow can expect significant numbers of digital screens in multiple formats and locations. For many city dwellers and visitors, digital poster screens in various shapes and forms will become a normal part of everyday life. Through sheer impact and interactive capability, however, many of these screens will provide brands with a level of consumer engagement that will add substantial value and transform OOH poster advertising strategies beyond all recognition.

Modern use of ambient media

Just about everything we are surrounded by that moves – arguably including ourselves – is a media channel!

A slogan on a T-shirt can be an effective ambient media channel as can the nozzle of a fuel pump when you go to fill up the car; the lid of a pizza box that's delivered to your home for a takeaway night in, or a message on a recycling skip in the supermarket car park when you go to get rid of your empties.

Other ambient media channels that are often used by advertisers to get their messages across include car park tickets, shopping trolleys, floor posters, umbrellas, car bumper stickers and branded sports bags. However, the fastest growing use of ambient media is via mobile phones and OOH poster advertising activating quick response codes.

Future use of quick response (QR) codes

The evolution of mobile technology has created a renaissance in OOH poster advertising, where it has moved from being a mass medium to one that can directly engage with the individual consumer in a highly targeted way using QR codes that are readable by a range of mobile devices. A QR code can direct the consumer to a landing page made especially for those who interact with that particular OOH poster advertising.

QR codes can provide immediate access for consumers to:

- information on the brand or product;
- a money-off voucher;
- a website landing page;
- exclusive content;
- directions to the nearest shop or outlet for the purchase of the goods advertised; and
- a video or interactive poster advert.

According to research by Kinetic Worldwide, most industry analysts regard the interactivity between digital posters and smartphones as the single biggest opportunity and challenge for the industry in the years ahead.

Consumer familiarization with the PC, mobile phone, smartphone and now tablet and other devices has created a tipping point for accessibility to more meaningful communication. If the OOH poster advertising industry can develop a consistent and effective approach to poster-to-mobile brand campaigns, it could spawn a new segment within the OOH advertising medium – 'interactive OOH'.

According to the latest Communications Market Report (2011) published by OFCOM, there are 81 million mobile connections in the UK, double the number reported in 2000. It's the massive growth in mobile computing, whether in the form of smartphones or tablet computers, that's the key driver in this development.

Research by Nielsen (2012) suggests that the number of people aged 15 and over accessing the internet on mobiles has more than doubled in the space of five years, and Kinetic Worldwide estimates that smartphone penetration is around 34 per cent, suggesting that UK consumers are ahead of other European markets. Almost half of Vodafone's contract customers have a smartphone (49 per cent) and 70 per cent of new customers joining Vodafone UK opt for a smartphone, compared with 43 per cent across Europe.

A recent report by Enders Analysis estimates that, by 2015, 75 per cent of consumers will carry a smartphone and 28 per cent of time spent online will be via a mobile handset. This is in line with OFCOM's research, which shows the number of mobile connections able to access third-generation (3G) mobile technology increased by 6.2 million in 2010 to 33.1 million in 2011, more than double the number three years earlier. During 2010, 2G connections fell by 5.3 million connections (9.9 per cent) to 48.0 million, in part driven by the growth in take-up of smartphones, which use the faster data connections provided by 3G networks.

It's against this background that advertisers have started to embrace QR to engage with these mobile populations.

Uptake in use of QR technology

The key to unlocking successful OOH poster advertising to mobile campaigns will depend largely on the mechanism used to exchange data.

Systems that can deliver data instantly as consumers pass or touch their handset to a surface could become viable in low-dwell time but accessible locations. Others that require a deliberate pause or a more time-consuming action only have a future in high-dwell time locations. Interactive poster campaigns are already very common across many territories globally.

QR codes originally came from Japan and were used to track separate car components in the production process. Today, they are a visual matrix barcode readable by camera phones that deliver a text message, URL or other data. There's no messing with search results, no clicking on wrong links and when it works it's fast, direct and efficient in delivering a link to exactly what the advertiser wants you to see. QR codes commonly appear on posters as well as product packaging. Most mobile handset brands also offer users QR code reader apps to download for free.

In the UK, QR codes haven't matched the awareness level in Japan, although it's expected to accelerate rapidly with the proliferation of smartphone usage and consumers become more familiar with QR codes. According to research by Kinetic Worldwide, nearly half of all mobile phone users have seen a QR code in situ and 12 per cent have actually used one – 20 per cent among 18–24 year-olds. Much of this usage has been on a product and in a media context. For example, a wine lover can scan a QR code with his or her mobile device and access special recipes that match the wine.

However, not everyone involved in online advertising and marketing sees QR codes as being the solution for all environments. Some of the drawbacks include lack of a mobile signal or connection to a wi-fi hotspot, poor experience of downloading a reward, and the time and trouble involved in scanning the QR code in the first place. Care must be taken as to what sites are being accessed and what's being downloaded – QR codes are often a portal to online content so the same rules about surfing the web apply.

In the United States, less than 5 per cent of the population has scanned a QR code, according to recent research by comScore. Jon Barocas, CEO of bieMedia, a Denver-based online marketing and media solutions company, argues:

> *Humans are visual animals. We have visceral reactions to images that a QR code can never evoke; what we see is directly linked to our moods, our purchasing habits and our behaviours. It makes sense that a more visual alternative to QR codes wouldn't only be preferable to consumers but would most likely stimulate more positive responses to their presence.*

Many analysts agree that standard black and white QR codes look awkward and will be replaced, but the functionality of QR codes may remain for a long time to come.

So rather than being a technology issue, it's all about the context, content and execution that allows for integration, multiple touch points, SEO, sharing and other benefits for the consumer that will make the adoption of QR codes more widespread in the OOH poster advertising environment.

Alternatives to QR codes

Mobile Visual Search (MVS)

Some online advertising and marketing analysts are talking about mobile visual search (MVS), which works on the basis of pointing a mobile device at a product or logo. Within seconds, the MVS application provides product or company information or even the option to make a purchase right there and then on the mobile device. Jon Barocas observes:

> MVS is a far more compelling and interactive tool to enable mobile marketing and commerce. In today's increasingly mobile world, instant gratification is the norm, and taking the extra step of finding a QR code scanner on your mobile device no longer makes sense. With MVS, you're interacting with images that are familiar and desirable, not a square of code that elicits no reaction.

Others are more sceptical and point to the context where image recognition will work best but as yet the technology is in its infancy and unproven. There's also no way to tell what is MVS-enabled and what isn't unless this is part of the poster advertising messaging. It's likely that in the future QR codes will be integrated into campaigns with MVS and near field communication (NFC) providing multiple options for audiences which will allow them to make use of the smartphone technology they feel most comfortable with.

Augmented Reality (AR)

Another current technology that's already in use in digital marketing, mobile apps and OOH poster advertising campaigns is augmented reality (AR). In its more basic form, AR creates a 3D image when an AR code is viewed through a mobile phone camera or PC webcam.

In 2011, Ford launched an AR OOH poster advertising campaign in the UK which enabled consumers to watch as its new C-Max model appeared in the palm of their hands. In this case Ford used a site with an in-built camera to track the viewer's movement and project the image. The 3D depth imaging technology campaign ran on mall six-sheets in the UK. The interactive technology allowed people to handle and explore mini 3D virtual models of the cars on screen and in the palm of their hands. The user interface was based on natural movement, and hand gestures allowed any passer-by to immediately start interacting with the car's features. (The video can be viewed on the Kinetic YouTube channel.) More sophisticated screen-based AR techniques overlay additional visual information on top of the view of the real world, which can be relayed onto mobile phone screens via the handset camera, or onto the lenses of glasses made with integrated AR systems.

For example, experimental campaigns have already run in the United States where consumers have been directed to locations via social media and, using an AR app, been able to view and shop at 'virtual stores'. The same technique has created virtual celebrity hot spots, where fans can pose and take pictures of themselves with AR celebrities. It's easy to picture the signposting role OOH poster advertising can play in a new AR marketing world.

Personal care brand Lynx recently launched a large format AR campaign: Lynx Angels seemingly fell from above and onto the Transvision screen at Victoria Station in London. The feed from the camera was augmented with falling angels that interacted and engaged with people in a high dwell-time environment. The video achieved over 1 million views on YouTube, plus an amplification of social media interaction.

Nigel Gwilliam, Head of Digital at the Institute of Practitioners in Advertising (IPA) in the UK, sees AR in the long term as both an opportunity and a threat to OOH media:

> When augmented reality makes the leap from novelty 3D image to a head-up display projected onto your designer glasses and when that becomes mass market it opens up a range of interesting and challenging possibilities. On one level you could reach a point where people are walking around and seeing other people's Facebook profile details bobbing around over their heads, which they can swap or even flirt with. In a foreign city you'll see directions to the airport, or if you're on a night out, you'll get recommendations for restaurants. Now in a sense what that does is create alternative ways for consumers to see commercial messages. In another, it's possible that OOH media almost becomes a blank canvas for AR projections which could be tailored to individuals.

Near Field Communications (NFC) and Radio Frequency Identification (RFID)

Both NFC and RFID technologies may have the biggest impact on mobile interaction with OOH poster advertising in the medium to long term. Both technologies use short-range wireless frequencies, typically operating over a distance of several centimetres, which opens up the possibility of hassle-free transmission of information from digital OOH poster advertising sites to mobile handsets with one swift swiping action.

Evolving RFID technology means that the cost of transmitter tags has fallen to a few cents and they're becoming small enough to insert into almost any surface, prompting predictions that many objects and surfaces in public surfaces will become mobile interactive. NFC, which is more versatile than RFID, is expected to enable consumers to use their mobiles to purchase goods in-store as an alternative to credit and debit cards.

Applied to OOH poster advertising in a shopping mall, NFC systems would enable consumers to easily collect a promotional offer flagged by the site or to download content and ultimately to make a purchase. Critically, while consumers make a positive decision to interact, the experience takes seconds to complete and could be done without stopping. The system could also register and recognize each individual consumer interaction. NFC poster sites could also be programmed to react to an interaction.

As a result of the speed of transmission, it's conceivable that consumers walking past OOH poster advertisement carrying a promotion or attractive content could pause for a moment or swipe as they pass, and download the content. That content can then be instantly passed from handset to handset by touching phones together, opening up the potential for a vast range of viral, social, location-based, interactive marketing experiences.

NFC- and RFID-enabled sites are some way off in the future, but they will have significant long-term potential as handset manufacturers incorporate the technology.

The future of OOH advertising

The OOH advertising sector globally is entering a transformative period. While it's perhaps easy to overestimate the impact of digital screens, it's also possible to underestimate the impact of technology in the long term.

The next decade will see a series of waves of investment in screens rolling through enclosed environments such as shopping malls, transport networks, shops, gyms and other leisure environments, as the research by the OMC and Kinetic Worldwide demonstrates. In the UK, digital OOH advertising will have become a national medium by the end of 2012, but restricted to major conurbations.

In parallel, the largest proportion of the billboard universe, what's currently categorized as roadside OOH poster advertising, will initially see far slower digital development. Over the next five years in this sector, the UK can expect to see perhaps no more than a couple of hundred high impact bespoke sites appear in major conurbations. However, in the medium to long term, say from 2015 to 2025, far more significant levels of deployment is possible.

Digital 6-sheets are likely to become ubiquitous in pedestrianized city centres and digital technology in screen-form and hosting technology enabling poster-to-mobile interaction could spread rapidly across 6-sheet networks on major thoroughfares.

In the long term, perhaps approaching 2020, media owners and new entrepreneurs may be enabled by falling screen costs to tackle the deployment of large format digital screens in the roadside environment. By necessity, the majority of these will be static, but the opportunity to drive sales volumes and offer advertisers infinitely greater flexibility could by this stage make this deployment viable.

The clear implication of these physical changes in inventory is that the OOH poster advertising industry will diversify beyond all recognition over the next 25 years.

References

Books

Gobé, M (2001) *Emotional Branding*, Allworth Press

Kolah, A (2013) Guru in a Bottle, *Essential Law for Marketers*, 2nd edition, Kogan Page

Kolah, A (2013) Guru in a Bottle, *The Art of Influencing and Selling*, Kogan Page

McDonald, M, Kolah, A *et al* (2007) *Marketing in a Nutshell*, Butterworth Heinemann

Ries, A and Ries, L (2002) *The Fall of Advertising and the Rise of PR*, Harper Business

Zyman, S (2000) *The End of Marketing As We Know It*, Harper Business

Zyman, S (2002) *The End of Advertising As We Know It*, Wiley & Sons

Websites

Outdoor Media Centre: http://www.outdoormediacentre.org.uk (accessed 14 February 2012)

Kinetic Report: The Future of Out of Home Media in the UK – The Industry, consumers and technology to 2020: http://www.kineticww.com (accessed 16 February 12)

Augmented Reality (AR) examples on the Kinetic Worldwide YouTube Channel: http://www.youtube.com/watch?v=InDEcb1VSdU&list=UUUeyWLfVbC8mOG ZQ6r2VqMg&index=7&feature=plcp (accessed 20 February 2012)

WARC Report: Planning for New Interactive Possibilities of UK Out of Home Media: http://www.warc.com (accessed 16 February 2012)

WARC Report: Asia's Outdoor Future: http://www.warc.com (accessed 16 February 2012)

Why QR codes won't last: http://mashable.com/2012/02/15/qr-codes-rip (accessed 16 February 2012)

Department for Communities and Local Government – Guide to Outdoor Advertisements and Signs: http://www.communities.gov.uk (accessed 18 February 2012)

Introduction

This chapter is wide in scope as there are parallel lessons to be drawn between e-marketing, m-marketing and direct marketing and to some extent these techniques are interchangeable. Through this journey we are going to focus on what we consider to be important in terms of high impact marketing that gets results.

In a recent interview published in the *McKinsey Quarterly* (2011), Steve Ridgway, CEO Virgin Atlantic, said 'Before we start marketing anything or talking about our brand proposition, we ask ourselves, are we being brave enough to get ahead of consumer expectations?' Arguably, this line of thinking has helped to fuel the incredible success of the Virgin brand through diversification of its business interests that are designed to satisfy customer needs that previously weren't being catered for. The same could be said about those brand owners that have embraced e-commerce and created new and innovative business models that are 'outside-in' rather than 'inside-out' – in other words, these business models are first and foremost customer- rather than product- or service-centric.

John Hayes, global chief marketing officer at American Express, adds:

> *If you really have a great product or a great programme, it can catch fire in the marketplace. That's exciting. But the challenge for most people who are marketers today is how do you remain accountable for the success of this when you don't control what somebody might say or contribute? I haven't met anybody who feels they have the organization completely aligned with where this revolution's going, because it's happening so fast and so dramatically. Marketing is touching so many more parts of the company now. It touches service; it touches on product development. We need to organize a way that starts to break down the traditional silos in the business.*

It's precisely this tidal wave of change that has pushed e-marketing, m-marketing and direct marketing to the top of the engagement agenda, and not just for American Express but for all brand owners as they struggle to come to terms with managing these constantly changing channels.

Research over the last decade shows that e-marketing, m-marketing and direct marketing have an important role to play in achieving customer retention as well as driving customer lifetime value (CLV) and customer equity within the business. For example, a study that calculated the value of customer equity of Ameritrade, E*TRADE, Amazon, eBay and Capital One found a close correlation between the value of customer equity and market capitalization – a ratio that's relevant today.

The study found that a 1 per cent improvement in the customer retention rate would increase the customer equity value between 3 and 7 per cent, depending on the individual company analysed. The researchers also found that a 1 per cent increase in sales margin would generate a 1 per cent increase in customer equity value, while a 1 per cent reduction in acquisition cost would generate an increase in customer equity value of just 0.3 per cent. In other words, customer retention for these brand owners had more impact on the customer equity value than sales margin or customer acquisition costs. (For more on customer and client acquisition strategies, refer to Guru in a Bottle®, *Art of Influencing and Selling*.)

In the above examples, the findings were largely predictable because brand owners such as eBay and Amazon have frequent and direct interactions with their customers and therefore score more highly on customer retention rates.

Tough times need not be bad times

Those companies that use marketing creatively to deepen relationships with existing customers and clients and recruit new ones will emerge stronger despite today's tough trading environment.

As a management discipline, marketing is changing faster than ever with both the web and mobile opening up new possibilities almost on a daily basis. That's good news for small and medium-sized companies because it's creating a level playing field for them to compete with much larger organizations.

Marketing is no longer about the size of resources that a company controls but about how marketers can be more innovative and creative in deploying those resources. One of the biggest shifts in consumer behaviour has been the use of web and mobile devices to make purchases of goods and services – in the UK the run rate is around £600 million a week. Increasingly, modern marketing is not so much in 'transit mode' and more about leveraging the value of a whole range of 'receive' media. For example, consumers swapping information about products and services on Facebook and Twitter can be more influential in the buying decision-making process than exposure to a full page ad in a newspaper – although interactive technologies such as QR codes have started to penetrate these traditional media channels to create two-way communication. (For more information on QR codes and other inactive technologies, see Chapter 5.)

As a result of the measurability of these new tools and techniques, marketing performance has graduated to the status of lead generation with a measurable impact on the bottom line. And with the increased use of social media, boardrooms are now required to take account of the views of their customers and clients much more in order to drive sales. Jo Causon, CEO of the Institute of Customer Service in the UK, advises:

> Looking back to the 1980s, we thought the United States was the best country in the world for customer service. But I would argue that customer service has fundamentally changed and our requirements as consumers are very different to back then. I'm starting to see boardrooms taking this a lot more seriously. When I talk to CEOs they say that obviously they are focused on financials but more and more it's about customer satisfaction. They are all chasing the same customers,

so one way to differentiate themselves is through the service and experience they are able to deliver.

The rise of in-bound marketing

The changing nature of consumers' shopping habits means that instead of continuing to 'push' messages out, marketers must now adapt to consumers' behaviour by creating marketing campaigns that 'pull' people into their business; this is known as 'in-bound marketing'. In-bound marketers offer their customers useful information, tools and resources to attract them to their websites while at the same time interacting with them and developing relationships on the web.

The nature of e-marketing

This is a catch-all description of a wide variety of digital marketing tools and applications that include:

- website marketing;
- e-mail marketing;
- search engine marketing;
- search engine optimization;
- viral marketing;
- blogging;
- microblogging;
- podcasting;
- vodcasting;
- photo and video sharing;
- social networking; and
- virtual reality.

In different ways, each of these tools and applications provide businesses with the opportunity to communicate with a vast, global audience at relatively low or no cost.

There are several advantages for using e-marketing:

- comparatively inexpensive for the target audience numbers involved;
- allows brand owners to create instant, high impact campaigns on popular or current topics of interest to their market and customer segments;
- can deliver a much more engaging and rich media experience where photographs, diagrams, images, videos and other content can be managed relatively easily;

- can try different forms of advertising and assess the results;
- allows for personalization where visitors can tailor their experience to find products and services they are interested in rather than searching through a whole catalogue;
- can provide a sense of community by sharing comments and reviews on products and services;
- can provide a useful 'receive mode' channel;
- can easily measure and monitor responses to a campaign; and
- can see exactly how many visitors opened an e-newsletter and what further action they took as a result.

On the flip side, there are many disadvantages and potential pitfalls in using these channels that need to be carefully considered. For example, legal and compliance issues on privacy and electronic communication as well as the EU regime of opt-in are extremely important as there are significant sanctions if these regulations and laws aren't observed. (Refer to Guru in a Bottle®, *Essential Law for Marketers*, 2nd edition for a discussion of the laws and regulations that apply in e-marketing, m-marketing and direct marketing.)

Other negative issues include the fact that delivery of e-mail marketing may be blocked or simply end up in junk e-mail rather than the in-box, and not all products or services lend themselves to being experienced through these tools and applications. For example, you may be able to change the metallic finish on a new BMW model but you'll still need to book a test drive to experience the product irrespective of how slick the website may be.

However, on balance, the advantages outweigh the disadvantages and the potential gains achievable means that e-marketing is one of the fastest growing disciplines worldwide.

Building a mouse trap

A website is like a mouse trap, except the idea isn't to trap visitors against their will!

It's important that you have answers to the following questions before commencing website development:

- How will the website fit within your overall marketing and communications activities?
- What budget can you allocate for website development, content, maintenance and hosting?
- Who are your customers, clients and prospects and what will be the compelling reason why they should visit your website?
- What do you want to say to them and what response (from a behaviour perspective) do you want to create as a result of them visiting the website?

- How much time can you allocate?
- Who in the organization can manage and monitor this activity?
- What's the likely payback (if it's a website with an e-commerce engine) and timing for this?

Web development is a skill that many marketers may not have and it's likely that if you work in a large organization the company website was out-sourced to a specialist company.

Technical assistance in building a website is a good idea even if you're a small or medium-sized business because it can be done more quickly and efficiently by a competent website developer, provided that you agree a detailed site plan for the website based on clear objectives and what you want to achieve from the outset. Although you may be able to outsource the construction, design and search engine optimization (SEO) of the site, it's likely that you'll need to maintain its content yourself on a regular basis.

Search engines like Google send 'robots' to sites to create a ranking, so that in a natural search (as opposed to a paid-for search) a higher ranked website will appear further up in the list of answers, making it easier for prospective customers and clients to find the 'best ranked' sites. To ensure that you register and stay registered with these 'robots' you must continue to keep your site's content up to date and fresh, otherwise you'll not only fail to maintain your ranking but you won't provide a compelling reason for customers or prospects to return to the site.

Writing copy for a website

Good copywriting existed well before the web was conceived or direct mail had ever made its way through a single letter box! In the opinion of British copywriter Andy Maslen, it all comes down to one thing:

> Good online copywriting must sell, first and foremost. The paradigm may have changed from promotion to education, but the underlying purpose remains unchanged. And that means holding people's attention and stopping them clicking off your site.

Ideally, copy that will produce results needs to grab the attention of visitors, hold their interest, create desire for the products or services that you deliver, assure them that they can do business with you in confidence, and lead them to take some action, such as landing on the check-out page to complete a transaction.

Headlines
Whether writing copy for a website or a news release, the headline is probably one of the most important – and perhaps the hardest – thing to get right. A headline is basically the hook for what follows next. You'll quickly lose the readers' interest if the headline doesn't grab them by the throat.

Table 6.1 SEO strategies that work

SEO Factors	Details
Title tags	These are the tags at the very top for each page on the website and should contain detail of what the page is serving rather than say 'home page'. These are the first things that search engines look at. If the key phrase shows up in the title tag, search engines flag the page as relevant to that phrase.
Keywords	As the name suggests, these are important words and your website should contain them, depending on the nature of your business.
Key phrases	In addition to keywords, it's also important to have key phrases and reuse these key phrases in proper sentences throughout the website.
Matching your competitor's title tags, keywords and key phrases	There's no reason why you can't have a look at competitor sites to understand how they are managing to drive more traffic than your own website and to beat them at their own game.
Headings on the website	It's important to have headings as these show up in search results when the robots from search engines crawl over your website. Remember, if the target key phrase shows up in a heading that demonstrates relevance in the search.
Paragraphs on the website	Keeping paragraphs short and using short sentences and simple words will make your website easier to rank.
Site map	This is essential as search engines like to see a map to determine where everything is connected.
Links	Links to other sites are useful but what's more powerful is that other sites independently link to your site. Search engines are now so sophisticated that some ignore out-going links and only rank in-coming links to your site. This is one reason why Twitter is so important – you could write a blog on your site, tweet it and then followers could retweet, which leads back to the blog on your website.
Social media sites can act as a funnel for traffic to your website	Adding tweets to Twitter or answering questions on LinkedIn that contain your web address can be effective in driving traffic to your website.
Captions	As websites become much more visual, having captions for pictures will help with image search results.
Error pages and broken links	Sometimes internal links within a website are broken and pages that should be there come up as 'error pages', which has the effect of not making your website relevant and impairing the ranking it can achieve with the search engine.
URL	Keyword-rich web addresses can help to drive traffic to your website because every link to your site that uses the URL as the link text creates a link.
Submit your website to the search engines	Don't forget to submit your website to Google, Bing and Yahoo as they are unlikely to find you among the billions of websites if you don't.

- Take the longer-term view when engaging with SEO for your website – there are no short-term fixes that will propel your website to the number one spot – and in fact older websites tend to get higher rankings than newer ones.
- Track the number of unique visitors to your website as a result of natural search results – any half-decent web analytics tool will be able to provide you with this data.
- Track the number of key phrases that are driving traffic to your website.
- Track the number of in-bound links to your website.
- Track the number of indexed pages by search engine.
- Try to link traffic data with number of sales successfully transacted on your website (where this is relevant).

Websites of tomorrow

Back in June 2011, the Internet Corporation for Assigned Names and Numbers (ICANN) decided to allow the radical liberalization of internet domain name endings – technically known as generic top level domains (gTLDs). The future of websites will effectively change post-January 2013 when this free-for-all becomes a reality and brand owners attempt to embed a marketing message as an integral part of their IP address.

New gTLDs will change the way people find information on the internet and how organizations can plan and structure their online presence. Internet address names will be able to end with almost any word in any language, offering organizations around the world the opportunity to market their brand, products, community or cause in new and innovative ways.

ICANN declared that its decision will usher in a new internet age and provide a platform for the next generation of creativity and inspiration. However, it's as yet unclear whether the security, stability and resiliency of the internet will in any way be compromised by such a move.

Dot gone?

This liberalization of gTLDs could be the curtain call for the ubiquitous dot com that today commands over 100 million registrations, far outnumbering all other suffixes and more than five times more popular than Germany's second-ranked 'de' suffix. So, instead of coca-cola dot com, the new URL could be therealthing dot coca-cola.

Before joining the stampede for these new suffixes, consider the evidence that suggests there's been a marked decrease in the importance of the web address in recent years, largely due to the power of search engines driving activity online. Then there's the cost and time involved in making such an application. The process for creating a dot brand includes an application of more than 200 pages and an administrative check, amongst other things. Significantly, ICANN is charging a US$185,000 fee for each registered dot brand address and a fee of US$25,000 annually over the course of a 10-year licence. A priority system established by ICANN also gives preference to public bodies filing gTLDs over consumer brand owners.

Additional cost considerations for dot brand owners include the establishment and maintenance of infrastructure, and the maintenance of original domains through a transitional period, along with related legal fees, likely to top US$1–2 million even before the website is operational. Going down this route isn't for the faint hearted or those without deep pockets!

Predictably, not everyone is happy and the Association for National Advertisers (ANA) in the United States has formed a sub-group with over 100 major brands including Wal-Mart, Kraft Foods and Toyota under the snappy title 'Coalition for Responsible Internet Domain Oversight' (CRIDO) that's opposed to such moves. Its main beef is that the ICANN system will undermine trust and erode confidence among consumers. In addition, the Interactive Advertising Bureau (IAB), which comprises more than 500 leading media and technology companies that sell 86 per cent of online advertising in the United States, are also campaigning against these changes, claiming that it could cause incalculable financial damage to brand owners as they are forced to spend considerable sums defending their positions by making multiple registrations as part of a brand defence strategy.

The beneficiaries of this new world order will be those who rely on driving sales of their products and services through the web:

- Entertainment and consumer brands that often rely on unique URLs to communicate a new campaign, property or attraction, such as a new movie. This gives them the status of standalone presence but they almost always tie back to the mother brand in their content.

- Brands with complex or reorganized structures, which could use a gTLD strategy to align offerings. Merging companies, for example, could benefit from the cohesiveness.

- Brands leasing internet 'real estate' to individuals and businesses. For example, eBay could provide each of its online sellers with a personalized URL with a dot eBay suffix, economizing online addresses while adding stature to the host brand.

- Those brand owners with an endorsed brand architecture for their sub-brands may be tempted to purchase a gTLD for their sub-brands to drive equity back to the parent brand. For example, Microsoft might wish to pursue xbox dot microsoft to draw attention to its innovative consumer products.

If a brand owner doesn't currently invest significantly in creating an online destination experience, securing a gTLD won't be sufficient in itself to capture attention and build loyalty. Yet for others, securing a new gTLD could signal a significant change in how brands approach their online experience as a whole. Committing to the change means using it as an opportunity to maximize a presence in this critical communications channel. It's going to be fascinating to watch what happens over the next 12 months and beyond.

Social e-marketing

Facebook, Twitter, Google Plus, YouTube and LinkedIn are just a few of the social networks and now represent the fastest way to disseminate a message to a global audience instantaneously, and increasingly are being used for social e-marketing purposes. Social e-marketing comes in a variety of flavours as can be seen in Table 6.2.

Do you exercise in the morning? It's not a trick question! Monitoring your social media presence for 10 minutes every morning should become a routine exercise before you reach the office. Try the following five simple steps as part of your daily workout:

Step 1: Check Twitter for chat about your company/brand (2 minutes). Use tools such as TweetDeck or Twitter Search to monitor conversations about your company in real time.

Step 2: Scan Google Alerts (1.5 minutes). Check for your company name, products, executives or brand terms. To set this up, enter your search terms in Google Alerts and select to receive updates as they happen or once daily. Now, when people blog about your products

Table 6.2 Social e-marketing channels

Channel	Description	Examples
Social networking	Where people can interact online.	• Facebook • Google Plus • MySpace
Blogging	Allows you to compose an opinion piece or article on a subject with relevance to many other people.	• Word Press • Blogger
Micro blogging	Where you are limited to a short sentence of 140 characters.	• Twitter
Media sharing	Where you can upload and share videos, pictures and audio content.	• YouTube • Flickr
Bookmarking sites	Allows you to save bookmarks as you would in a browser but accessible from any computer.	• Delicious • StumbleUpon
Popularity sites	Where you can collect bookmarks and then let visitors vote on them.	• Digg • Reddit

or services, an alert is sent to your inbox. You can read the articles and comments and respond in real time.

Step 3: Check Facebook stats (1 minute). Visit your company page Facebook Insights. This can be found under the page's main photo if you are an administrator for your page. Scan your active users and interaction stats. Check out your wall posts or new discussions if you have them enabled for your page.

Step 4: Answer industry-related LinkedIn questions (3 minutes). Search for questions on LinkedIn that you or members of your organization can answer. You can set up an RSS feed for specific question categories to go to your Google Reader as well. When you find a relevant question, respond and include a link to your website or a relevant blog post that might be helpful to your audience.

Step 5: Use Google Reader to check Flickr, Digg and other social network sites (2.5 minutes). Also set up RSS feeds for searches on your company name and industry terms in other social media sites. Similar to monitoring LinkedIn and Twitter, your Reader will serve as a great place to centralize your other searches too!

It's less about 'push' and more about 'pull'

Social e-marketing isn't about pushing messages and expecting sales leads to follow. It's about engaging with customers, clients and prospects in a meaningful way that adds value for those involved in the conversation. It's about empowering them as true collaborators in the sales and marketing process. Reaching your desired customer segments without engaging with them through social e-marketing is a bit like dancing in the dark. Sooner or later you trip and fall over.

Social e-marketing can't be ignored. For example, Facebook is on track to exceed 1 billion users and if it were a country it would be the world's third largest, after China and India. That's incredible given that Facebook has only been around since 2004. And it's also a huge opportunity for marketers.

Twitter, launched in 2006, has amassed over 100 million subscribers worldwide who have no trouble in communicating within the confines of a 140 character limit. More than half of Twitter's users log in every day, but about 40 per cent prefer to read messages rather than tweet. Outside of Twitter subscribers, an audience of 400 million people regularly visit Twitter.com – the vast majority of people reading tweets haven't signed up to the service.

Without doubt, Facebook and Twitter are responsible for changing the way marketers can communicate with consumers. For example, a 2011 research study in the UK found that 80 per cent of companies of all sizes were using social media to market their products and services. Out of that same group, nearly 40 per cent of business executives found social media to be very effective at influencing brand reputation and increasing brand awareness. In the same year, research by the Aberdeen Study Group found that those companies using social e-marketing enjoyed a 5 per cent average year-on-year improvement in customer profitability compared with just 2 per cent for non-e-marketers. In addition, companies that used social e-marketing gained an average 4 per cent year-on-year improvement in return on marketing investment compared with a 1 per cent improvement for those that didn't.

Research by WPP-owned media buying agency Group M in 2011 showed that consumers exposed to a brand's social e-marketing campaigns were 50 per cent more likely to click on paid search ads on the web than those who hadn't been exposed to social e-marketing.

The influence of social media will develop and expand in the coming decade as its role of watchdog of corporate behaviour becomes more pervasive. As a result, brand owners must become more transparent in their communication with consumers. (For the new rules on PR, see Chapter 7.)

'If things go spectacularly wrong, it comes out and goes on Google Plus and Twitter. That kind of transparency hasn't happened before and it's now searchable and enduring,' reflects Dr Nicola Millard, a customer experience futurologist at telecoms giant BT in the UK.

One high profile example of this is a 2009 YouTube video posted by a disenchanted United Airlines passenger who battled with the customer service department over the issue of a broken guitar. The video clocked up more than 10.5 million views, spawned several additional versions and has been widely profiled in the mainstream media – none of which has strengthened the reputation of the airline.

As a result of social media, every customer now has an instant, global, searchable means of transmitting his or her feedback, good or bad. In addition, customers are also more willing to complain about bad service than ever before. Sites such as TripAdvisor (http://www.tripadvisor.com) have become much more important for businesses such as hoteliers and holiday resorts that fear poor or negative reviews will damage future bookings; they need to have an active engagement with such sites.

The Institute of Customer Service (ICS) in the UK runs an annual customer satisfaction index, which has charted this rise in the propensity of customers to complain. 'In 2000, 50 per cent of people were willing to complain. By 2010, 75 per cent of people were willing to do so, while people are also more likely to tell others about bad service too,' observes Jo Causon, CEO of ICS.

All this is accelerating the move away from mainstream media acting as a consumer watchdog towards a more 'crowd-sourced' approach, and word of mouth is forcing brand owners to up their game if they want to remain competitive by becoming more attentive to the quality of their products as well customer service.

Social e-marketing guidelines

These guidelines apply if you:

- work within an organization and engage with customers, clients and prospects through social e-marketing;
- actively blog or micro-blog (Twitter) on behalf of the company;
- contribute comments, reviews and content to forums, social networks, websites or blogs on either a personal or professional basis; or
- maintain a profile page on one of the social or business networking sites (such as LinkedIn, Google Plus, Facebook or MySpace).

Key principles:

- Be transparent.
- Be honest about who you are and who you work for, while remembering to be careful about disclosing other personal information. Disclose your identity as an employee and make sure your profile makes it clear that the views you express here are your own views and not necessarily those of the company.
- Don't use social networks in a cynical way to push a product or service. If you're using your social networking contacts to promote your company, a product or service, be open about the fact that you are an employee of the company.
- Observe the relevant laws and regulations as they apply to making statements on the web.
- Ensure that any advice given is sound and reasonable and genuinely helps to solve a problem that a correspondent may have.
- Never tell a lie or attempt to deceive or obfuscate the truth.
- Acknowledge mistakes made. Once you've posted content to the web, your mistakes have become a matter of public record. There's no point trying to cover it up, so the quicker you reverse the mistake made, the better it will be perceived to be by those reading what you have to say.
- Be constructive, not destructive.
- Ensure that you aren't defamatory or fall foul of any law that protects the rights of others (see Guru in a Bottle®, *Essential Law for Marketers*, 2nd edition).
- Don't post other people's materials without getting permission and, better still, link to the original source.

In addition to all of the above, an organization that permits its employees to engage with customers, clients and prospects should be clear as to what topics are sensitive and need to carry a health warning. This would include confidential information, price-sensitive information, product development or trade secrets, business strategy, litigation proceedings, personal and sensitive information.

Framework for measuring social e-marketing

It's important from a marketing perspective that you have a clear vision and purpose, and this needs to be a core driver for any social e-marketing that you're contemplating. Far too much loose thinking surrounds brand owners deciding to engage with social e-marketing and it's no surprise that it often fails to achieve its full potential. As with all marketing activities, social e-marketing must be linked to business goals and objectives (see Figure 6.1).

Brand health

This is a measure of how people feel, talk and behave towards your brand – this is one of the most popular measures used in social e-marketing. Applying social insights to your brand can add a further data set to existing research activities and could even mitigate or prevent reputational damage as well as expose threats and opportunities.

Arguably, advertisers withdrew their advertising in the now defunct *News of the World* newspaper in the UK because of the backlash they received on social media networks for seemingly condoning the illegal behaviour and harassment of people from all walks of life in the phone hacking scandal that was rife at the paper.

Figure 6.1 Framework for measuring social e-marketing

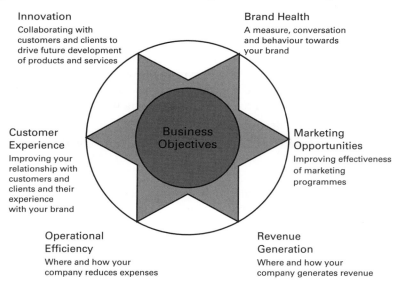

Innovation
Collaborating with customers and clients to drive future development of products and services

Brand Health
A measure, conversation and behaviour towards your brand

Customer Experience
Improving your relationship with customers and clients and their experience with your brand

Business Objectives

Marketing Opportunities
Improving effectiveness of marketing programmes

Operational Efficiency
Where and how your company reduces expenses

Revenue Generation
Where and how your company generates revenue

Source: Altimeter Group (2011)

Monitoring can also add an additional layer of insight to common business metrics such as the Net Promoter Score (NPS), which is a ratio of advocates less detractors. Table 6.3 is an approach to measuring brand health.

Marketing optimization

Social data is invaluable input as it can drive social e-marketing in terms of new content and campaigns. An emerging best practice according to recent research by the Altimeter Group in the United States is to integrate measurement strategy into the initial planning of a marketing campaign to facilitate learning, accountability and continuous improvement.

Table 6.3 Brand health metrics

Themes	Insights	Metrics	Actions to consider
Conversation and sentiment drivers	• How people feel about your brand, product or service • What words or values they associate with your brand, product or service • Where the conversations take place on social e-marketing channels • Frequently shared topics	• Sentiment over time • Source of positive, negative and neutral sentiment • High performing topics, brands, regions • Number of fans/ followers, brand mentions • Top keywords • Top 'shared', 'like' and retweeted	Conduct real-time market research and scenario and crisis planning. Use the research to support marketing strategy for the brand, product or service.
Location, time and impact of conversations	• Top social e-marketing channels • Sentiment variation by social e-marketing channel • Location of conversations about your brand, products and service • How far your conversation reaches into desired customer and client segments • Content speed and resonance with desired customer and client segments	• Where people talk about your brand, product or services • Sentiment by social e-marketing channel • Time-parting analysis by conversation topic	Conduct real-time market research and scenario and crisis planning. Use the research to support marketing strategy for the brand, product or service. The research informs competitive moves and can help to identify and develop relationships with advocates and detractors.

Table 6.3 *continued*

Themes	Insights	Metrics	Actions to consider
Competitive implications	• How people talk about your competitors • Competitive position in industry/product area/topic • Competitive opportunities and threats	• Sentiment by company/competitor • Social share of voice over time versus competitors • Share of total conversation by industry, product, service or topic	Conduct real-time market research and scenario and crisis planning. Use the research to support marketing strategy for the brand, product or service.
Issues identification	• Emerging issues • Issue sentiment • Sentiment drivers	• Accelerating key words, volume, sentiment	Conduct real-time market research and scenario and crisis planning. Use the research to support marketing strategy for the brand, product or service.
Influence	• Influencers, whether advocates or detractors	• Influencers by topic (segmented by followers and/or reach) • Sentiment by influencer	Conduct real-time market research and scenario and crisis planning. Use the research to support marketing strategy for the brand, product or service.

American Express (2011)

In 2011, American Express partnered with YouTube and VEVO to live-stream a Duran Duran concert as part of its 'Unstaged' series. It incorporated Google Plus to better understand how many people talked about the concert and, if so, whether they referenced American Express in their comments. The goal was to determine whether and how the live-stream experience influenced purchase intent and brand perception to better understand how to tune future initiatives. American Express wanted to use the analytics to help influence the type of content it creates.

It's important to note that not all campaigns, channels and metrics are equal. Some are designed for awareness (such as building the marketing funnel), while others are focused on revenue or other goals (such as return on marketing investment and sales). The appropriate metrics need to be chosen with care, depending on your brand, products and services.

In addition, some channels, such as YouTube, can generate more negative sentiment than other channels, such as Twitter, which tends to generate positive sentiment. While social media measurement offers insight into campaign performance, it can also be used to tailor communications to specific customer or client segments (see Table 6.4).

Table 6.4 Marketing optimization metrics

Themes	Insights	Metrics	Actions to consider
Overall social e-marketing performance	• Performance of social e-marketing compared with traditional advertising and offline campaigns • Level of fragmentation of audience reach when using social e-marketing (impact on offline channels)	• Revenue, conversions, leads per dollar spent compared with advertising and other offline channels	Develop and plan future campaigns based on these insights. Review advertising and offline channels to ensure these are integrated with social e-marketing channels.
Content performance	• How many people viewed, shared, 'liked' your content • How videos and other social e-marketing content drove 'calls to action'	• Visit loyalty by content (pull metrics) • Sentiment, retweets, 'likes', fans and followers by content • Revenue, conversions and leads by social e-marketing content	Develop social e-marketing programmes that will capture highest value customer or client segments based on social and lifestyle insights.
Channel performance	• Effectiveness of social e-marketing channels: Facebook, Twitter, YouTube and others	• Visit loyalty, views and click-through by social e-marketing channel • Sentiment by social e-marketing channel • Retweets, 'likes', fans, followers by social e-marketing channel • Revenue, conversions and leads by social e-marketing channel	Plan social e-marketing channel investment based on insights.
Timing impact	• Optimum time to post social e-marketing content and to engage with desired customer and audience segments	• Time-parting analysis by conversation topic	Identify and develop relationships with advocates and detractors.
Influencer identification	• Where to find advocates and detractors	• Most active advocates and detractors • Sentiment of influencers	Identify and develop relationships with advocates and detractors.

Table 6.5   Revenue generation metrics

Themes	Insights	Metrics	Actions to consider
Sales	• Effect of social e-marketing channels for conversion and revenue generation • Extent to which social e-marketing influences purchasing behaviour	• Leads by social e-marketing channel • Conversions and sales by social e-marketing channel • Visit loyalty and intent to purchase • Revenue by product review rating (where appropriate) • Revenue per product across social e-marketing channels • Revenue streams from social e-marketing compared with offline channels	Develop social e-marketing programmes that will capture highest value customer or client segments based on social and lifestyle insights.
Search	• Impact of social e-marketing on search results on Google and other browsers	• Improved search engine placement that drives increased traffic to website	Make marketing investment decisions based on social e-marketing channels performance.
Relationship	• Whether social e-marketing helps to increase customer loyalty over time	• Customer or client lifetime value (CLV) • Average transaction size • Average transaction frequency	Develop social e-marketing programmes that will capture highest value customer or client segments based on social and lifestyle insights.

Revenue generation

Using social e-marketing isn't usually the most efficient strategy for direct revenue generation, but it can have a measurable impact on lead generation and conversion. The key is to understand the role social e-marketing media plays in the purchase process and then fine-tune it to support the ways that consumers use social platforms in the context of your brand.

Brand owners such as Dell look beyond the transaction relationship with its customers and attempt to build a dialogue with them. This means looking at social media as a way of engaging with customers rather than looking at it as just another sales channel (see Table 6.5).

Operational efficiency

While social e-marketing requires up-front investment and ongoing resources, over the long term it can save the organization money. For example, customers can 'market' to each other, which doesn't require intervention from the brand or marketing department. Also, answering a specific enquiry on Twitter that's also read by other customers and clients can reduce time in dealing with the same or identical enquiry.

Social media measurement can also deliver significant insight into the most cost-effective ways to address a particular product or service issue.

Best Buy (2011)

In the United States, Best Buy noticed a trend in which many customers from Latin America were calling the toll-free Spanish number to order products from Latin America for pickup in the United States. To facilitate this process and help its Latin American customers buy products for US family and friends, the company posted detailed instructions in its blogs and forums, but saw that this content didn't resonate well with its website visitors. In response, Best Buy created a video in Spanish to demonstrate the ordering process, placing it with a call to action on the landing page of its Spanish-language website.

As a result, the company decreased calls on this topic to its Spanish-language toll-free number by more than 50 per cent. It also made a second video in English and now, whenever customers come to the English-language website from an international IP address, they are served with a pop-up box that offers help with international ordering – a strong example of operational efficiency in practice.

Table 6.6 provides an approach to measuring operational efficiency through social e-marketing.

Customer experience

For many customers and clients, the first interaction with the brand, product or service is through some form of online presence such as a company website or social e-marketing activity. This virtual experience has become incredibly important within the total customer experience as it can turn up the dial on brand health, cost savings and increased revenues.

Customers and clients will have different expectations of how brand owners behave based on where they are interacting. For example, there's a higher expectation of asynchronous conversation on community channels, so many brand owners cultivate engagement by hanging back a bit to encourage customers to help each other in the first instance (Table 6.7).

Innovation

Brand owners such as Starbucks pioneered the idea of 'crowd-sourced' innovation on websites like MyStarbucksIdeas.com. But not every organization has the resources to devote to the implementation and maintenance of purpose-built innovation platforms. That said, all brand owners can benefit from monitoring the social web for feedback (see Table 6.8).

Table 6.6 Operational efficiency metrics

Themes	Insights	Metrics	Actions to consider
In-bound sales calls	• Potential cost savings achieved through utilizing social e-marketing compared with costs for outbound telesales calls	• Percentage of enquiries from customer and clients that were resolved on social e-marketing channels that didn't require call centre intervention	Align website and social e-marketing content to customer and client questions, issues and enquiries about products and services.
Advocates identification	• Identify who are the advocates and brand fans • What topics do they prefer • Who are the most influential	• Improved search engine placement that drives increased traffic to website	Develop an advocacy and brand fan network.
Relationship	• Whether social e-marketing helps to increase customer loyalty over time	• Most active advocates • Sentiment or hot topics by advocate • 'Likes', shares and retweets by advocate	Develop social e-marketing programmes that will capture highest value customer or client segments based on social and lifestyle insights.
Cost efficiencies for serving customers and clients	• Which product and service issues are best answered online without requiring intervention from the call centre • Where are the knowledge gaps	• Most frequently asked questions (FAQs) online versus in-bound calls	Align website and social e-marketing content to customer and client questions, issues and enquiries about products and services.

Table 6.7 Customer experience metrics

Themes	Insights	Metrics	Actions to consider
Attitudes	• How people talk about your brand, product and service without your being present on social e-marketing channels	• Common keywords • Common topics in social e-marketing compared with those covered in traditional offline channels	Service levels should take account of this insight.
Intensity	• Momentum of an issue or topic that is 'trending'	• Acceleration of keywords or phrases	Align content on social e-marketing channels with service.
Context	• Sentiment and emotion of customers and clients and prospects	• Most common words associated with keywords 'love' and 'hate' in respect of your brand	Directly engage and address service issues.
Continuous improvement	• Areas that need attending to that are dragging down the net promoter score and advocacy score	• Net promoter score and customer satisfaction	Identify and act on emerging issues and crises.
Issues and crises	• Issues with products and services • Emerging crisis	• Volume of sales of products and services	Identify and act on emerging issues and crises
Service levels	• Performance of social customer relationship management • How rapidly can your organization respond to issues online	• Number of service issues addressed in social media • Percentage escalated and resolved in social media compared with offline • Number of positive ratings and reviews • Number of retweets	Service levels should take account of this insight.

Table 6.8 Innovation metrics

Themes	Insights	Metrics	Actions to consider
Opportunities and threats	• Product and service opportunities and issues as they impact marketing, design and service • Competitive opportunities and threats • Emerging crises	• Keywords that are positive such as 'I love' and keywords that are negative such as 'I hate' • Acceleration and unusual volumes of new terms, trending terms and top keywords	Identify the likes and dislikes of customer and client segments and feed this into the service development and customer experience development.
Idea acceptance	• Which insights and ideas appear to gain rapid acceptance and resonate with desired customer and client segments	• Volume of new ideas • Number of retweets, 'like' and shares	Shape the agenda by identifying and engaging on issues and topics that are important to customer and client segments. Use social e-marketing to thank customers and clients for their collaboration.

The world of Twitter for business

Twitter is the real-time information network that connects users to the people and topics they find most interesting. Users tweet a maximum of 140 characters of information but can attach photos, videos or links within the details pane. There are a billion tweets posted every week, making it one of the most effective ways of reaching customers or clients very quickly, particularly if they 'follow' you.

From a marketing perspective, Twitter can be successfully used to increase traffic to a website or blog; create links to content on the web; increase brand awareness by highlighting news and developments; drive conversations as well as assist in establishing thought leadership on issues that matter. The key is to attract influential followers by providing valuable content that can be retweeted and shared across a wider community of interest.

In 2012, Twitter introduced a raft of changes to the website and mobile apps for brand owners and users in a bid to make it more appealing as a promotional tool for marketers. The new look pages were introduced to give brand owners more creative control and personalization, which includes the ability to insert a large header image and select one tweet to highlight at the top of its tagline. The changes aim to encourage users to access Twitter from its desktop site Twitter dot com and not just from apps like TweetDeck and Hootsuite.

Research by Econsultancy (2011) questioned 993 respondents about their interactions with brands on Twitter. The findings concluded:

- Over half of all consumers who took part in the survey (52 per cent) followed brands and companies on Twitter, demonstrating its usefulness as a business channel.

- When asked why they follow brands, 47 per cent of consumers reported that they used the channel to keep informed of the latest offers and discounts.

- About 42 per cent used Twitter to keep up with the latest news from brands, whilst 32 per cent were simply fans of the brands they were following on Twitter.

- The survey showed that overall, sentiment about brands on Twitter is largely positive.

- Only a quarter of consumers (26 per cent) had complained on Twitter, while over half (58 per cent) were very positive about brands on Twitter.

- Around 66 per cent of consumers who gave feedback received a response from brands, compared with 34 per cent who didn't receive any feedback.

- As a proportion of those consumers who use Twitter, 25 per cent said that they considered Twitter to be highly useful, 41 per cent said they found it slightly useful, and 21 per cent said that they didn't find it that useful.

About 77 per cent of Fortune Global 100 companies use Twitter to communicate with market and customer segments, with the highest number of companies in Europe (83 per cent), compared with United States (72 per cent) and Asia-Pacific (67 per cent).

Twitter works particularly well for small and medium-sized companies that want to deliver a highly personalized service. It's also a no-cost way of reaching your customers and prospects in a social e-marketing context. Twitter also works particularly well for those brand owners that want to develop deeper relationships with their customer segments and interact with them, such as Innocent Drinks, Nike, Adidas and Starbucks.

Use Twitter to drive traffic to your website

Provided you've something interesting to say or have a free download or a tool that can be used by your desired customers and followers, tweet about this and embed a link to the landing page for that content. If the content is prized by the community, people will start to retweet it and share it with their own followers. This will start to create a 'thought leader' profile for you within the influencer community you seek to be part of.

Conversely, Twitter can be used to collect opinions about changes to your products and services and act as an excellent 'crowd-sourcing' tool. It can be used to solicit views and opinions about new services and products that you may think about developing and in doing so could be useful in exploring new revenue streams.

Monitor your brand on Twitter

Using the Twitter search tool (http://search.twitter.com) you can search and track what people are tweeting about your company, products and services, competitors and anything else that might be on their mind.

Set up an RSS feed to receive all search results in Google Reader. If you find someone tweeting about your products or a person who's looking for a solution that your product or service provides, then let them know – but resist the hard sell! If customers don't like something, they now have a greater opportunity to make this clear in a very direct way.

Comments on Twitter are indexed by Google and other search engines within hours and can rank highly for keywords, which can improve your search profile. And an RSS feed from Twitter can be used to update other social media channels including Facebook and LinkedIn.

Drive footfall from online to offline ('clicks and mortar')

If you're in the retail sector, Twitter can be used to complement other sales channels, including offline. Creating a buzz online can then translate into a high volume of customers visiting the physical store or retail outlet.

Use Twitter as a search engine

If you're researching a particular topic then a keyword search can tap into real-time community insight.

Use Twitter to promote your events, seminars and latest campaigns

Tweetups are typically an event specifically organized for Twitter users to meet up and network. You should also consider using the hashtag (#) which is unique to Twitter and is a tagging system that is used to aggregate the conversation about the event, seminar, topic, theme or campaign. Hashtags can easily be created by combining # with a word, acronym or phrase and used as a tag within your tweets.

During an event, people often use the hashtag while live tweeting (what they see and hear in real time). The hashtag will tag and aggregate the event's tweets, building an online conversation about the event. The additional benefit is that people who aren't at the event may see your hashtag and want to follow or join in the conversation too. A popular hashtag often sparks curiosity and people will go to http://search.twitter.com to participate in the conversation. (For further discussion on the new rules of real-time public relations, see Chapter 7.)

E-mail settings for Twitter

Twitter allows you to customize your settings for notifications and you can be notified every time someone retweets you or follows you. The default settings on Twitter send e-mail notifications every time:

- a new direct message is sent;
- a reply is sent or you're mentioned;
- you get a new follower;
- someone retweets or 'favourites' one of your tweets;
- Twitter sends an update or newsletter; and
- Twitter sends specific updates such as reminders and suggestions to your account.

Commercial enterprise-wide solutions for managing Twitter

With thousands of tweets, Facebook posts and Google searches per second filling the blogosphere, it can be a struggle to keep abreast of everything that's being said about your brand, products and services!

Organizations like United States-based ExactTarget have developed enterprise solutions to address this, such as the Interactive Marketing Hub, which is a cross-channel interactive marketing platform giving marketers the ability to engage in real-time marketing, consolidate all data streams to create a common view of the customer as well as deliver targeted messages across all social e-marketing channels.

Think of Twitter as a signpost to other destinations and a way for people to find out what you have to say by using the limitation of 140 characters to your advantage. If you follow people, people will follow you back and, provided you have a point of view or something interesting to say (no corporate jargon please!), you'll become a valued member of the Twitter community. You can also join in conversations on Twitter with your followers by replying to them with an @ sign. This allows you to engage with the followers of your Twitter friends.

Measurement

Many marketers are getting to grips with Twitter and other social e-marketing channels so it's important that appropriate metrics are understood and used to measure the value and return on investment (ROI) these channels deliver to the organization, so that senior managers can be convinced that it's worth the effort. (For a detailed discussion on the marketing mix, see Chapter 3.)

There are two main types of metrics that can be used to measure the value of Twitter: site-specific metrics that relate to Twitter itself, and site-specific metrics that aren't present on Twitter. With respect to Twitter, metrics can include:

● number of followers, including follower:following ratio;

● retweets;

● number of replies or engagements; and

● number of lists.

With respect to non-Twitter site-specific metrics, for example where people make use of the custom URL shortener TinyURL.com, which can be used to tweet links and allows marketers to see:

● how many people clicked on links;

● where they were referred from;

● where they are located; and

● the time of day they clicked on the link.

Site-specific metrics are a good indicator of the effectiveness of social media but as with other types of measurement, the data must be combined with other metrics to create an accurate overview.

Traffic

One of the most straightforward ways to measure social e-marketing is to examine traffic to the website and take note of referrals from social media sites. Traffic is a good starting point – it may not be the metric that relates most to your objectives but nevertheless it does provide a good indication of how many people are reading your tweets and clicking through to your website. The effectiveness of measuring traffic also depends on the nature of the business and your business model.

Engagement

Having measured how many visitors have come to your website, it's worth looking at what they're actually doing there and how they're engaging with your brand. Engagement metrics will vary from organization to organization and by product or service, but could include customer loyalty, satisfaction, comments, forum posts and the likelihood of a customer switching to another brand. Customer engagement metrics could include:

● duration of visit;

● frequency of visit;

● percentage of repeat visits;

- recency of visit;
- depth of visit (percentage of site visited);
- sales; and
- lifetime value.

Customer engagement could also be measured through actions such as:

- replies;
- comments left;
- ratings and reviews;
- downloads on site;
- bookmarking links; and
- customer enquiries.

Sales

It makes sense to track sales through Twitter and if you're also tracking sales from other channels it's relatively simple to compare the performance of each social e-marketing channel. Marketers need to track sales over an extended period to appreciate the true impact on the bottom line and how this changes over time.

By focusing on customer service, engaging with customers and resolving customer issues, brand owners can reduce customer churn, which will indirectly result in more business. Increasing positive word-of-mouth will often result in higher levels of customer acquisition. It's important to remember that the impact on sales may not be felt straight away and it may take some time, forming part of a longer-term strategy.

Customer retention

As we've said elsewhere in this book, it's usually seven times more expensive to acquire a new customer than it is to retain an existing one. An effect of increased customer engagement can be better customer retention, and it's worth tracking customer retention rates and the percentage of orders that come from repeat customers.

Leads

Marketers who work in market sectors where the transaction takes place offline may be able to measure direct sales through Twitter. However, this can only be achieved if they capture leads depending on the 'call to action' that happens online. For example, this could be a catalogue that's downloaded and the customer then makes a purchase as a result in a store. The level of interaction as well as the context of the communication could be an indicator of lead generation through Twitter.

Brand

Undertaking consumer research will enable brand owners to assess the impact of social e-marketing over the long term. Social e-marketing may result in a shift in how consumers perceive the brand along the following standard advertising metrics:

- awareness;
- brand equity;
- recall;
- reputation;
- favourability;
- propensity to consume; and
- propensity to recommend.

Public relations

Given the impact of social media on PR, measuring PR can be a good way to benchmark social media activity.

Blogging in real time

Arguably the most important thing to do when writing a blog is to be authentic. Blogging isn't about corporate-speak but part of the broader marketing communications mix where thoughts, ideas, points of view, issues, challenges, commentary and observations can be freely shared to encourage dialogue. It's about belonging to a community and having a point of view. It's about universal exchange.

Basic ground rules when blogging

Rule 1: When you start, keep it up!

It's important you follow through with frequent blogs or tweets as regular customers and followers will think you're off the radar if you start and then suddenly stop. If you're not prepared to commit to frequent postings or tweets, then it's best not to do it at all.

If you decide to stop blogging or tweeting, you should tell your followers you're doing so – its good etiquette and you may want to restart again sometime in the future.

Rule 2: Be personal and friendly

Many organizations make the mistake of trying to control their employees in terms of what they can and can't say. It's far better to provide them with support and guidance and trust them to be good ambassadors for the organization. Transgressions from these sensible approaches can be dealt with after the event, but being too prescriptive defeats the objective of a blog and people can see through the mist of corporate-speak very quickly. The blog needs to be written in the first person by a real person. It must be authentic.

Rule 3: Give people a reason to want to read your blog

This is all about providing interesting, engaging content. Have a plan in your mind as to what you want to talk about and always try as hard as you can to provide genuine insights. Sometimes, these can come from a reflection on what someone else may have said in another blog. Always consider the audience you're writing for before you hit the keyboard – you should have a particular audience segment in mind.

Rule 4: No hard sell!

I'm not sure the hard sell ever worked, but if you think you can do the hard sell thing through a blog – and ironically many sales consultants have almost turned the hard sell into an art form – *don't!* It's the surest way to be a big turn-off.

The old adage: 'If it sounds too good to be true, it probably is' applies to hard sell claims. For example, you guarantee to make people rich as they sleep if they sign up for this exclusive training programme... People will think you're running a scam and you'll damage your reputation in the process.

Rule 5: Don't think a blog is a web page – it isn't!

There are some social network experts who say that you should never have a blog connected to your website but use a different platform such as WordPress (http://www.wordpress.com), which offers one of the best content management systems for writing a blog. That's a view we have some sympathy with. However, some websites label an area where visitors can read a blog and, provided it has some genuine quality as a blog, it should work just as well.

Rule 6: Provide a mechanism for soliciting responses to your blog

As marketing professionals, we are generally very good at the 'transmit mode' stuff but less good at being in 'receive mode', so it's good practice to ask questions or even run a survey to engage with those reading your blog. For example, on the special interest groups on LinkedIn, you can talk directly to the community you are part of and you could start a discussion on a topic where you genuinely want to solicit other points of view.

Rule 7: Keep it simple, use plain language and avoid hyperbole and jargon

As we've discussed earlier, good use of colloquial English will massively improve the flow of the blog and help to build your reputation.

Rule 8: Don't be frightened or take criticism personally

Provided comments aren't abusive or simply vexatious, you can choose to publish them, which may encourage others to post their comments too.

Expect that your company, brand, products and services will be subject to negative comment; develop a thick skin and don't feel compelled to respond in every case. You'll end up not doing your day job and will start to go stir crazy!

In any blog, ensure that people can't post their responses straight away and that your settings are such that you get to moderate what gets posted. This is simply a common sense approach to help manage your own reputation. This would be particularly pertinent if you decide to record a Vlog (a video blog) or make a short film for YouTube.

Rule 9: Make recommendations

As part of the community, it's good to once in a while make recommendations, retweet links to interesting articles as well as provide honest feedback on products and services (good or bad).

Rule 10: Don't forget to have fun!

You're not writing an exam answer or a learned dissertation for an academic journal – that's not what a blog is there to do. Follow the school of thought of 'entertain, inform and engage' – notice that 'entertain' comes before 'inform'. You'll get engagement as a result!

Managing your reputation with other bloggers

One of the greatest fears that most senior managers have is opening the floodgates once they start blogging and inviting others to comment. The fear is that they'll be deluged with feedback and possibly negative sentiment about their brand, products or services. It's this fear that causes a knee-jerk reaction in those not prepared to see the benefits of this form of social e-marketing and who remain unconvinced as to the business value of doing it. This is a grave mistake.

A major fact that's often overlooked is that it's much better to know what's being said about your brand, products and services than to be in the dark and, if it's not that complimentary, there's an opportunity to listen and engage with detractors so that issues and problems can be rectified. This is what the management of reputation is all about.

United States Air Force

An excellent approach to the management of reputation with other bloggers comes from an unlikely source – the United States Air Force (see Figure 6.2).

Figure 6.2 Blog assessment tool

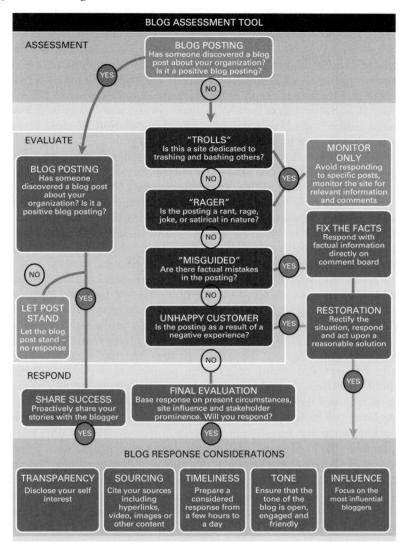

Source: United States Air Force, 2011 with author's modifications

The blog assessment model is based on the US Air Force Web Posting Response Assessment Tool devised by the public affairs directorate of its emerging technology division. It provides a framework for how US Airmen should assess, evaluate and respond to both positive and negative blog posts.

The world of Facebook for business

Arguably, Facebook has become synonymous with social e-marketing leaving Twitter, Google Plus, YouTube, LinkedIn, Tumblr, Foursquare, Ustream and Dailybooth in its shadow as it's grown to be the dominant online social network, topping over 1 billion users worldwide. Facebook makes its money by leveraging the social graph – the individual's online address book. Add together all social graphs of Facebook members and you end up with a world of social connections bigger than the entire population of most countries outside of China and India.

Facebook predicts that most of us make decisions based on 'crowd-sourcing' – we are more likely to buy and do something if our friends, family and colleagues do the same. With an unprecedented dataset of preferences and 'likes', Facebook has been rapidly producing the next generation of algorithms based on group influence and is offering a tempting gateway for brand owners eager to get their hands on this data to drive sales of their products and services.

But not everyone's happy in Facebook-land. Serious privacy, data protection and even psychological concerns dogged Facebook ahead of its IPO in 2012. For example, it's almost impossible to delete personal information once it's on Facebook because complex content delivery networks manage data and distribution and don't always synchronize at the same time, leaving a trail of ghost data still accessible for all to see many years later. Recently, Facebook had to improve its privacy protection after it was found that e-mail addresses and phone numbers of people who weren't members of Facebook were being culled from friends' details, and private messages were being stored after having been deleted from a member's profile.

The latest psychological research suggests that Facebook and other social networking sites are transforming people inside as well as out. Dr Elias Aboujaoude (2011) of Stanford University fears that people who belong to Facebook are developing e-personalities as alternative personae. 'Yet for all the change wrought by the virtual world and thoroughly incorporated into our lives at this point, the more subtle reconfiguring of our psychological landscape that has taken place along the way is often lost on us,' he observes in his book, *Virtually You*.

Pressure group Europe-v-Facebook.org is attempting to bring the social network giant to account but despite the concerns, many brand owners have embraced Facebook when looking to reach a global audience rather than build their own database that could take many years and millions of dollars to achieve.

Coca-Cola (2010)

In 2010 Coke used YouTube, Twitter and Facebook as part of its distribution strategy for its 'Happiness Machine' video. The video, featuring a vending machine in a college campus that delivers flowers, pizzas and unlimited Coca-Cola, is the company's most successful viral campaign to date, with nearly 3 million views on YouTube.

At its peak, the Facebook Page was nearing 11 million members. Coke fans posted an array of content including photos, videos, stories and even song lyrics. While maintaining a global Facebook Page (40.1 million 'likes' as of March 2012), Coke lets individual markets execute what they think is right under the global umbrella. However, the brand owner moderates all content to ensure that it's decent and inoffensive and in keeping with its family values. 'We not only make sure the content is clean but make conversations more meaningful by either responding or driving it in the first place and prompting users to generate their own content,' explains Carol Kruse, vice-president of global interactive marketing at Coke.

If you plan to use Facebook for business, you should select a business account. Our publisher Kogan Page has one and profiles its forthcoming titles and authors on it. Facebook Pages allow brand owners to share information, to interact with customers and fans and to create a brand presence on Facebook.

Facebook Pages are useful because they are indexed and generally rank well in search engines. Most of Facebook is hidden behind a log in, but Facebook Pages are available to everyone. Links can be added that can drive traffic to your blog, website or other online presence, creating further opportunities for viral marketing. However, it does require you to build your database of fans and you may want to start connecting with Twitter followers first, especially if they retweet your appeal for Facebook followers.

Facebook Pages are also very popular with search marketers looking to market on Facebook. These Pages have had a makeover by Facebook to be more brand-friendly. When compared to a basic ad that goes directly to a home page of a website, 'liked' ads may generate a bigger audience and steadier traffic with returning visitors. The advantage of Facebook is that it gathers lots of personal information about its members and allows brand owners to target advertising to specific users by:

- location;
- age (18 years old and over);
- birthday;
- gender;
- keywords;
- education;
- company, organization or other workplace;
- relationship status; and
- hobbies and interests.

The following are tried and tested Facebook features that will deliver a higher impact for your marketing efforts:

Facebook ads

These are demographically targeted text and image ads that can target users based on a number of variables including likes, age, gender, education and other indices. These ads can be cost-per-thousand (CPT) or cost-per-click (CPC) and traditionally have a low click-through-rate (CTR). Unlike search ads, Facebook ads are targeted by demographics, not by keywords. Brand owners can target desired customer or client segments by a range of demographic factors such as geo-location, 'interests' and so on.

Unlike search advertising, which uses keywords to target searchers, Facebook advertising tends to target who the person is, based on demographic and declared interests. It's an important distinction, as these differences tend to capture Facebook members at different locations within the purchase funnel. (For a discussion on creating an effective sales pipeline, refer to Guru in a Bottle®, *Art of Influencing and Selling*.)

Location tagging

This allows Facebook members to tag locations and share where they've been, where they are now and where they are going. It's mainly used on mobile devices and from a brand owner's perspective can be useful data as part of a location-based advertising strategy. Facebook members can also add location to photos they've already posted. The Facebook application competes with Foursquare, which has over 15 million members worldwide.

Facebook events

These can be set up by a member on their Facebook profile or by a brand owner on their Facebook Page and allows members to communicate with each other in a specific location. Members can respond to an event by confirming, declining or offering a 'maybe' to the host. Events can be used much like a Facebook Page for specific activities and are only open to profiles to attend, not other pages. Event creators can communicate directly with the mini-community that's been invited and share images, videos and files. Facebook events can be public, closed (by invitation only) or private.

Facebook groups

These allow like-minded Facebook users to communicate with each other. Groups can be public, closed or hidden; only profile accounts can be included in a group. Groups operate like Facebook Pages, but the default settings allow users to be notified of new threads.

Group chats can be conducted and documents created. The marketing potential for Facebook Groups is much lower than Facebook Pages but can be effective in specific scenarios.

Since Groups only allow individual profiles to participate, any messaging must come from an individual instead of a brand owner. If you do choose to market in groups, you need to be transparent in disclosing your sales and marketing motives. (For a discussion on the data protection and privacy issues that these activities raise, refer to Guru in a Bottle®, *Essential Law for Marketers*, 2nd edition.)

Best practice in m-marketing

Mobile device adoption is growing exponentially and if you look at almost any industry metric the trajectory for mobile growth over the next five years is stratospheric.

Currently, there are 5.9 billion mobile subscribers, equivalent to 87 per cent of the world population and around 10 per cent of all website hits and page views come from a handheld device. As a result of this rapid take-up, over a third of all mobile users now expect websites to load faster than or just as fast on their mobile devices as on wired computers, and nearly a fifth of all users expect websites to load nearly as fast on their mobile devices.

Recent research by Bytemobile (2012) shows that video content accounts for 50 per cent of overall global mobile traffic and amongst certain networks this can be as high as 70 per cent. For example, YouTube was found to account for about 350 times as much traffic as Facebook despite actual usage levels being similar for the two platforms, with the average smart-phone user spending 9.06 minutes on Facebook, 4.57 minutes on Twitter and 8.51 minutes on YouTube.

Vodafone and Visa (2012)

In February 2012, Vodafone and Visa joined forces to create the world's largest m-marketing partnership to allow customers to pay for items directly from their handsets. The Vodafone branded 'mobile wallet' covers 30 countries spanning five continents and allows users to pay for goods with near field communications (NFC) enabled SIM cards by waving their devices in front of payment terminals to purchase low-value items from the balance in their Visa pre-paid accounts. They also have the ability to make higher-value pur-chases when combining this with a secure password.

As can be seen from these examples, technology is rapidly enabling change in this field, which is making it increasingly difficult for marketers to keep up. In fact, the rising penetration of smartphones and tablets is compressing IT innovation cycles to between 12 and 18 months, forcing companies to review their m-marketing strategies every 6 to 12 months. We advocate that marketers focus on behaviour as the key driver for m-marketing activities, rather than any particular mobile device such as a smartphone or tablet. A common misconception is that a mobile device is a desktop made smaller. It isn't. It's a completely different medium requiring a different content management and design approach to that used for the web. And apps aren't the default solution for m-marketing.

M-marketing is best understood as a way of moving experiences around for the user rather than just being confined to a specific mobile device. Conversely, many people who use a mobile device may be immobile themselves but choose to interact through the mobile medium. So whether m-marketing is less about the device and more about the experience, it's clear that people engage with these experiences in a multitude of ways that aren't desktop-driven.

Mobile devices and platforms

The main mobile devices used globally are notebook PCs, feature phones, smartphones and tablets.

Notebook PC

This is a laptop personal computer for mobile use which integrates most of the typical components of a desktop computer, including a display, a keyboard, a pointing device or touchpad and external speakers into a single unit.

Feature phone

This is a mobile phone which at the time of manufacture wasn't considered to be a smartphone but nevertheless has additional functionality over and above a basic mobile phone. It's marketed to customers who don't want the full functionality of a smartphone or to spend that much on a mobile phone.

As a result of the pace of change in technology, a previous smartphone model that's 18 months old could now be considered a feature phone. Typically, a feature phone will have a personal digital assistant (PDA), portable media player and capabilities such as a camera, touch screen, GPS navigation, wi-fi and mobile broadband access.

Smartphone

This is a mobile phone built on a mobile computing platform, with more advanced computing ability and connectivity than a feature phone. A smartphone typically has a high-resolution touch screen, web browser that can access and properly display standard web pages rather than just mobile-optimized sites, and high-speed data access via wi-fi and mobile broadband.

The most common mobile operating systems (OS) used by modern smartphones include Apple's iOS, Google's Android, Microsoft's Windows Phone, Nokia's Symbian, RIM's BlackBerry OS, and embedded Linux distributions such as Maemo and MeeGo. Such OSs can be installed on many different phone models, and typically each device can receive multiple OS software updates over its lifetime.

The distinction between a smartphone and a feature phone can be vague and there's no official definition for what constitutes the difference between them. One of the most significant differences is the advanced application programming interfaces (APIs) on a smartphone for running third-party applications allows for better integration with the phone's OS and hardware than is typical with feature phones. In comparison, a feature phone more commonly runs on proprietary firmware, with third-party software support through platforms such as Java ME or BREW.

Tablet

This is a mobile computer that's larger than a mobile phone or personal digital assistant, integrated into a flat touch screen and primarily operated by touching the screen rather than using a physical keyboard. It often uses an onscreen virtual keyboard, a passive stylus pen, or a digital pen. Since 2010, the most popular tablet mobile device globally has been the Apple iPad.

There are four varieties of tablet models available at the time of writing:

1 *Standard format* – this is called a slate, which doesn't have an integrated keyboard but may be connected to one with a wireless link or a USB port.

2 *Convertible format* – this does have an integrated keyboard that can be hidden by a swivel joint or slide joint, exposing only the screen for touch operation.

3 *Hybrid format* – this has a detachable keyboard so that the touch screen can be used as a stand-alone tablet.

4 *Booklet format* – this has two touch screens and can be used as a notebook by displaying a virtual keyboard on one of the screens.

Of all of these formats, almost half a billion smartphones were shipped globally in 2011 compared to over 1 billion feature phones.

According to the latest research by the Gartner Group (2012), sales of tablet devices will outstrip desktop PCs by as much as 60 per cent by 2015 – with Apple's iPad dominating almost half the market by then. It's also predicted that the popularity of Google's Android as a tablet operating system will wane unless Google can address barriers for adoption that include high prices, poor user interface and limited tablet applications.

According to Google's own 2011 study of the behaviour of smartphone customers conducted across 30 countries:

- 79 per cent of people turn to their mobile phone to help them shop;
- over 70 per cent of people use their smartphones in shops to compare prices;
- 88 per cent take action on that information within a day;
- 70 per cent of all mobile searches result in action within an hour; and
- unlike the desktop computer, the mobile phone is always on, always with us and always connected.

It's important to remember that smartphones aren't a prerequisite for mobile web use and the distinction is fast losing its usefulness as feature phones improve.

Those brand owners who ignore feature phone owners do so at their peril. It's vital that any m-marketing strategy doesn't overlook large sections of users of non-smartphone devices and that any mobile website is optimized for all handsets, not just smartphones.

Another issue to consider is whether to go down the native app route for separate operating systems or to produce a mobile website that covers all the bases. Either way, increasing numbers of consumers now reach for their mobile before anything else and brand owners must think 'mobile first' as the mobile platform can be the connective tissue between all channels – offline, online and social (see Figure 6.3).

Google, Amazon and eBay (PayPal) have all seen a dramatic increase in the volumes of payments for goods and services being made via mobile over the previous 12 months. In the case of Amazon, that amounted to more than US$1 billion of products being ordered using a mobile device. In 2012, m-payments made globally for all goods and services will exceed US$100 billion in value, and by 2015 global mobile transactions will top US$1 trillion, according to research by the Yankee Group.

Device detection

With a vast array of screen sizes, operating systems and capabilities, it's essential for any mobile-enabled website to detect and react to the specific device each mobile visitor is using.

Figure 6.3 Mobile support for consumers throughout the buying cycle

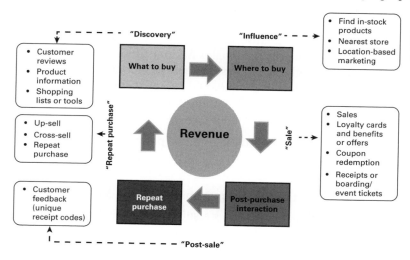

Source: Forrester Research (2012)

There are at least 6,500 different models of mobile device that are capable of accessing a mobile website, so it's important that the mobile website can identify the handset used by each mobile visitor in order to optimize their experience accordingly. This not only makes your customer's visit as pleasant as possible; it also allows you to make assumptions about the visitor based on what handset they use and target services, promotions and advertising accordingly.

Most mobile phones will struggle or fail to render (display) a desktop-oriented website. The vast majority of people around the world today don't have a smartphone so it's important that your mobile website works on these lower-end handsets. Even on smartphones, most mobile sites will give a much better user experience if the content is adapted to the device. This doesn't just mean making things smaller to fit the small screen or speed up the time it takes for the page to load; the content supplied should also be more relevant. While PC users are usually sitting in an office or at home, mobile users are often out and about – their context means they have different requirements. No matter how great a mobile device is, web surfing can only ever be as good as the performance of the mobile network at the point of use. The connection is rarely going to be as good as a PC on a fixed broadband connection. So reducing the page and picture sizes can really improve the user experience, even for smartphone users, and if the customer has a limited or pay-as-you-go data package then a streamlined site will save them money too.

Twin track for native apps and mobile web growth

There's a clear growth trend for content consumption via mobile web rather than via native apps. This is due to several factors, all of which tend to suggest that this trend will continue.

Apps provide an unassailable advantage in terms of control over the user experience and this will remain the case even with the growth of the next generation of HTML website programming language (HTML5) that allows web pages to store data, work offline, look fantastic and use rich interactions. However, native apps simply have a different goal: in simple terms, apps are for loyalty and mobile-enabled websites are for discovery. Most brand owners need both, but for many it makes sense to focus first on getting the customer and then on how to retain them.

An effective mobile strategy embraces all of the mobile devices out there, not just the ones of the well-heeled audiences. Remember, too, that each mobile ecosystem has its own submission procedures, rules and idiosyncrasies. Each time you update your app you will run up against these issues. Right now, the mobile web is the only way to reach the whole audience in one fell swoop. The mobile user benefits too – there's no need to repeat the download each time the app is updated.

With browsers now being embedded in a vast array of devices as standard, mobile users have moved from going online to living online. The net effect

Other issues to consider when specifying the requirements for a mobile-enabled website are the flexibility of the content management system (CMS) that's used. Most aren't configured for the website to live in the mobile world and at best are a compromise in helping to create a contextually-appropriate experience. For example, a mobile plug-in will strip down page templates, reduce menus and resize images that are delivered to mobile devices. But this will fall far short of treating the mobile platform as something that needs to be considered at authoring time where more added value can be built in.

If you're outsourcing the build of the website/mobile website:

- Clarify with the agency what range of devices it's expected to work on.
- Remember to include recent iOS and Android devices as well as feature phones and Windows Phone.
- Make sure that the agency tests the site(s) on multiple devices.
- Check that the analytics you receive will also track feature phone use and not just smartphone use, as some analytics tend to under-report traffic delivered by certain classes of mobile device. One way to check how well mobile devices are currently supported by your site is to measure the bounce rate with actual devices.

The following is a checklist to ensure that your m-marketing campaign is successful:

- Segment you desired customers and prospects with care.
- Pay attention to timing and frequency issues.
- Test m-marketing campaigns prior to roll-out.
- Keep communication personal and relevant and consider using rich media where appropriate to capture interest.
- Keep up to date with changes in data protection and privacy laws within the relevant territories of the m-marketing campaign.
- Seek guidance on m-marketing best practice from professional bodies such as the Mobile Marketing Association, the Direct Marketing Association, the Interactive Advertising Bureau and dotMobi.

Best practice in direct marketing

Storm clouds are gathering over direct marketers irrespective of where they may be on the planet. And the reason is this: revenue per message is shrinking – whether delivered by physical direct mail through the letter box or by e-mail to an individual's PC, laptop or mobile device. As a result, marketers feel they must send more and more messages to compete. However, volume is a detriment, not an asset, in the battle to win the hearts and minds of recipients, and relevance has become even more important in the war of words.

Table 6.9 Average direct marketing response rates

Type of direct marketing	Typical response rate	What you can expect
Direct mail letter individually addressed to a named recipient	6.7% of the names mailed to	67 responses per 1,000 pieces posted
Direct mail B2C campaign	7.1% of those mailed to	71 responses per 1,000 pieces posted
Direct mail B2B campaign	6.2% of those mailed to	62 responses per 1,000 pieces posted
Door drop to households but named individuals ('junk mail')	5.0% of those who receive the mail	50 responses per 1,000 pieces posted
Door drop to households but named individuals ('junk mail')	40% is put in the recycle bin unopened	Of the 60% that does get opened by the householder, a further 20% doesn't get read
E-mail campaign	Open rates for segmented and named individuals versus non-segmented campaigns can vary as much as 20%	A carefully segmented and named e-mail campaign will perform 20% more effectively in the first 30 days

In many respects, direct marketing – whether in physical print form like a printed flier or an e-mail – can be relatively quick and inexpensive to produce. But it's often hard to beat the odds of it actually being opened and read (see Table 6.9).

From reviewing the table, it's clear that typical response rates from any type of direct marketing are likely to be low. Making realistic predictions before deciding to invest in any form of direct marketing is a sensible precaution.

In the remaining part of this chapter we'll look at how high impact direct marketing both offline and online can outperform typical direct marketing response rates. (For a discussion on out-bound telesales marketing effectiveness, refer to Guru in a Bottle®, *Art of Influencing and Selling*.)

Traditional direct marketing

Back in 2009, commentators in the UK were busy writing the obituary of direct mail, the Cinderella of the marketing world that most people preferred to call 'junk mail'. It's not easy not being wanted! The doomsayers claimed that the dip in items being sent through the post – 1.4 billion from the previous 1.5 billion – was evidence of this long-term malaise. The web and e-mail were going to kill direct mail and consign it to the history bin. Fast forward to 2012 and far from being in terminal decline, direct mail in the UK is in rude health and hovering just below 2 billion items being sent by post every year. TV didn't kill the radio star, and the web didn't kill direct mail!

Given the all-singing, all-dancing web content that a targeted e-mail campaign can deliver to millions of people instantly and at relatively low cost, why should traditional direct mail be making a comeback? One reason is that customer concern about junk mail has now shifted to the inbox.

Old fashioned and trusted delivery systems, such as the postman, are having a disproportionate effect on influencing behaviour, claims Anthony Miller, head of media markets at the Royal Mail in the UK. 'People open about 95 per cent of what comes through the front door. Consumers and business customers respond positively to messages arriving via the friendly postman.'

E-mail fatigue has certainly contributed to the renewed interest in direct mail but increasingly the channels should be seen as complementary rather than competing with each other. All organizations, large or small, private, public or voluntary sector use direct mail as a way of creating a useful database of customers and supporters. (For a discussion on how to interrogate a database, refer to Guru in a Bottle®, *Art of Influencing and Selling*.)

Given that it's possible to segment your desired market and customers on an individual basis, there's never a need to send a piece of direct mail that begins 'Dear Sir or Madam'. It's never been that effective in any event. And if you are to use lists of people who have opted in to receive information it's prudent to double-check that they really have opted in! (For a discussion on the privacy laws and data protection regulations that impact direct marketing, refer to Guru in a Bottle®, *Essential Law for Marketers*, 2nd edition.)

Increasing the chances of being read – outside

There's been a lot of trial and error over the years in the way in which an envelope can turn on and off the recipient of a piece of direct mail. This may sound bizarre, as you would have thought that direct mail was all about the contents of the envelope rather than what's on the envelope itself. But remember, this isn't a letter from your mother whose handwriting you can decipher from the envelope, which will encourage you to open and read it (or not!)

There are four 'envelope types' most commonly used in direct mail:

1   'Creative envelope' type – this is where marketers can start to think laterally about messages, colour, images and even the shape of the envelope, which can all be combined to make this a distinctive-looking item.

2   'Special offer' envelope type – this is more common and is a bit *Reader's Digest*, but has a high response rate when tested! This includes envelopes that tell you there's a free sample of a new coffee or fragrance inside plus a money-off purchase.

3 'Benefits envelope' type – you may decide to give the compelling proposition top billing – on the outside of the envelope! Typically, some envelopes scream 'OPEN NOW!' but recipients are more sophisticated and are likely to consign this to the recycle bin if you do.

4 'Stealth envelope' type – making the envelope look like personal mail is disingenuous and is only likely to irritate the recipient rather than help influence their behaviour in a positive way to your message. Best avoided.

Increasing the chances of being read – inside

Assuming the piece of direct mail hasn't ended up in the recycle bin, your next big challenge is to grab the recipient's attention when the piece of mail is opened and read.

Often, an existing customer will have made a purchase and this has been logged, but very rarely will the retailer send a polite 'thank you' and start to reward the customer's loyalty by offering them something else to buy with an enticing discount. Media and cable TV companies frequently do this as it's more profitable if they can sell you a bundle of cable/satellite, broadband internet and phone services.

The production costs of a piece of direct mail can be 10 or more times the cost of an e-mail – but it could also be 10 times more effective. A brochure has a tangible quality and production values that can't easily be replicated in an e-mail; it could also drive a recipient to visit the website, for example, to watch a film or demonstration of the product or service.

The quality of the mailing database is extremely important in targeting the messages accurately. For example, insurance companies tend to send car drivers direct mail at the point when they know they're looking to renew their car insurance, so this stuff tends to get read. It has some value. It's timely, appropriate and targeted. Some car insurance companies go one step further and promise to beat any quote, including from the existing insurer.

To greatly improve your chances of being read, follow this checklist:

● Carry out segmentation analysis to improve the chances of the direct mail being opened and read. It's important to have a handle on the attitudes, values, beliefs and behaviours of the recipients and preferably address them by their correct name. You could build a target list for a direct mail campaign by analysing what they click on when visiting your website, how often, and what they've done before. This will help to integrate the offline marketing activity with any online marketing activity, and vice versa.

● One of the best times to contact customers is after they've interacted with you or your website. Focus on marketing automation, where most of your mail is sent out in response to enquiries and site visits, rather than 'spamming' people who may or may not be interested.

● Treat different people differently and don't treat every customer the same – some are more valuable than others. Make sure you address their personal and business needs in a relevant and meaningful way, based on what you know about them.

- Allow recipients to respond to your offer online. You may be sending the communications by post but people will probably want to respond via e-mail or through the website, provided you make it easy for them to do so. In such cases, provide a landing page with a trackable URL to visit and provide a mobile option too.
- Consider using QR codes (see Chapter 5).
- Track all responses to the campaign via post, web visits and e-mails, which will allow you to test all elements of the campaign.
- Don't treat direct mail as a standalone channel – using the creative to drive through a consistent message across all media will reinforce rather than dilute that message. Use the unique personalization benefits of direct mail to tailor the message.

E-mail marketing

S&P and the US Treasury

On the morning of Monday 1 August 2011, officials in the US Treasury building, neighbour of the White House, were preoccupied with whether President Obama could secure enough votes to get a debt deal through the House of Representatives and the Senate. Without a deal within 24 hours, the United States was on course for a default on its sovereign debt for the first time in its history. While they fretted over this, another crisis was stirring a few blocks away. A phone call from Standard & Poor's, one of the world's leading credit rating agencies, demanded to see the numbers showing how the United States could cut US$2.1 trillion from federal spending over the next 10 years. Four days later, S&P pressed the send button on a global e-mail announcing it had downgraded US sovereign debt from AAA to AA+, declaring that the United States was now less likely to meet its debt obligations than the Isle of Man. What made global financial markets convulse wasn't as a result of a Reuters or Bloomberg news flash. It was an e-mail.

In an age of information overload, e-mail still has enormous power, as the above story illustrates. But as a form of direct marketing, e-mail marketing is getting itself a bad rep and its potency may be on the wane.

Cognitive overload

A new field of behavioural research known as 'decision science' is attempting to unravel why the mind appears to give equal attention to an e-mail selling timeshare apartments and a message about a family bereavement.

According to researchers, the brain automatically gives credence to the latest input, not necessarily the most useful. Angelika Dimoka, director of the Center for Neural Decision Making at Temple University in Philadelphia, warns that the huge volume of data we now handle in our wired lives is rapidly becoming counterproductive: 'The web is creating cognitive overload and when we face that we make the poorest decisions in every aspect of our lives.'

Joanne Cantor, a psychologist and author of *Conquer CyberOverload*, says the brain can juggle only seven items at a time, and often e-mail arrives in mass batches that can overwhelm judgement: 'If you let things come at you all of the time, you can't use additional information to make a creative leap – you need to take a break.'

One famous experiment pitted two groups of business students against each other in an exercise in playing the stock market. One group was given every conceivable piece of information on the markets while the other received only simple stock prices. The latter easily outperformed the former.

Atos ban of internal e-mail by 2014

The boss of IT and systems integrator giant Atos, Thierry Breton, signalled that the company will ban all internal e-mail in its business by 2014 as part of its 'Wellbeing at Work' policy. There were several reasons advanced in defence of such a policy: graduates hired by the company weren't using e-mail but social networking; on average each employee received 100 e-mails a day of which only 15 were deemed 'useful' and as a result there were productivity issues that the company wanted to address.

Interestingly, Atos hadn't banned external e-mail use and accepted that this would continue to be used as an important direct marketing tool – although its use would be smarter.

According to Henry Smith, strategic global accounts director at US marketing consultants E-mailvision, 2012 will be the year when marketers raise their game in the use of outbound e-mail:

> Greater relevancy, driven by customer intelligence, should be foremost in the minds of marketers. We all understand the need to create compelling and relevant campaigns to ensure a return on investment, but as e-mail inboxes become smarter, so must our understanding of customers. There's an exciting opportunity to turn customer data into usable, intelligent information that can help marketers to go beyond traditional segmentation and truly personalize their customer communications.

In 2011, global e-mail marketing grew substantially, with revenues increasing 26 per cent and the number of e-mails sent increasing by 17 per cent compared with 2010. The prediction for 2012 is that e-mail usage is set to increase by over 30 per cent globally compared with 2011. However, turning off has become the challenge, typified by the view of Atos and others. The key to success for direct marketers is to focus their efforts on performance optimization, better targeting and effective adaptation of e-mail for mobile.

Traditional e-mail marketing

Due to its low cost and easy execution, e-mail has long been used as a tactical channel. But despite its popularity with marketers, diminishing returns have dented its popularity.

This type of direct marketing is used to encourage recipients to click through to a website or online store to take some further action, such as request a download, make an appointment or order a good or service. Amazon does this particularly well. It knows what purchases you've made in the recent past and will often (without bombarding you) send an e-mail suggesting products that other users have purchased which you may like to consider, plus forthcoming books or albums not yet released that you can pre-order, based on your own purchasing behaviour. This isn't hard-sell and is done with the intention of being information-friendly. And it works!

Intelligent e-mail activation

Three areas need to be addressed:

1 delivery – landing in the in-box and being read;
2 relevancy – needs to be a message and content that the recipient will welcome; and
3 engagement – needs to have a compelling reason why someone will take the time to read it.

(For a discussion on customer and client segmentation, refer to Chapter 1.)

One-to-one marketing

Where e-mail can score is its ability to deliver a highly relevant communication targeted at individuals in terms of their attitudes, values, beliefs and behaviours. At a basic level, the communication needs to be addressed to someone by their name. Many brand owners that rely on e-mail direct marketing techniques to drive their business are successful because they regularly engage with their desired customer and client segments through surveys, polls, games, downloads and money-off coupons to drive the propensity to purchase. They also integrate e-mail with other aspects of their marketing activities, for example linking to a landing page, a micro-site or a Facebook profile. In this regard, e-mail is a gateway to the brand rather than a single, standalone piece of communication.

Spam filters are now very sophisticated and complex algorithms look for patterns in an e-mail message that will reveal it as spam and stop it being delivered either at the internet service provider (ISP) end or at the user end on the computer.

Many brand owners send e-mails during the night to save on server load, but research shows that e-mail will tend to have the greatest impact if it arrives in the recipient's in-box while they are using the computer. The optimum time for sending a direct marketing e-mail can be determined from reviewing your website statistics. For example, many B2C brand owners' websites tend to have their peak volume of visitors on a Tuesday, suggesting that Tuesday may be the best day for a newsletter. However, rather than attach a newsletter to an e-mail, consider using an e-newsletter software program and type only an abstract of the articles you wish to write. The abstract should be sufficiently compelling to encourage readers to click through to your website to read the article in full.

Although it's almost impossible to generalize, research shows that for many B2B brand owners, Monday is the worst weekday compared with Tuesday to Thursday. Sending an e-mail on a Friday could work, although it may be viewed by home users at the weekend. Business users tend to wind down on a Friday and are more likely to read a newsletter or respond to a viral campaign. The key is to test and compare the results for each day and time of the e-mail campaign.

E-mailing the full text of articles to a subscriber may discourage them from reading them – remember that people are time-challenged and want to be able to judge quickly whether something's worth reading in full before committing to do so.

In 2011 in the UK, the Privacy and Electronic Communications (EC Directive) (Amendment) Regulations (2011 Regulations) provided marketers with a 12-month window to comply by May 2012 or risk legal action by the Information Commissioner. These regulations affect direct electronic marketing on laptops, desktops, digital and mobile devices and the security and confidentiality of such communications. The 2011 Regulations amend the Privacy and Electronic Communications (EC Directive) Regulations 2003 and make a number of important changes to safeguarding of data, spam e-mails and third-party information notices. (For more guidance on the impact of these regulations, refer to Guru in a Bottle®, *Essential Law for Marketers*, 2nd edition.)

- Keep e-mail marketing messages short, to the point, and offer useful hyperlinks that add value rather than become a distraction to the core message you want to deliver – remember the person reading the e-mail message has many more to get through, so you need to capture his or her interest fast.

- Pay attention to subject lines: these are the headline for capturing the interest of the recipient. Consider using powerful keywords at the beginning and restricting this to 40 characters to avoid Outlook or other e-mail programs truncating the headline.

- Don't exaggerate or make wild, unsubstantiated claims that will make the e-mail look like spam – spam filters look for patterns in e-mail that can identify it as spam and it will go directly into the junk e-mail folder.

- Avoid bulk e-mails and comply with data protection, privacy and EU electronic communications regulations (refer to Guru in a Bottle®, *Essential Law for Marketers*, 2nd edition for guidance).

- Always follow a 'permission based' direct marketing approach, where the recipient has actively opted in to receive communication and, ideally, there's an established relationship in place, such as being an existing customer or client. A sign-up to a free newsletter or useful download can be a good way to gain permission where no goods or services have as yet been purchased.

- Remove names and addresses immediately from your list when people request their details to be deleted. Remember that not allowing users to opt out even after they've opted in is unlawful and risks action from the legal authorities in your territory.

- Remember that responsibility for checking a purchased e-mail list for legal compliance rests with you, as well as the list agency. It's good practice even with opt-in lists to send a short pre-qualifying e-mail that could contain an offer based on a request for further information, provided this isn't onerous. Remove bounce-backs as well, as they don't want to hear from you.

- Keep all communication open and transparent, and always make it easy for someone to opt out of receiving further e-mails from you.

- Regularly update your e-mail lists.

Mobile e-mail marketing

This is one of the most important tools available for use in any direct marketing campaign since it provides a cost-effective technique for reaching the desired customer or client segment via a channel that's open 24/7.

According to the latest industry research, the number of consumers who access e-mail on their mobile devices will top 1 billion by the end of 2013. To succeed in this new environment, marketers must rewire the customer experience of the web and adopt a new set of e-mail marketing tactics for the mobile generation.

One of the first issues that marketers need to face is finding out the preferences of customers and clients when they first sign up for an e-mail newsletter; they also need to be able to update those preferences. As we discussed earlier in this chapter (see the section on m-marketing), it's important that marketers employ technologies that detect what device recipients are using to read e-mail messages. For example, if a retail brand owner knows that its customers always open their e-mail using a webmail program on Tuesday to Thursday but tend to use a mobile device to read e-mails on Friday to Sunday, the retailer may consider sending an online or website promotion such as a money-off offer earlier in the week and sending a mobile offer at the weekend that's designed to drive traffic and sales offline at its physical stores. It could use different design strategies to optimize campaigns for both desktop and mobile experiences, depending on the day of the week and the user's behaviour.

Given the smaller screen size compared with a computer, a mobile e-mail needs to have a powerful subject line and a compelling 'top of the fold' message to engage with the recipient. The most common techniques to gain attention are:

- teaser – intended to intrigue the recipient and often combined with a question;
- question – usually alludes to the benefits of the product or service being marketed, working on a need or a problem the recipient may have (could be financial or time-based);
- event tie – relates to different types of events, which can include annual holidays or company-type events;
- direct approach – clearly states the offer or benefits without attempting to be intriguing or humorous; and
- personalized – where the name of the recipient is incorporated into the start of the subject line, which has the effect of grabbing attention as it's not that commonly used, although it can appear to be insincere if not done appropriately.

Industry best practice is to avoid multiple columns, wide graphics or tables in the e-mail, making sure users can view the entire message by scrolling down – not to the right; and keeping the size of the e-mail below 20 kb so it can be accessed without needing to download a large file that could take time and as a result cause the user to click away.

Measurement and evaluation

Setting sales goals for direct mail campaigns is routine, because the cost of mailing must be recouped by the value of the response. It seems that because e-mail is cheaper, specific response goals aren't always set, but for major campaigns it is best practice to set specific goals for e-mail marketing campaigns.

Often e-mail marketing is measured on the open and click-through rates, but equally valuable is looking at engagement through the customer life cycle:

- conversion of prospects into buyers;
- conversion of first-time purchasers to repeat buyers;
- reactivation of lapsed customers; and
- increased penetration among key desired customer segments.

You may also want to evaluate the relative value generated from a mobile e-mail campaign. This is best achieved by normalizing value by 1,000 e-mails – number of leads, sales, revenue or profitability per 1,000 e-mails. These are also known as 'subscriber figures', which are either for a single campaign or over a time period, such as 12 months.

References

Books

Aboujaoude, E (2011) *Virtually You*, Norton
Akins, J and Hanlon, A (2009) *Digital Marketing*, Oak Tree Press
Frank, C and Magnone, P (2011) *Drinking from the Fire Hose*, Portfolio Penguin
Garrett, J (2003) *The Elements of User Experience*, AIGA
Kolah, A (2013) Guru in a Bottle, *Essential Law for Marketers*, 2nd edition, Kogan Page
Kolah, A (2013) Guru in a Bottle, *The Art of Influencing and Selling*, Kogan Page
Maslen, A (2006) *Online Copywriting that Sells*, Sunfish
Rogers, M and Peppers, D (2005) *Return on Customer Currency*, Doubleday

Articles and reports

Interview with Steve Ridgway, CEO, Virgin Atlantic, in *McKinsey Quarterly*, July 2011
Service 2020: Megatrends for the decade ahead, BDO/Economist Intelligence Unit, September 2011
The social habit II, Edison Research/Arbitron, 2011
A framework for social analytics, Altimeter Group, 2011
Social marketing for search marketers, *Search Marketing Now*, 2011
How to Use Twitter for Business, HubSpot (2012)
Personalized targeting: don't get personal, get social, *ADMAP*, March 2011
Personalized targeting: the race for relevancy, *ADMAP*, March 2011
Delivering intelligent e-mail, *Alterian*, 2008
The ROI of mobile, *Forrester*, January 2011
Implementing your mobile strategy, *dotMobi*, 2012

Websites

Google provides guidance on how to register your website, update your settings, monitor and manage your site, add a sitemap to the webmaster tools account and how to keep up to date: http://www.google.com/webmasters/checklist (accessed 26 February 2012)
Microsoft provides guidance on how to register your website, update your settings, monitor and manage your site, add a sitemap to the webmaster tools account and how to keep up to date http://wwwbing.com/toolbox/webmasters (accessed 26 February 2012)
Ardi Kolah wrote the copy for this sports marketing website powered by YouGov: http://smg-insight.com
Three mobile e-mail marketing challenges – and what you can do about them: http://www.unica.com (accessed 25 February 2012)
E-mail Marketing Best Practice Guide: http://econsultancy.com (accessed 25 February 2012)
Twitter for Business: http://econsultancy.com (accessed 25 February 2012)
Pressure group against Facebook: http://www.europe-v-facebook.org (accessed 3 March 2012)
How to build your e-mail list: http://www.internetmarketingacademy.com (accessed 4 March 2012)

eBay has an excellent process in place for communicating reassurance to the customer to be able to purchase products from the website with peace of mind: http://www.ebay.co.uk (accessed 26 February 2012)

Location based mobile services: https://foursquare.com (accessed 4 March 2012)

Trade industry bodies that represent the interest of mobile operators and mobile marketers include: GSMA http://www.gsma.com; dotMobi http://mtld.mobi; the Mobile Marketing Association http://www.mmaglobal.com; the Direct Marketing Association http://www.the-dma.org and the Interactive Advertising Bureau http://www.iab.net (accessed 4 March 2012)

The United Nations Agency for Information and Communication Technologies: http://www.itu.int (accessed 3 March 2012)

All the world's a stage, but most of us
are desperately under-rehearsed...

a public body, an NGO, a charity, a government department, a famous celebrity or a brand owner.

According to the Chartered Institute of Public Relations (CIPR) in the UK, reputation is defined as:

> *the beliefs or opinions that are held about an organization or an individual. These beliefs or opinions are formed through expectations (what and how it will deliver and how it will behave), experiences (what it has actually delivered and how it has behaved, which builds trust), the messages people are exposed to and the conversations they participate in or observe. An organization's constituencies therefore determine and 'own' its reputation.*

Today, all organizations are judged not simply on the quality of their products or services but on how they are managed, governed, what steps they take to safeguard their employees, financial performance, compliance with regulations and their overall contribution to the communities they serve and society in general. Failure to manage reputation can lead to catastrophic results.

Research by RepTrak Pulse (2012)

This research surveyed over 10,000 British consumers and found that public confidence in utility companies was lower than for any other sector.

British Gas, Scottish Power and Southern Water were all in the bottom 12 of the 262 UK firms ranked for corporate reputation, behind banking and telecoms overall, with Royal Bank of Scotland named as the individual organization with the worst corporate reputation. 'Many issues have yet to be resolved with some corporations flying in the face of public opinion and expectations, particularly in relation to executive remuneration and bonuses paid to employees of the big banks,' says Spencer Fox, MD at the Reputation Institute UK.

The most favourably viewed sectors were consumer goods manufacturers and food and drink companies. The most trusted brands were Dyson, Rolls Royce and Boots. Chief executives typically take their own role as the face of the organization very seriously and surprisingly a high number spend more than half their time communicating with stakeholders in one form or another.

In many organizations, the director of communications reports to the CEO, which gives an indication of the importance placed on the function as a whole. However, the relative importance that both CEOs and chairs place on individual disciplines within the communication function varies considerably, with notable differences between sectors and operating environments.

For example, in the retail sector, considerable emphasis tends to be placed on media relations as this is seen as a direct way of building corporate reputation and an important channel for customer engagement. However, media relations doesn't appear to have the pre-eminence it once enjoyed and a growing number of organizations now place communication with other stakeholders such as government, investors and employees as of equal or in some cases greater importance in managing corporate reputation.

Those firms operating in highly regulated environments, such as financial services or pharmaceuticals, or with government as a shareholder or customer tend to put more emphasis on government relations, but across all sectors this discipline appears to be rising in overall importance. With the turbulence in the global economy, more governments are prepared to be interventionist and this is forcing brand owners to work harder at building stronger relationships with them and regulators. In the future, directors of communication will need to have more input into strategy discussions with those running day-to-day operations whilst retaining an external perspective on the reputation of the organization.

Google (2012)

Every minute of every day, millions of searches are typed into the Google search engine. Users flock there because Google, more than its rivals such as Yahoo and Microsoft's Bing, tends to deliver more pertinent results for its users. This is reflected in its market share: in the United States, two out of every three internet searches are performed through Google, rising to more than 9 out of 10 in Europe. Its dominant position has produced gigantic rewards for the 13-year-old company. In 2011, it reported a US$9.7 billion profit and almost all of this came from adverts and sponsored links that flank Google's search results.

Google, whose corporate mantra is 'Don't be evil', is accused of using its near monopoly to promote its new services, and is now subject to one of the biggest anti-trust investigations by the European Commission and the US Federal Trade Commission. Eric Schmidt, Google's redoubtable chairman, has to fend off allegations that the search giant rigged the system and cooked its own results showing that it achieves better search rankings than its competitors.

All these claims have been vehemently denied. But irrespective of the outcome of these investigations, the corporate reputation of Google has been tarnished and it will take a focused effort to restore this to its former position where it was once seen as the 'David' to Microsoft's 'Goliath' Internet Explorer browser.

London 2012 Olympic Games

Many sponsors of the London 2012 Olympic Games spent millions enhancing their corporate reputation globally. In some cases, such as with Dow Chemical, the company had been under attack for its link with Union Carbide and the Bhopal disaster, and various pressure groups campaigned against the company to have its sponsorship revoked by the International Olympic Committee.

Arguably, Dow Chemical missed an opportunity to engage with all stakeholder groups by considering how it could use social media and the global interest in the magic of the Olympic Games to reconnect with these audiences in an appropriate, meaningful and interesting, way which would have gone a long way in restoring its reputation. Instead, Dow Chemical decided to keep a low profile despite being a global Olympic sponsor.

Another global Olympic sponsor, Coca-Cola, whose 94-year association with the Olympic Games has also been criticized by pressure groups and anti-obesity campaigners, took a very different approach to dealing with attacks on its reputation. Instead of diving for cover, it agreed to submit its US$70 million sponsorship to scrutiny in the first independent measurement of such promotion's social value, a brave move and one that has strengthened its corporate social responsibility credentials. Dow Chemical, please note.

The British government has strenuously defended the role that sponsorship plays in supporting the Olympic Games where the majority of the cost is borne by the commercial activities of brand owners like Coca-Cola rather than through taxation or public finance.

Other brand owners take a radically different approach and rather than spend millions trying to persuade media outlets to carry their content or shape the media's opinion about the company, they are exploring the option of distributing and promoting their own content directly to the audience.

Brandcasting

The wave of brand owners becoming broadcasters is likely to accelerate as brandcasting and advertiser-funded programming (AFP) becomes much more attainable than it was back in the late 1990s, when brand owners were still fixated with the old interruption model of communication (advertising) and hadn't switched onto the power of embedding messages in TV-type content.

This new chapter in the evolution of PR is spurred by digital developments that are removing barriers between TV programmes and online content, creating new and exciting ways for brand owners to get their messages across to desired customer and client segments. (For a detailed explanation on the law and regulation in this area, refer to Guru in a Bottle®, *Essential Law for Marketers*, 2nd edition.)

In the UK, catch-up services such as BBC's iPlayer, 4oD and ITV Player have created opportunities for consumers to search for traditional programmes online. The next generation of smart TVs that allow viewers to surf the internet alongside TV channels and online streaming services such as Netflix are creating the momentum for change in the viewing habits of the next generation of consumers.

Within a couple of years, smart TV will compete with everything on the web, providing a huge opportunity for brand owners to create their own content and their own channels. 'Brands already invest heavily in getting their content into other media owners so why don't they take this expertise, passion and knowledge and become their own broadcasters,' observes Howard Kosky, chairman of PR broadcast specialists Markettiers4dc.

For example, YouTube already attracts more views than content broadcast on traditional TV channels and it makes sense for brand owners to create content and channels that reach demographics who don't watch traditional TV.

Red Bull

As discussed at the top of this chapter, Red Bull is sponsoring the exploits of Felix Baumgartner and has occupied the role of content producer of the 'Stratos campaign'. At every stage in the campaign, Red Bull is gathering content – from the testing of the modified astronaut suit through to 'fly-on-the-wall' meetings with Felix Baumgartner and NASA. This exclusive content is being released regularly, helping to build a global audience and will be packaged into a full blown programme about the record attempt when the time comes.

In the future, the trend will be for brand owners to produce a variety of short- and long-form content for all media platforms. 'Behind the scenes' content that augments traditional TV shows will also grow in popularity, and TV viewing will leave behind the history of being a solitary experience and will enter the realm of being a social experience of one-to-many and integrating seamlessly with the power of the web. Technical standards for making this a totally HD or 3D experience are around the corner, heralding a new dawn for channel broadcasters, brand owners and audiences. The internet will never look or feel the same again.

Power of the narrative

What all of the above demonstrates is the need for a good storyline to engage with the audience that a brand owner may seek to influence. One of the most famous business success stories of the past 50 years is global athletic brand Nike.

Nike

In 1964, Phil Knight was a fledgling athletic-shoe salesman whose high career point had been selling US$8,000 worth of imported Tiger running shoes out of his Blue Ribbon Sports store in Eugene, Oregon. Within the next seven years, Phil Knight had sold nearly US$1 million's worth of Nike product. And the rest, as they say, is history.

Runners probably had little idea that Nike was the winged goddess of victory in Greek mythology but Phil Knight had a vision and purpose to turn the humble running shoe into one of the most desirable consumer products in the world, explains Scott Bedbury, brand guru and former Nike head of advertising:

Andrew Griffiths takes up the story:

> *You've just read one of the most successful urban legends of the past 15 years.*
>
> *The kidney heist is a story that sticks. We understand it; we remember it and we can re-tell it later.*
>
> *If the story is true, it might change our behaviour permanently, at least in terms of accepting drinks from strangers!*
>
> *The story is effective because it works on a number of different levels.*
>
> *It's simple. It's easy to recall. It's unexpected: man goes for a drink and loses a kidney. It's concrete: ice bath, tube protruding from back. It's credible: we're already familiar with stories about dating and drugs. And finally, it's an emotional story: conveying anger, fear and disgust.*
>
> *In all organizations senior leaders struggle to communicate everything from strategy to getting new ideas accepted and acted out. It's no surprise with the amount of information we process daily, initiative overload and the constant of uncertainty that getting people to behave differently is a huge task. So the challenge for senior leaders is to think differently about the big ideas they have and how they can make them stick.*
>
> *This is very difficult for experienced leaders who've immersed themselves in company logic, constructs and conventions over a long time. It's time to re-learn how to take big ideas and transform them. Should the CEO who communicates the top priority to 'maximize shareholder value' be surprised when the call to arms fails? Take the example of John F Kennedy's famous 1961 call to 'put a man on the moon and return him safely by the end of the decade'. Simple? Yes. Unexpected? Yes. Concrete? Amazingly so. Credible? It seemed like science fiction but coming from the President of the United States it seemed credible. Emotional? Well it motivated millions of people for a decade. Had John F Kennedy been a CEO he could have said: 'Our mission is to be recognized internationally as the leading country for space exploration, innovation and strategically targeted space initiatives.'*
>
> *Fortunately John F Kennedy knew that empty words don't inspire and captivate people. But sticky stories do.*

To create a compelling story that delivers a distinctive, highly memorable message that can influence not just awareness or perceptions about a brand, product or service but also motivate behaviour, consider the following points:

- Start with a deep understanding of the demographics and psychographics of the audience you want to reach with the story – their attitudes, values, beliefs and behaviours.

- Be clear what it is you want to deliver as a message.
- Do your homework and gather facts, figures and statistics that will help to tell the story.
- Use business judgement to incorporate or ignore research data.
- Think about what the audience will be doing when you're delivering the story as well as the format for that piece of communication.
- Have a variety of versions of the same story that will transmit well on the page and as a picture and piece of film or video content.
- Entertain, inform and engage.
- Remember that there are only seven great storylines and whatever the story you want to tell, it will fall into one of those basic plotlines!

Creating powerful PR 'products'

The key outputs of any proactive PR programme can usually be broken down into these 'products' that have been put together for use by journalists:

- news release;
- background brief;
- case study; and
- visual image.

(The aspect of social media and PR activities outside of dealing with journalists is dealt with in a separate section in this chapter.)

News release

The news release is one of the most powerful statements that can be issued by a brand owner when it wants to transmit its news to a wide audience, rather than just the print media, which is why it isn't called a 'press release' anymore! It's also one of the major areas of weakness for those working in PR who've never experienced working on a busy news desk or don't have an insight into the pressures that journalists face on a day-to-day basis in print, broadcast and web-based media.

There are certain 'hygiene factors' that a news release should comply with, as discussed below.

Date of the news release

The date of the news release should be immediately clear to the recipient and not buried in the body of the text or at the end. This may sound like a basic PR principle but if the news story really has news value, then the date is critically important for the journalist. Is the news story for today, tomorrow or for next week?

All journalists work to deadlines and the last thing they have time for is working out whether the news story should get their attention right now when they receive it or it can wait for later.

Headline of the news release

This is an art in its own right as it's the hook for the journalist. Ideally, it should be fairly short and encapsulate the essence of the news story. It's more likely to get read if it's interesting, otherwise it will end up in the recycle bin. Even business news stories can benefit from a 'tabloid newspaper approach' to headline writing.

First paragraph of the news release

This should be the main guts of the news story. Short, punchy and not wasting a single word. Ideally, a compelling number, fact, figure and/or statistic should be included. Avoid hyperbole, exaggeration and flowery language and actually have a point of view, backed up with evidence. Facts are so important, along with interpretation and insight.

So many 'news' releases in fact don't contain anything new but recycle what we already know. Fundamentally, a news release must comply with news values.

Avoid the temptation to label something a news release unless it really is news. It doesn't do your organization's reputation any good as it's very poor PR practice to call everything you send out to the media a news release when it's patently anything but newsworthy.

Body of the news release

Try not to go over the top but actively look for other contributions to the story – expert opinion, new research data, perspectives of customers and clients, even a government minister or leading and respected authorities in their fields such as an academic that has a good reputation and credibility. Quotes provide 'colour' and also seek validation through numbers and data. They help to tell the story.

Using quotes in a news release

The worst thing a PR professional can do is to ask for a quote for the news release. As the storyteller, it's your job to write that story and then seek approval for the quote that you've attributed to that person.

Always think about making the news release as strong and robust as possible as well as making the contributor look good. Any person or body quoted in a news release needs to be saying something that patently adds value rather than something generic and boring that has no media value.

End of the news release

Think how a business piece is written in a leading business newspaper, periodical, trade journal (both offline and online) in your market and you'll notice that there's usually a strong point to finish on, or a conclusion that can sometimes be an expert quote or even a call to action.

Note to editors

This comes at the end and should be in numbered bullet format. This could be a link to the research paper (online), a key background fact to something in the news release, further data that supports the insight shared in the news release and a link to a photograph or video. You may want to make a commentator quoted in the news release available for interview for broadcast media or a photo-call for national press. You may want to refer to a webinar with the precise date and time or any other event where something may be taking place on the day that's relevant to the news release.

Media contact

It's important to have the media contact person's name, title and contact details including an out of office hours contact mobile number.

Background

This is also referred to as a 'boilerplate' and is a paragraph of what your organization is, how many employees and markets it operates from, what products and services it delivers and other data. Although it's unlikely that a journalist will reprint a boilerplate in the news story, it does help to emphasize the significance of the information as coming from you rather than a much smaller or less impressive organization.

Other considerations

Make sure that if someone is prepared to be quoted in the news release they are prepared to speak to the media. Many journalists prefer to conduct a short interview rather than 'cut and paste' the quote taken directly from a news release.

It's not good form for a news release to be issued when a person that's quoted in it isn't available to speak to the media, for example immediately it's issued he or she goes on holiday. That simply pisses off journalists in the broadcast media where they may want to interview the commentator for TV or radio. You run the risk that they'll not come back to you again in the future if they feel you can't deliver.

Always consider whether the news story can be encapsulated as a picture – thinking in this way will amplify the opportunities to view the news story you're creating with the potential to be much bigger than you may at first have recognized.

Style of writing

This depends on the market and customer segments you're trying to engage with. News releases for the music industry will use language and cultural references not found in releases about the insurance or medical sector.

All writing should be straightforward and to the point. *The Financial Times*, Associated Press and *The Economist* have all produced excellent style guides. Good writing never goes out of fashion!

Tone of voice

Again, this depends on a number of factors:

- nature and culture of your organization;
- type of news you are trying to convey;
- the use of language your audience feels comfortable with; and
- what feels appropriate – formal versus informal, technical versus colloquial, etc.

Length of news release

In an ideal world, one or one and a half pages is the norm. It would need to be a cracking news story for it to cover two pages! The exceptions to this rule of thumb include financial news announcements that need to comply with certain financial rules and regulations and as a result can often run into five or more pages.

Background brief

Not every organization will always have 'hard news' to issue on a daily basis and the skill of a PR professional is to create 'talking points' with the media and other audiences.

Where there isn't a hard news story, then an issue, problem or challenge facing an industry or customer or client could become the basis for a background brief for a journalist. This needs to be carefully researched as the point of view, opinion or insight that you want to share needs to sit within a broader context, and it is the job of the background brief to set the scene, so to speak. Typically, the background brief will:

- identify the issue, problem or challenge;
- provide data and statistics that are both historical and forward looking;
- provide a summary of viewpoints about the issue, problem or challenge and a point of view that can be substantiated; and
- suggest an interview, follow-up meeting or other 'call to action' with the journalist.

The objective of the background brief is to encourage the journalist to want to cover this area in the first place or to adopt a line of enquiry being mooted, so it must also be topical, relevant, timely and of interest to the audience the journalist is writing or broadcasting to.

A background brief is really useful because it can avoid having to go through an interminable internal approval or sign-off process; for example, where a news release may be generated in Europe but will need clearance in the United States where the HQ of the parent company is based. This can be very frustrating and slow things down. Preparing a background brief may be one way to avoid this situation, although it shouldn't be misused!

The background brief can be a useful one page or double-sided one page (effectively two sides) that can be handed to a journalist over a lunch with a CEO, director or manager to help stimulate discussion and debate about a point or issue that's relevant for your organization and market segment.

However, a background brief should clearly state 'not for publication' or 'draft' or 'strictly confidential' so that the journalist doesn't use this as a de facto news release by mistake as it may not comply with internal policies and procedures that a news release would need to go through. You should cover your back and always follow internal company policies.

Case study/testimonials

Case studies and testimonials are really useful media assets and tend to have many more uses than simply PR. They can be used in:

- presentations;
- printed materials;
- website;
- annual reports;
- conferences, seminars and exhibitions;
- books, articles, journals and academic papers;
- marketing collateral;
- internal communications and employee engagement;
- third-party communications;
- the customer or client's internal communication channels;
- pitch documents and proposals;
- credentials presentations;
- business plans; and
- teaching and training materials.

The art of creating a compelling case study or testimonial is that it should be a memorable story; it should be evidence of what your organization actually delivers as opposed to what it says it offers and it should in large part be in the voice of the customer or client, so it's externally rather than internally focused. It should always be supported by powerful photography and can be part of a case study library on an organization's intranet so that when a business presentation or pitch has to be prepared, an appropriate case study can be found and used. In this way, a case study is a useful media asset.

Many case studies and testimonials available on the web really are nothing more than hard sell advertising masquerading as a case study or testimonial, and they tend to have little or no real value.

All the material used for the case study or testimonial should be signed off by the customer or client and they should be encouraged to distribute the case study within their own organization, maybe in their own internal newspaper or intranet. This helps to demonstrate the close relationship each party enjoys and shares this with a much larger audience, encouraging more business interaction as well as enhancing reputation and encouraging myth building.

Case study template

There are many different approaches and uses for a case study. Some are designed to support products and services and so the hero of the case study may be the product or service being launched. However, all successful case studies share key characteristics in the way in which they are put together (see Table 7.1).

Table 7.1 Case study template

1. Identify the problem, issue, challenge, opportunity	• Describe this clearly and succinctly in business terms.
2. What did the customer or client do about this?	• For example, did they research the market; draw up a short list of potential solution providers?
	• Need to explain.
	• Why did they choose you compared with others?
	• Need to explain this in rational and unemotional language.
3. What did you do?	• What was your response?
	• Did you map out a strategic plan?
	• Did you scope the problem/issue?
	• Did you do some initial analysis (what were the findings)?
	• Did you undertake a short research study or programme?
	• At this part of the case study you need to create quotes from the customer or client and quotes from your own organization that provides some 'colour' to the story.
	• This is where emotional language can be used.

Table 7.1 *continued*

4. What did you deliver?	• Here you need quotes from the customer or client.
	• 'The Influencer' quote could be a chairperson or someone very senior within the customer or client organization but who didn't authorize the contract.
	• 'The specifier' could be a boss within the customer or client who sets the framework or direction for the work to be done but who may not personally sign off the invoice.
	• 'The authorizer' within the customer or client is someone who was responsible for the scope of work to be done and who also signs off the invoice.
	• It's also important to have numbers or statistics (measurable stuff) that back up and validate what is said you have delivered. This is the evidential basis part of the case study and in many respects one of the most important ingredients.
5. Did this work?	• This is also evidential in nature.
	• Where possible, it's useful to find an external third party who can give an objective perspective/ endorsement on the work you have done.
	• Input from an institute, professional body, recognized university or academic can be extremely powerful and add a level of credibility and authority to the case study.
6. What are the measurable benefits for the customer or the client?	• Need to describe the benefits delivered.
	• Benefits should be from the perspective of the customer or client (B2C or B2B).
	• For example, the expression of benefits can be in terms of cost savings, income generation, new product development, or opening a new facility.
	• It's also important to have numbers or statistics (measurable stuff) that back up and validate what is said you have delivered.
7. Within a B2B context, how did this impact the customer or client's own customers?	• Here you need to get some insight from the customer or client that validates the decision to use you rather than another organization.
	• This part of the case study is with quotes from the customer or client's own customers or clients and other stakeholder groups.
	• This is often ignored or forgotten in case studies and yet could be the most interesting bit.

Table 7.1 *continued*

	• Using these stakeholders' own quotes will be powerful (and permission from the customer or client will be required).
8. (Where relevant) what can the customer/client now do in terms of its market segment that it couldn't do before?	• Where relevant, you may have empowered the customer or client to be able to do something that is important for them.
	• Explain what this is.
	• This part of the case study is about delivering a competitive advantage to the customer or client or some other advantage that has value for them.
9. (Where relevant) what are the future opportunities for the customer/client?	• This is a forward-looking bit of the case study.
	• This can be described in terms of competencies, capabilities, market position, market share, new product development, increase in productivity, decrease in risk or other such measurable benefits that link back to the other parts of the case study.
10. (Where relevant) what experience and capability do you now have as a result of this work?	• This is a more sales-oriented type of case study.
	• This bit could be a useful round-up of your own competencies, capabilities, market position, market share, new product development and other meaningful 'sales' type messaging.
	• This part of the case study ends on you so it's much more selling-focused.
	• Try to make this bit more future-oriented.
	• Include contact details at the bottom.
11. How can all of the above be encapsulated by a photograph or video or film?	• Need to break away from linear thinking and consider expressing the case study through the medium of photography, video and film.
	• This helps to add emotional intelligence in the way the story is told.
	• This is the most powerful way to help in getting the audience to engage with the case study.

You may not be able to satisfy each of the suggested elements of the case study template, but don't panic! It doesn't have to be rigidly followed and much will depend on the amount of space you have at your disposal to tell the story.

It's useful to use a small tape recorder or similar to go through a list of questions for each of the sections of the case study that you want to build with each of the contributors in your story. In this way, you focus on the answers being given rather than worrying about taking notes. If this is being done over the phone, be sure to ask the interviewee whether he or she minds being recorded for note-taking purposes only.

Visual images

The cult of celebrity can be traced back to the 19th century and the rise in popularity of photography. Celebrities were put on pedestals and the photograph was a means of capturing their image and making it portable and affordable. As small cameras and fast presses created the dream factory and turned people into celebrities, the introduction of the movies in 1895 made stars out of the celebrities.

The old adages 'that every picture tells a story' and 'a picture is worth a thousand words' hold true today as pictures are the common currency of communication around the world. A visual image:

- can reach out and touch someone in a way that words never can;
- is instantaneous;
- doesn't require linguistic interpretation;
- doesn't need to be heard;
- doesn't always require additional explanation;
- can be understood in a matter of nano-seconds or within the blink of an eye;
- has the power to change the way we feel;
- remains in our subconscious for the rest of our lives; and
- can be recalled at will depending on our emotional state.

Some of the biggest moments of the 20th century have been captured for prosperity not in words but in pictures. For example, on 24 November 1963 Jack Ruby shot Lee Harvey Oswald as he was being transferred from one Dallas jail to another at about 11 am in the morning. Captured on NBC TV, it was the first time that millions of US viewers had witnessed someone being killed live on their TV screens. Disturbing as this was, it's the still photograph of Jack Ruby pulling his gun on Lee Harvey Oswald who's flanked by two detectives that sticks in our collective consciousness. US photographer Vicki Goldberg observes:

> *Every photograph is an artificial present; it implies a past and a future, a moment before and a moment after. Rarely has a photograph held the future in such suspension as this one does. The knowledge of how momentous the next few seconds would be makes this image seem to have captured history holding its breath.*

Photography is important within PR and yet many brand owners often ignore its significance when putting together presentations or even the website, where using a stock photograph is often the default solution. This sloppy thinking doesn't help the attempt to create a distinctive image of the brand, the products and services – the same stock image may appear elsewhere. It could even be the exact same image that's used by the competition. Such a coincidence isn't just unfortunate but also serves to confuse those customers and clients into thinking there's a connection between the two brands, services and products when this isn't the case.

Working with a professional photographer and producing images that the media can use (these will have to be a minimum of 300 dpi resolution) can get the news release, case study or a picture story greater coverage than had an image not been used.

PR and its relationship with public affairs

The relationship between business, politicians and government is often the lead news story wherever you may be in the world.

In the UK, the British Government became embroiled in the 'lobbygate' fiasco that turned it into a running news story for over six months:

- October 2011 – Dr Liam Fox resigns as defence secretary ahead of Sir Gus O'Donnell's report of his investigation into whether he had allowed his personal and professional responsibilities to become blurred as a result of the lobbying activities of his friend and special adviser Adam Werritty.

- December 2011 – *The Independent* newspaper publishes The Bureau of Investigative Journalism's undercover operation into Bell Pottinger. It claims to have caught the UK's largest PR agency secretly boasting about its access to the Government and how it uses the 'dark arts' to bury bad coverage.

- January 2012 – the Government launches a consultation on a statutory lobbying register.

- March 2012 – Conservative Party co-treasurer Peter Cruddas resigns ahead of *The Sunday Times* 'cash for access' investigation that claims donations of £250,000 a year can give 'face time' to senior ministers and that 'premier league' donors could lobby the Prime Minister David Cameron directly.

- May 2012 – former News International CEO Rebekah Brooks and her husband Charlie Brooks were charged with attempting to cover up evidence in the *News of the World* phone-hacking scandal. The charges are hugely embarrassing for the Prime Minister who already admitted that his relationship with Rebekah Brooks got 'too cosy', with text messages regularly signed 'LOL'. Her husband is an old-Etonian and close friend of David Cameron.

Whether or not lobbyists Bell Pottinger went beyond accepted practices is the subject of much debate and an independent professional practices committee at the Public Relations Consultants Association (PRCA) found there wasn't any evidence of malpractice. Francis Ingham, Director General of the PRCA, observes:

> You can't expel members just because The Independent will give you a good headline if you do. The issue of how the public affairs industry regulates its activity is much wider than this case. The biggest lobbyists in the UK aren't consultancies. They are charities, think-tanks, and business groups and trades unions. A statutory register needs to include all of those who lobby or it will be an expensive failure.

In a survey of 2,000 members of the public conducted by global research agency OnePoll for industry newspaper *PR Week*, fewer than half of the respondents understood what lobbying is and 40 per cent believed that companies shouldn't be able to pay for advice on engaging with government.

What's clear is that the outcome of the British Government's consultation on a statutory register of lobbyists must first define the act of lobbying if it's going to work. Yet despite the hostile environment around lobbying, it remains an important part of PR practice and an essential and legitimate activity that's part of the democratic process.

For example in Europe, Brussels is home to over 1,500 European business organizations or trade associations that play a prominent role in EU public affairs. Their composition, vocation and outreach vary considerably due to their particular histories and the growing breadth and depth of EU competencies. By far the largest constituency that appears in the EU Transparency Register is trade associations and they tend to consider Brussels as their natural HQ: the necessary platform from which to seek to influence EU decision- and policy-making.

To be a successful lobbyist, the public affairs professional shares a lot in common with the PR professional:

- excellent communicator;
- strategic leader;
- persuasive diplomat;
- industry expert;
- energetic networker; and
- competent manager.

The work of the public affairs or government relations professional often overlaps with his or her PR counterpart, although the public affairs professional may be looking for PR support for a particular policy document, positioning paper or research that needs to be shared with a wider stakeholder audience rather than just policy makers at the heart of government. Transmitting this clearly to the media is the job of the PR professional.

Many organizations ensure that the director of communications and the director of public affairs/government relations work closely and in an integrated way. This ensures consistency in messages as well as appropriate and timely external and internal communications on issues that affect the organization as a whole, such as the 'licence to operate', particularly in regulated markets such as energy, pharmaceuticals, healthcare, food and beverage, transport and financial services.

Offline versus online media

When the Titanic sank a century ago, it was a news story that swiftly took on global dimensions. Built at Belfast's Harland and Wolff shipyard, the world's largest ocean liner was a potent symbol of the British Empire. But rather than the story of its demise breaking in a national newspaper, it was the humble local paper, *The Halifax Courier*, which landed the scoop of the decade. Fast forward 100 years and *The Halifax Courier* is itself fighting for its own survival, moving from daily to a weekly title.

The fact remains that in possibly the most competitive media market in the world, British national, regional and local newspapers face an uncertain future as sales of newspapers skydive and media owners are forced to diversify their interests, increasingly to online media. And this trend is being replicated around the world.

For example, the Mail Online is the most visited newspaper site in the world, registering nearly 4 million unique visitors to its website a day, trumping its venerable rival, the New York Times. This contrasts sharply with its offline sister publication, the *Daily Mail*, whose British readership is predominately women aged 50 and over. The website attracts a much younger global audience for a completely different diet of endless salacious celebrity picture news stories. So while advertising in the *Daily Mail* is heavily skewed towards the likes of Tesco and M&S shoppers, a US visitor to Mail Online is served up ads from local US brands.

Yet for all the soul-searching about online media strategies, it's unclear which titles, if any, are going to prosper as the internet becomes ever more pervasive and the circulation of printed newspapers continues to tumble. One reason is that reading a newspaper is no longer a common habit. Whereas a decade ago, 25 million newspapers were either bought or given away in the UK, as a result of broadband and smartphone penetration that number has dropped to below 19 million today and falling.

At the same time, the internet has supplanted newspapers as a space for advertisers who are able to target customers and prospects with a higher degree of accuracy on social networking sites such as Facebook and Google +1, and often more cheaply as a result of the endless supply of web pages.

Although digital is growing rapidly, it's not growing quickly enough to offset the falls in print revenues for newspapers.

The most prudent approach for PR professionals to adopt is a dual media strategy – offline and online media – to reach and influence desired customer and client segments rather than putting all of their eggs into the online media basket. The relative advantages of key offline versus online media channels are summarized in Table 7.2.

The overwhelming benefits of online media are that it's excellent at building trust, developing conversations in real time and informing customers and clients via third-party credibility on social networking sites. It can also be a useful early warning indicator for trouble ahead and allow the PR professional to manage communications to avoid the issue becoming a crisis later.

Social media and PR strategy

Most published data tends to show roughly a third of all organizations are heavily involved in social media within a PR context while just under two-thirds have either experimented with social media and do an average amount with it. About 1 in 10 brand owners are in the minority for having not done anything about it at all. Not surprisingly, those brand owners with annual turnovers in excess of US$200 million are the heaviest investors in social media, whereas those with turnovers of less than US$1 million tend to fall into the category of those still playing catch-up.

The organizations that are very active in using social media in PR activities are: around 12 per cent for B2B brand owners; around 26 per cent for B2C brand owners; and about 16 per cent for those that are B2B and B2C brand owners. Part of the slow take-up isn't as a result of a lack of interest on the part of the PR professionals but often the reticence of senior management, who don't believe in spending resources to communicate through the medium of social networks. This view is partly understandable.

In 2011, global research company TNS surveyed 72,000 consumers across 60 countries about their attitudes to social media and digital behaviours. The findings showed that the majority of consumers in developed markets didn't want to engage with brands via social networks, and in the UK that sentiment was felt by 61 per cent of respondents surveyed. This may appear to be an 'inconvenient truth' given that some brand owners invest considerable PR budgets in social media channels, but it doesn't automatically lead to the conclusion that brand owners shouldn't bother at all. Rather, the take-out from the research is that all forms of customer and client communication must be appropriate if it's going to be successful.

'Many brands have recognized the vast potential audiences available to them on social networks: however, they are failing to understand that these spaces belong to the consumer and brand presence needs to be proportionate

Table 7.2 Offline versus online media channels

Media channel	Advantages	Disadvantages	What it's especially good at doing	What it's not especially good for
TV	High impact in terms of audience reach; can turn a story into a powerful narrative with strong pictures. When added to online media can deliver a rich media experience.	Hard to target specific demographic groups with the same accuracy as online media. Can suffer from lots of clutter as often competing with other brand owners' messages.	Where the news story, case study or issue needs to be brought alive and to create the most powerful impact with the desired audience segment.	Not so good at engineering a direct 'call to action' response compared to more direct channels such as online media.
Radio	Easier to segment the audience – certain genres of music, talk stations and those that appeal to certain demographics. More immediate than TV as radio can break news stories much more quickly. Great for reaching local communities and audiences. Useful for supporting an above-the-line advertising campaign.	Lack of visual stimulation could be a disadvantage if the essence of the news story or message is very visual, such as an art exhibition or the opening of a new building. Another disadvantage is that the audience reached by radio is highly likely to be doing something else at the same time, such as driving a car, working in a shop or factory, reading other media or engaging on online media.	Traditionally, radio was used to support impulse purchases, such as special offers in certain localities. Increasingly, internet radio is gaining deeper penetration but this tends to be music-based rather than news-based.	Can't be used as a standalone media channel as it will only reach a percentage of the total audience.

Table 7.2 *continued*

Media channel	Advantages	Disadvantages	What it's especially good at doing	What it's not especially good for
Newspapers: national, regional, local	A permanent record that can be turned into other marketing communications outputs, such as a collection of news coverage available on the website or intranet. Lends itself to the use of pictures, graphics, charts and diagrams for getting the message across.	Shrinking audience and need to target based on demographics and geography. Web versions of newspapers offer greater degree of segmentation but content may not always be the same or treated in the same way as the offline version of the title.	Supporting advertising with news stories that genuinely have news value and are reported objectively by reporters on the newspaper. Also good at generating a response to a 'call to action'.	Shelf life of the story is very short unless the story also appears on the newspaper website and can be found that way for later retrieval.
Trade press	Excellent for talking to the peer group within your market segment. Highly targeted and very little wastage. Excellent for B2B PR activities.	Subject to other industry news that's happening at the time and can be easily bumped off the news agenda particularly if the trade media are reporting another piece of news about your company in the same title as this could be seen as undue prominence by the trade press editor.	Where there's a new product or service launch and you need to engage with intermediaries as well as help B2B purchasers that also read the trade press, so it's a highly influential channel.	Can report your exciting new product or service in a very flat, information-only way and tends to have a large number of similar news items, which creates clutter in the pages of the trade press title.

Consumer or specialist B2C magazines	Highly targeted and motivated audience that is hungry for the new and latest information, such as financial services, hi-fi, music, parenting, food, beauty and health and fitness titles.	The frequency of such titles (monthly) with long lead times for print variants, although online websites can carry more recent news. Editors like to tie in advertising with editorial through 'advertorials' which don't always help to build a durable reputation with readers as it is advertising masquerading as editorial.	Excellent media for creating brand advocates, particularly when linked with social media such as blogs and social networks of consumers with a common interest.	Where a spike in news coverage is needed and you want to reach a wider audience than those who subscribe to a specialist magazine or website.
Blogs	Bloggers are now some of the most influential commentators on the web and often have thousands of followers who share the same or similar attitudes, values, beliefs and behaviours.	There's absolutely no guarantee that any PR effort that's aimed at reaching bloggers will result in any positive coverage or comment and in some cases can actually backfire where the blogger feels that he or she is being manipulated.	Where the communication is about you genuinely listening and understanding a blogger's point of view and then respecting this input, it can help build rapport and dialogue.	Companies should be wary of entering into commercial arrangements with bloggers as the McDonald's example given in this chapter illustrates.

Table 7.2 *continued*

Media channel	Advantages	Disadvantages	What it's especially good at doing	What it's not especially good for
Twitter	Real people providing a real point of view and signposting followers to a full article elsewhere on the web. The 140 character limit helps to concentrate the mind about the news story and some journalists now only want to be reached in this way.	Once you start to tweet and build a following, you can't then simply go quiet. It needs to be managed carefully and again, it's a great 'receive mode' channel rather than transmit mode.	Tracking trends in real time, being used to canvass public opinion in real time with instant results. Good for checking on image and perception of the organization at any given point in a 24-hour news cycle.	Where there are complex and complicated thoughts, issues and ideas that need a detailed explanation will need to use Twitter as part of the communication process, rather than being the primary communication channel. Twitter is best used in 'receive mode' rather than 'transmit mode'.
Wiki	The internet's free encyclopaedia that can be edited anonymously.	Notoriously inaccurate and open to abuse. Often PR professionals feel the need to use Wiki as a promotional tool, which is not what it's designed to do.	It often comes up in natural searches and enquiries and scores high page rankings, so it's useful to check that any page(s) on your organization is as accurate and up to date as possible. There's also an opportunity to provide links from these pages to other websites.	Promotional copy has no place on Wiki and it's very easy for the page to be deleted or amended without any recourse to you.

RSS	A web feed format to publish the latest news, views, blogs and podcasts as they happen, making it easy for users to keep up to date without constantly having to check back with the website.	Requires the user to subscribe to the RSS feed by entering a link into their reader or by clicking an RSS icon that automates the process.	Updating information to users by checking original sources regularly and downloading the updates. You can tweet your news headlines by Twitterfeed and push your blog's RSS feeds directly to Twitter, which effectively gives your blog a route for 'breaking news'.	RSS relies on technology working. RSS also needs to be combined with other social media activities, such as blogs and tweeting.
Podcasting	Audio programmes, news bites or features that are syndicated almost exactly in the same way as an RSS feed. Easy to set up and subscribe to podcasts that can be delivered directly to a user's iPod or MP3 player.	Requires sound recording and computer-based editing kit to produce to a professional standard. Many trade magazines broadcast podcasts on their websites and often these are taken from interviews conducted down a phone line, so quality of audio can be variable.	Allows the audience to hear the news story for themselves rather than just sending a news release to a journalist and waiting for them to print it. Podcasting has more immediate potential impact.	Podcasting relies on mastering production and technical techniques to produce to a satisfactory standard, so unless this competency exists within the organization, can use external agencies to create and distribute podcasts or alternatively work with individual news sites that offer podcasts to their visitors.

Table 7.2 *continued*

Media channel	Advantages	Disadvantages	What it's especially good at doing	What it's not especially good for
Social bookmarking	Allows the user to save bookmarks as they would in a browser but accessible from any computer they are using anywhere in the world. These bookmarks can be shared with other users and can be sorted chronologically, by category or by tags.	Need to send news releases, case studies and pictures that have appeared on your website or other websites to social bookmarking sites such as Delicious, Digg, reddit and StumbleUpon, otherwise these won't necessarily become bookmarked.	Social bookmarking systems offer a different way of organizing and searching content on the web from search engines that use automated programs known as web-bots or spiders to find content.	The web classifications are created by human beings with intuition, as opposed to programs that use algorithms to attempt to determine what a site is about. In practice, users discover and bookmark web pages that haven't yet been discovered or indexed by search engines.
Social networking	The success of Facebook now makes it obligatory to have some presence on the social networking site as it looks odd if you don't.	Absolutely no control on what others may say about your brand, services or products, although Facebook is working on giving a better user experience for brands that have Facebook pages. YouTube is also developing more brand-centric channels for social networking.	Provided the presence of the brand owner is through a real person and this is transparent to all the other members of the community, it's a good way to listen and learn about the attitudes, values, beliefs and behaviours of customers, clients and prospects.	It's less about being in 'transmit mode' and more useful for being in 'receive mode'. Facebook and other social network sites aren't always the best channel for B2B or B2C messaging, although this is slowly changing.

and justified,' warns Matthew Froggatt, chief development officer at US media research company TNS.

Social media tends to suggest communication between real people in a social rather than business context. It's therefore extremely important that there's total transparency and that the person representing the brand owner is there to understand different points of view rather than try to hijack the debate – this will only result in alienation and antagonism from social network members. According to UK brand consultant Mark Ritson:

> As more brands attempt to grab attention and start social media conversations with disinterested consumers, more of them will switch off. That's probably why the sample in developing countries in the TNS research were more positive about brands on social media than those in developed markets – they have yet to be switched off.

Get it wrong and this will result in a Facebook account with no friends and blogs that no one reads.

Business case for social media in PR

Subject to the caveats above, an effective social media and PR strategy will allow you to understand what people really think about your organization, its products and services. This is vital if you're going to be successful at managing the reputation of the organization you work for.

There are several reasons why a social media and PR strategy is essential in the management of PR and these include:

- Assisting in search engine optimization (SEO) and helping to drive more traffic to the organization's website.
- An effective way to 'receive' messages in real time and invite two-way rather than one-way communication with desired customer and client segments.
- Making the organization more transparent and in turn breeding trust and confidence and having a positive impact on reputation.
- Allows the organization to learn and appreciate what attitudes, values, beliefs and behaviours are shared among its customers and clients, which in turn can improve messages, the use of media channels and the understanding of how these can affect behaviour.
- Identifying detractors and critics as well as brand ambassadors and advocates.
- Allows you to take remedial action quickly and show to be caring and responsive to complaints and criticisms rather than just ignoring them in the hope they'll go away.
- Excellent for relationship building.

- As the internet becomes increasingly fragmented, social media can assist in identifying the most appropriate customer and client segments to engage with.

What's clear is that one-way communication that was the preserve of a public relations officer (PRO) dealing with a journalist is long dead and gone.

Important as engaging with the media is, particularly for big organizations that tend to be newsworthy, the vast majority of PR activities can be much more targeted to individuals and groups who share common attitudes, values, beliefs and behaviours across a wide spectrum of forums.

To a large extent, this has removed the guesswork from assessing whether the latest news release or photo-opportunity will actually achieve and sustain the interest it deserves. Such content can now reach the intended audience without passing through the filter of a journalist's point of view.

Creating a social media and PR strategy

Rethinking what should be included in a social media and PR strategy is relatively straightforward as it's based on established PR best practice:

- segmentation analysis;
- behavioural objectives;
- profile of users on social networks;
- online PR tactics;
- listening and monitoring; and
- responding and engaging.

Segmentation analysis

In the context of B2B brand owners, the following information on users is relevant:

- age;
- level in the customer or client company (authorizer, specifier or influencer);
- job title and role;
- internet use and habits;
- when they access the internet;
- how they access the internet;
- particular social and professional networks they belong to;
- other media they engage with;
- existing attitudes and perceptions about your organization; and
- existing attitudes and perceptions about your competitors.

In the context of B2C brand owners, the following user information is relevant:

- age;
- social demographics;
- income level;
- internet use and habits;
- devices used to access the internet;
- other media that they engage with;
- existing attitudes and perceptions about your organization; and
- existing attitudes and perceptions about your competitors.

(For further discussion in market and customer segmentation, see Chapter 1 and also refer to Guru in a Bottle®, *Art of Influencing and Selling*.)

Behavioural objectives

The purpose of engagement through social media and PR activities is to influence behaviour. This can be achieved by getting a prospect customer or client to:

- make an enquiry about a product or service;
- place an order for the product or service;
- request a demonstration or test drive;
- visit your website;
- enter a promotion or competition;
- take part in a promotion;
- write a blog about their experiences of attending an event or using the product or service;
- create a piece of user-generated content (UGC);
- recommend a friend; or
- engage in another 'call to action'.

In all of the above, there needs to be an incentive for this to happen. So the messaging about the offer or opportunity must be clear, unambiguous and compelling. (For further discussion in best practice in digital marketing see Chapter 6, and for the use of promotions see Chapter 8.)

Profile of users on social networks

In the context of B2B and B2C brand owners, the following information is relevant:

- Social media areas that the desired customer and client segments access.
- The frequency of that access.
- The level of engagement when on these social networks.
- Any particular times or days of the week where customers and clients are at their most active on social networks.
- The relative importance of key social network channels in influencing attitudes, values, beliefs and behaviours towards your brand, products and services (see Figure 7.2).

Competitor activities across social networks

Many brand owners use Twitter and blogging to reach desired customer and client segments but many don't respond to Twitter or blog comments.

In the context of B2B and B2C brand owners, the following information is relevant:

- Social media channels and tools that competitors are using.
- What competitors are doing to influence behaviour of customer and client segments.
- The degree of participation and engagement that competitors are trying to achieve with the same customer and client segments that you're trying to reach.

Figure 7.2   Audience profile on social networks

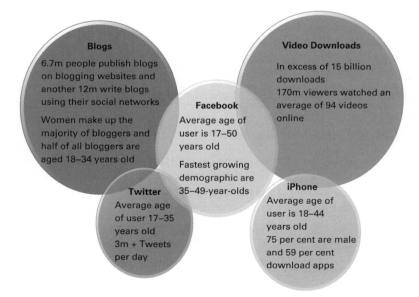

Source: Nielsenwire (2012)

- The relative success of these efforts compared with your own.
- The number of responses and mentions that competitors are achieving within these social networks compared to those that you're able to achieve.

Table 7.3 is a useful tool for social media monitoring and tracking of competitor activities.

Online PR tactics

Many brand owners continue to use traditional online media relations as part of their PR efforts, for example maintaining an electronic newsroom as part of the website where journalists have to register to gain access to high res (300 dpi) images, pictures, company information and previous news releases.

However, according to Econsultancy research, the trend for continuing traditional online PR activities is on the wane and in its place savvy brand owners are switching their attention to blogger relations as well as using and posting SEO news releases so that they get picked up and linked to by various social networking sites as a way of disseminating information across the internet. Other changes in PR tactics that are on the increase include online dialogue with other UGC/social media sites, ratings and reviews, and online crisis and issues management activities.

Many of the PR tactics now undertaken by brand owners can be sorted into the following activities:

- social network profile creation and management;
- creation of video and the use of video-sharing sites;
- corporate or brand blog;
- ratings and reviews;
- creation of mobile content applications;
- use of social bookmarking sites;
- creation of podcasts;
- use of social news sites;
- creation of widgets;
- use of location-based platforms; and
- social gaming.

A lot of these online PR activities accompany the kind of e-marketing and m-marketing activities described in the previous chapter, although brand owners are now becoming more focused on a few areas rather than trying to do everything and finding little return for their inflated expectations.

For example, ratings and reviews of products and services is one of the best conversation topics a brand owner can use to engage with customers

Table 7.3 Social media monitoring and tracking of competitors

Week 1 (...)	Total Volume/Traffic	Company Name	Company URL	Key Employees/Public Figures	Related industry websites	Product/Service Name	Product/Service URL	Competitors	Blog Comments/Posts
RSS									
Feedburner (Stats)	0								
	0								
Keywords and referrals									
Google Alerts	0								
Google Analytics	0								
HitTail	0								
	0								
Industry-related websites									
<Site 1>	0								
<Site 2>	0								
<Site 3>	0								
	0								

Authority websites							
Google	0						
Technorati	0						
Brand Republic	0						
Microblogs							
Twitter	0						
Identi.ca	0						
Plurk	0						
Social Bookmarks							
StumbleUpon	0						
Digg	0						
reddit	0						
	0						

and clients where this is integrated into people's Facebook pages and other social profiles.

Listening and monitoring

Most brand owners accept that they are still on a steep learning curve when it comes to using social media and online PR effectively, and in studies many feel that more improvement is required in the following areas:

- using Twitter generally;
- listening and monitoring;
- using Facebook generally;
- managing social media communities;
- engaging customers and clients in dialogue;
- having a content strategy for social media; and
- identifying and engaging with key influencers.

One of the keys to success is to have a content strategy for social media engagement. Successful brand owners like Zappos (see Chapter 3) are flexible and able to respond and react when things change.

It's essential to maintain a solid foundation of content in order to maintain dialogue with your customers and clients. Simply tweeting random stuff to keep pumping out information won't work.

The online PR effort needs to be structured and part of the overall PR strategy. As part of this process, it's useful to have identified the social media content that's relevant for your organization. That could include your products and services, key employees, senior figures within your organization with a high profile as well as industry-related terms, keywords and phrases. With respect to search terms within social media areas, a number of tools can be used (see Table 7.4).

Some brand owners also set up a timetable for monitoring each individual media area (see Table 7.5).

Table 7.4 Monitoring search terms within social media areas

Description	Monitoring tool commonly used in these channels
Journalists	RSS, Google Alerts
Industry figures	Google Alerts
Industry publications	RSS, Google Alerts, Twitter, Delicious
Industry websites	RSS, Google Alerts, Twitter, Delicious
Key bloggers	RSS, Google Alerts, Twitter, Delicious

complexity and cost of measuring may be prohibitive or not justified on the return expected.

All good PR strategies are made up of three core components: inputs, outputs and outcomes. All too often PR agencies will come up with a long 'shopping list' of outputs, such as the number of news releases and journalist one-to-ones as if by magic this equates with excellent PR. This is all output-driven and although useful, the key consideration for the organization or company is how this made a difference in a tangible way which, for a commercial organization, should have supported the sales and marketing effort.

Inputs. For example, background information and research including an analysis of current organizational and company perceptions can inform the initial planning step. Some of this information could provide benchmarks against which to measure later. For example:

- the PR brief (information on organization/sector);
- desk research and original research (to inform the content of PR materials);
- pre-testing (messages/materials understood).

Outputs. Literally, what messages go out from the organization or company? This is a measure of a quantified nature that can analyse the degree of exposure and audience reach, but can't explain to what extent people's opinions or behaviour have been influenced.

Many PR plans produced by PR agencies are built on outputs, but this isn't the complete picture and doesn't allow PR professionals to demonstrate the positive impact their work can have on an organization and its objectives. For example:

- News releases, background briefs, case studies and photographs issued and coverage monitored and evaluated.
- Website launched and traffic analysis compiled.
- PR event staged, and who and how many attended.
- Research survey conducted, which informed the organization strategy and plan in that market.
- Extent to which messages are received by the desired customer and client segment.
- Analysis of media coverage achieved.
- Online tracking of comments and feedback with customers and clients.

Outcomes. This is perhaps the most important element of any PR programme – and the toughest to satisfy.

Measuring outcomes should be the focus of PR measurement, so that the positive impact on the organizational or company's objectives can be clearly articulated. Measuring outcomes is about understanding the degree to which PR has changed people's awareness, opinion and, very important, their behaviour. This is the most valuable form of measurement:

- tangible incremental increase in sales;
- focus groups to confirm a shift in behaviour rather than just purchase intention; and
- the number of brand advocates in this quarter compared to the previous quarter.

Outcome is the strongest basis for calculating the return on investment from PR activities and is also a valuable source of information to be fed back into the research, planning and measurement process. (For a detailed discussion on various research and evaluation tools, see Chapter 3.)

Step 4: Ongoing measurement

Depending on the PR objectives, these can be short, medium or long term. The likelihood is that there will be a mix of these that will need to be satisfied. Where the PR objective is about shifting attitudes and behaviour, this is unlikely to happen overnight and will take concerted PR effort. In such cases it will be necessary to listen, gather input and feedback over a long period of time. Ongoing measurement will ideally allow you to track progress before, during and after the PR campaign. The advantage of this is that it allows for modifications and for adjustments to be made as the programme unfolds rather than waiting until the end of the programme to effect changes when it may be too late. For example, where the PR campaign isn't generating sales leads as expected:

- try to determine the pattern of enquiries and leads and whether PR is having any effect on the pipeline of opportunities;
- adjust the content accordingly; and
- identify other causes for the lack of sales enquiries, such as issues with the product or service or other factors.

Step 5: Results and evaluation

The benefit of having a formal planning process is that you can make a direct comparison between the objectives and the results. The more precise the objectives, the easier it is to quantify the outcomes, determine the return on investment and influence the core organizational and business strategy.

A large volume of apparently 'favourable' media coverage or positive conversations with influencers, specifiers and authorizers would only represent a successful outcome if it satisfied the communications objectives agreed at the start of the PR programme or campaign. If those PR objectives were to achieve a measurable shift in attitude, values, beliefs and behaviour then even quite sophisticated media measurement wouldn't provide that level of insight.

For example, a successful outcome for a pressure group lobbying to change government policy would be the policy change, not positive media coverage that might have swayed government opinion.

'Level substitution' – typically confusing outputs with outcomes – is one of the most common mistakes made in the PR measurement process. PR performance has to be in tangible terms against set objectives. It's also important to capture learning points and experience and feed this into the research, planning and measurement model. For example:

- How could we create a better PR brief or bridge information gaps?
- What information about market and customer segments could be reused for another PR campaign or to create better benchmarks?
- How realistic were the PR objectives and the strategy against the timeline?
- Which PR tactics worked best and which ones didn't do so well?
- What feedback from customers and clients has been received?
- How can the PR programme encourage more collaboration with customers and clients in order to improve products and service?

A planned and research-based approach to communications can also be an important tool or a valuable source of intelligence on competitor activities.

Media measurement

'Media' generally means press, radio, TV and the web, but it also extends to any published material such as report and accounts, government publications and news wires.

Media measurement can be conducted on its own or in conjunction with other forms of research, for example interviews with desired audience segments to see to what extent media relations has influenced levels of public awareness or public opinion.

However, media coverage on its own, whether it is traditional media or online, is of limited value. It's only when coverage is appraised in a systematic way, and according to a pre-agreed brief, that it has meaning.

To have true meaning, output analysis should be linked to outcomes (the impact on the organization or company). The approach should be repeatable, robust and relevant to the context of the organization's needs and requirements. It should be simple and understandable and the management reporting should be understandable to the board, who aren't PR experts.

The analysis of media coverage is a form of business intelligence that provides a systematic analysis of an organization's reputation, its products and services or those of competitors as reported in the media. It condenses quantitative and qualitative information into actionable insights. It also enables:

- the analysis of media clippings and transcripts to create a media coverage benchmark for a new PR campaign;

- the development of a radar by identifying trends in coverage such as indications of future issues or market intelligence of value to the organization; and
- analysis of competitors' media coverage.

Table 7.6 provides a breakdown of the typical PR analytical charts that are used to monitor and evaluate PR activities. There are several PR monitoring, evaluation, and measurement systems available; two of the most widely used systems are Gorkana and Vocus. Systems such as Vocus can automatically generate excellent graphs and charts as well as compile smart looking PDF booklets at the touch of a button.

Table 7.6 Typical PR analytics

Analytic chart	Description
Activity by category	This allows the user to see what percentage of activities have been assigned to each category of PR activity, such as journalist briefings, issue of news releases, background briefs, case studies, interviews with journalists and other activities across a particular time frame.
Activity by type	This allows the user to see what percentage of activities have been assigned to each type of PR activity, such as issue of a news release, journalist enquiry, call-backs, project tasks, media coverage opportunity and other activities.
Top reporters by activities and news articles	This can provide the Top 10 list of media contacts, based on the greatest number of activity records associated with them as well as the greatest number of articles written by individual journalists.
Top outlets by news articles	This can provide a Top 10 list of media outlets based on the number of reported articles on the organization or company. News outlets could include *Financial Times, Wall Street Journal, New York Times*, Associated Press, Press Association and Reuters.
Media contacts by media type	This pie chart breaks down the media contacts on the basis of the media: radio, TV, website, blogger, trade media, newspaper, consumer magazine, business magazine, etc.
Media contacts by subject matter	This is also very enlightening as it segments media contacts on the basis of subjects covered, such as corporate, mortgage insurance, lifestyle protection insurance, etc.

Table 7.6 *continued*

Analytic chart	Description
News by category	This shows what percentage of news has been assigned to each category, such as corporate and operating divisions within a company.
News by media	This allows the user to see which media channels are harvesting the news, such as newspapers, wire services, websites, bloggers, magazines, broadcast and others.
News by number of clips	This can be a pie chart or a linear graph with the number of articles mapped against a weekly or monthly breakdown.
News by tone of coverage	This is extremely useful as it segments all coverage in terms of positive, negative and neutral in tone, usually done by a sophisticated algorithm. It is possible to alter the tone of coverage in the way it's classified. Overall, the majority of news coverage will be neutral.
Coverage by source of news	This is interesting in terms of where the majority of coverage actually comes from, for example, self-generated through the issue of news releases as well as passing mentions in articles on competitors' activities.
Impressions by media type	This is a quantifiable number of impressions across online and offline media.
Average prominence in news coverage	Average prominence scores are assigned to each news article based on an algorithm that evaluates data gathered from news articles, including the number of mentions, placement of the mentions (headline, first paragraph), size of the article and exclusivity. The prominence chart can be presented as a comparison of the organization or company's competitors over a period of time.
Share of negative and positive voice	This combines a number of data sets: the media impact score of a news article in conjunction with the tone (positive, negative or neutral) of the article.
Overall tone of coverage	This chart measures whether the percentage of the news over a period of time was positive, negative or neutral.

Table 7.6 *continued*

Analytic chart	Description
Key spokespeople in the media	This always has a few surprises as it's very common to have a few individuals from the organization or company regularly featuring in the media and they may have a higher profile than some of the main board directors who appear infrequently.
News by country	This is extremely useful if you are managing PR across a large number of territories, such as countries within the European Union.
News by circulation	This segments the news picked up by the media on the basis of circulation figures for media outlets.

Measuring social media

Social media are having a profound impact on PR practice and in many ways are rewiring the way we think about engaging, communicating and influencing desired customer and client segments. The challenge is how to identify, track and analyse the thousands of conversations, tweets, posts, comments and other content to make sense of these inputs.

All of this stuff can have an impact on an organization's reputation as well as its sales and marketing efforts. But it's not just about tracking or trying to understand the influence of an individual commentator or blogger. It's about identifying what conversations the organization should participate in and understanding how all of these interactions and mentions (the 'outputs') impact the organization. In other words, what impact (outcomes) do these outputs have on the organization's goals?

The Barcelona Principles provide that: 'social media can and should be measured', followed by 'measuring outcomes is preferred to measuring media results (outputs)'. In other words, the principles that apply to online PR are the same as researching, planning and measuring of offline PR activities.

At first glance, the web appears to be the holy grail of PR evaluation. A piece of content was viewed or it wasn't. A link was followed or it wasn't. Either someone decided to 'like it' or 'become a fan' or 'click it' or rate it, or they didn't. Someone may have commented positively in response to a blog post or indeed posted positively about the organization. A comment may have been retweeted. If the organization is in the eye of a news storm, it may 'trend' overnight on Twitter, where thousands and potentially hundreds of thousands of people could be reading and sharing their own views about that story.

All of these things should be tracked and analysed, as they may be outputs of your PR efforts and impact your organization or company's reputation. By tracking and analysing these outputs, you'll gain an insight into influencer and audience perception and behaviour that can then feed into the research and planning of PR activities.

Use of social media monitoring tools. There is a wide range of social media and web analytic monitoring tools, most of which can be accessed for free on the internet. These tools can do a number of jobs:

- They can track blogs, forums, comments, tweets, online news, social networks and video for mentions of your organization or company, customers, clients and competitors.
- They can analyse these mentions and produce reports that summarize the number of Twitter followers, comment counts, tweet counts, retweets, @replies, DMs, comments, ratings, YouTube comments/ratings, media type and sentiment (positive, neutral or negative).
- They can segment this data by geography, media type, language and identify links and sources, or segment by keywords.
- They can present this information in various reporting formats, including 'dashboards' that summarize key data points.

This type of analysis can help to inform the PR programme by identifying what people are saying about your organization, your products and services and even your clients.

CIPR and AMEC research into best practice in social media

Research jointly conducted in the UK by the CIPR and the Association for Measurement and Evaluation of Communication (AMEC) has attempted to identify ways in which output analysis can be linked to outcomes, as this is the real measure of the success of online, indeed any, PR activity. The major stumbling block is trying to isolate only online PR activities that are responsible for the result.

The following online metrics are useful in creating a rounded view of the performance of PR:

- Did ratings or recommendations lead to an increase in online sales of products?
- Was there an increase in requests for further information?
- Did positive customer satisfaction scores or comments lead to an increase in sales or sales queries?
- Did the PR campaign lead to an increase in visits to the website?
- Did the length of the average visit increase as a result?

- Did you capture data about what these visitors did on the site and did this lead to orders being placed or transactions being completed?
- Did the PR activity drive more traffic to the website as a result?
- Were there more queries, sales, downloads, contributions to a campaign or signatures on a petition?
- Did online comments provide feedback that's been used to inform strategy and to improve products or services?
- Have perceptions or awareness levels changed as a result?
- Has this led to greater engagement between the organization and its stakeholders?

Influence and authority. Metrics such as the number of Twitter followers or Facebook friends don't actually measure influence per se. For example, a participant with 40 followers may be more influential for the customer or client segments you're trying to reach than someone who has a hundred times that number of followers but who isn't that relevant. Popular isn't the same as influential.

As with a traditional PR programme, it's essential to try to identify those bloggers who influence your desired customer and client segments:

- Are your customers or clients amongst your Twitter followers or Facebook friends?
- Are those media contacts that have influence quoting or linking to particular bloggers or twitterers?
- Does the journalist/blogger/commentator have an impact on purchasing decisions through recognized authority or through consumer reviews or by recommendations to family and friends? (It's important to note that authority is not a proxy for influence.)
- Does the journalist/blogger/commentator have authority?

The growth in social media has led to a raft of products and tools claiming to measure influence. The CIPR and AMEC warn that PR professionals should be clear that some of these tools have opaque ways of measuring influence that may provide little or no insight into real influence:

- PR professionals need to know how to speak to non-PR people such as members of the board or other teams within an organization.
- Clear links should be established between organizational objectives and PR outcomes so that non-PR people can immediately understand how PR has helped the organization to achieve key objectives.
- PR professionals should take part in business skills training so they're able to discuss PR outcomes and distil this information throughout the organization in a format and language that other teams can understand and engage with.

- Where possible, PR professionals should share research and evaluation resources and budgets across multiple functions. This can help to support investment in PR evaluation where typically the evaluation budget isn't ring-fenced.

- Given that many PR functions report into the marketing function, it's important to consider the measurement tools marketers are familiar with and to develop an integrated approach to marketing and communications campaign evaluation that includes PR.

References

Books and reports

Bedbury, S (2002) *A New Brand World*, Viking
Big Mouth Media (2010) *Social Media and Online PR Report*
Brennan, D (2010) Getting closer to television content – the advertiser benefits, *Journal of Sponsorship*
Brown, R (2009) *Public Relations and the Social Web*, Kogan Page
Chartered Institute of Public Relations (2011) *Research, Planning & Measurement Toolkit*, CIPR
Chartered Institute of Public Relations (2011) *Social Media Measurement Guidance*, CIPR
De Bono, E (1992) *Serious Creativity*, HarperCollins
De Bono, E (1992) *Lateral Thinking for Management*
Haig, M (2011) *Brand Failures*, Kogan Page
The Economist Style Guide (2005) Profile Books
The FeedRoom Inc (2009) *The Benefits of Video-enabling Your Virtual Press Room*
Financial Times (1993) *Financial Times Style Guide*, FT Books
Hill, S and Rifkin, G (2000) *Radical Marketing*, Harper Perennial
Kolah, A (2004) Will brandcasting succeed where advertising failed?, *Admap*
Kolah, A *et al* (2003) *Public Relations in Practice*, Kogan Page
Kolah, A (2013) Guru in a Bottle, *Essential Law for Marketers*, 2nd edition, Kogan Page
Kolah, A (2013) Guru in a Bottle, *The Art of Influencing and Selling*, Kogan Page
McCusker, G (2005) *Public Relations Disasters*, Kogan Page
Mathews, R and Wacker, W (2008) *What's Your Story?*, FT Press
Meerman Scott, D (2010) *The New Rules of Marketing & PR*, Wiley
Meerman Scott, D (2011) *Real-time Marketing & PR*, Wiley
Meerman Scott, D and Halligan, B (2010) *Marketing Lessons from the Grateful Dead*, Wiley
Nero, P and Patel, N (2003) *Creative Business*, FT Prentice Hall
Oliver, S (2010) *Public Relations Strategy*, Kogan Page
Ries, A and Ries, L (2002) *The Fall of Advertising and the Rise of PR*, Harper Business
Social Marketing for Search Marketers (2010) Third Door Media
Social Media & Online PR (2010) Econsultancy

Vincent, L (2002) *Legendary Brands*, Dearborn
Zyman, S (2002) *End of Advertising as We Know It*, Wiley

Websites

Vocus is a leading provider of cloud-based marketing and PR software:
http://www.vocus.com (accessed 8 May 2012)
JournalistTweets.com: http://www.journalisttweets.com (accessed 8 May 2012)
Technorati: www.technorati.com (accessed 9 May 2012)
Identica: http://identi.ca (accessed 9 May 2012)
Plurk: http://www.plurk.com (accessed 9 May 2012)
Ardi Kolah's Twitter: https://twitter.com/ardikolah (accessed 9 May 2012)
Delicious: http://www.delicious.com (accessed 9 May 2012)
Digg: http://www.digg.com (accessed 9 May 2012)
Reddit: http://www.reddit.com (accessed 9 May 2012)
StumbleUpon: http://www.stumbleupon.com (accessed 9 May 2012)
RepTrak Pulse Survey is conducted by the Reputation Institute:
http://www.reputationinstitute.com (accessed 12 May 2012)
Nielsen data on the internet and social networking:
http://blog.nielsen.com/nielsenwire (accessed 20 May 2012)

"Hop along to your nearest store - now!"

Using promotions

In this chapter:

- Objectives of sales promotions
- Use of creativity in sales promotions
- Off-the-shelf promotions
- Joint promotions
- Price promotions
- Premium promotions
- Prize promotions
- International sales promotions
- International Chamber of Commerce (ICC) Code 2011

Introduction

Sales promotions are one of the most popular marketing devices for driving customers to visit a store or website. The holiday season provides an ideal opportunity to think about running a sales promotion, although with the global economy struggling to pick itself off the floor, you could be forgiven for thinking that sales promotions have become a permanent feature on the high street or on the web, irrespective of your locality.

Harry Potter

Ahead of the pre-Christmas rush in 2011, Warner Home Video released the final instalment of the Harry Potter franchise: 'Harry Potter and The Deathly Hallows – Part 2' on DVD. To promote its release, HMV stores across the UK and Ireland opened their doors from 7.00 am to give fans one of the first opportunities to purchase a copy of the film. The first 200 fans attending each HMV breakfast opening received a highly collectible A3-sized Harry Potter poster featuring a scene from the new DVD, while the stores had a quantity of scarves in the Gryffindor house colours of orange and red to give away. Over 150 of HMV's high street stores took part in the breakfast launch, including the entertainment retailer's flagship stores in London's Oxford Street, Dublin, Belfast, Edinburgh and Cardiff as well as regional superstores in Manchester, Birmingham, Leeds, Liverpool, Newcastle, Glasgow, Norwich, Reading and Southampton, making it one of the biggest promotions of the year. As a result of the media hype around the promotional launch, the DVD, Blu-ray and complete collection box set were the Christmas bestsellers for HMV in 2011.

In the UK, sales promotions are governed by the self-regulatory CAP and BCAP Codes of Practice administered by the Advertising Standards Authority (ASA). (For a detailed discussion on the legal framework around the operation of sales; price promotions; prize promotions; incentives; product placement and sponsorship in the UK and Europe, refer to Guru in a Bottle®, *Essential Law for Marketers,* 2nd edition.) In this chapter, the term 'sales promotion' is being used in its generic sense; it covers consumer and trade promotions; incentive schemes as well as the promotional elements of sponsorship.

The relevant laws and regulations that apply in the jurisdiction where the sales promotion takes place need to be checked carefully as they are likely to apply to competitions, prize draws, instant wins, premium promotions and other activities (but not necessarily lotteries which, in the UK, come under the Gambling Act 2005). International promotions should also comply with the voluntary Code of Conduct established by the International Chamber of Commerce 2011. (For a detailed discussion on how the ICC Code (2011) applies to sales and marketing practice, see Guru in a Bottle®, *Essential Law for Marketers*, 2nd edition.)

A sales promotion can provide an incentive for consumers by employing a range of added-value benefits to a product or service to influence purchasing behaviour. Such sales promotions can include two-for-one offers, money-off offers, text-to-wins, competitions and prize draws. In this chapter we are only concerned with the mechanics of different types of sales promotions.

Objectives of sales promotions

The objectives of a sales promotion can broadly fall into four categories, which are not mutually exclusive:

1 To attract competitors' customers and clients where the promotion encourages the consumer to purchase a new brand or to switch supplier.
2 To attract new customer or client segments that have never bought the product or service in the past but are now more willing to give it a go.
3 To stimulate repeat purchases or renewals where the promotion helps to maintain loyalty.
4 To stimulate volume of sales of existing products, such as a buy one, get one free (BOGOF) promotion.

It's common to have volume of sales as an objective for the sales promotion and this may be linked to a call centre where the sales team need to handle more in-bound callers and the promotion is to be used to drive this traffic.

As with any marketing campaign, it's important to have clear and measurable objectives for any sales promotion so that the success can be related back to the business and the bottom line. The approach to be taken will ultimately be a combination of rational and emotional involvement with the promotion. As can be seen from Figure 8.1, the most successful sales promotions combine the emotional and rational appeal to drive sales.

A good example of such a sales promotion was the loyalty promotion run by British Gas that was shortlisted for the prestigious UK National Business Award in the Excellence in Marketing Category in 2011.

British Gas and Nectar (2011)

British Gas is a leading energy supplier in the UK, specializing in supplying energy to homes and businesses. Its services also include boiler installation, heating maintenance, security systems, micro generation and smart technology. The key objectives of the sales promotion in 2011 were to position itself as the energy provider that now offers Nectar points (previously offered by its competitor EDF) and to drive sign-ups in a way that would help to mitigate the short-term negativity of price rises for its services.

Nectar is the UK's largest loyalty programme with in excess of 18 million collectors who earn Nectar points when shopping at over 4,000 locations for groceries, DIY, booking a holiday, paying household bills, buying petrol or paying utility bills. Over 49 per cent of UK households earn Nectar points with over 500 online retailers participating, generating US$2.4 billion of rewards spent. Rewards include money off shopping, travel, eating out and general merchandise.

Figure 8.1 Two dimensions of sales promotions appeal

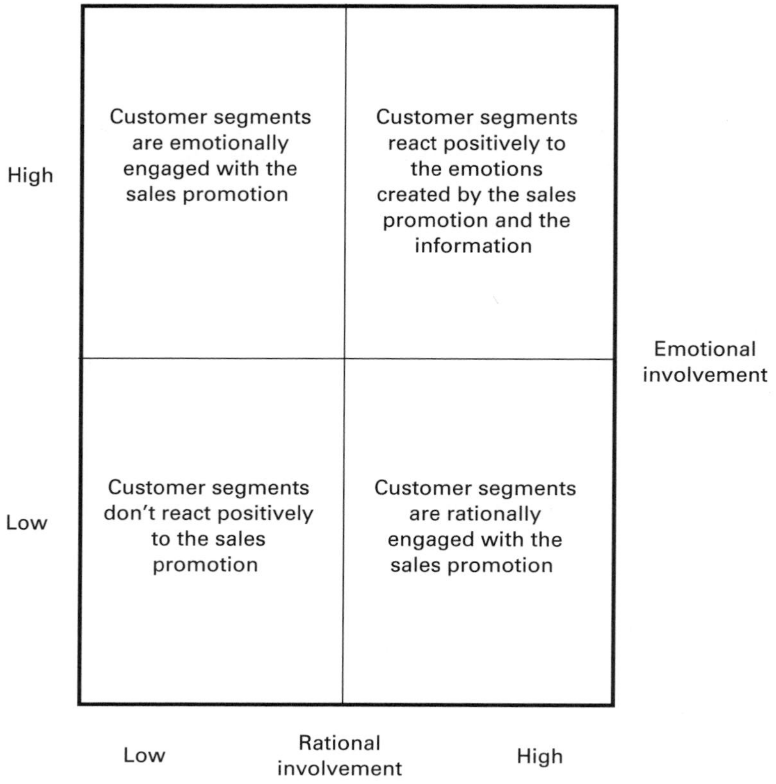

'To raise awareness of the British Gas/Nectar partnership amongst a wide audience we launched an above-the-line (ATL) awareness campaign aimed at maximizing reach and ensuring Nectar collectors knew that British Gas had taken over the partnership from EDF,' explains Chrissy James at British Gas promotions agency CHI & Partners.

At a time of increased prices, the universal need was to deliver more value – tangible and emotional. The tactical decision to launch Nectar delivered a tangible value but the way it was communicated pressed all the emotional hot buttons. Chrissy James adds:

> *Launching a reward programme could be pitched in a number of different ways, from focusing on ways to collect, to end rewards, to addressing value directly. This was as much an exercise in brand building as it was driving awareness and enrolment; we needed a campaign platform which would maximize the positive feeling towards British Gas. The basis for our campaign was a universal emotional insight focused around 'everybody likes to be thanked'.*

Pre-testing confirmed that such a platform had the ability to make everybody feel that bit better for being recognized in such a way. Results surpassed expectations, particularly given the brand negativity post-price rise. The results of the promotion included:

- An increase of 20 per cent customer net promoter score (NPS) for Nectar/British Gas sign ups immediately post campaign.
- A 60 per cent increase in prompted awareness and 20 per cent spontaneous awareness among the UK population after six weeks.
- Within eight weeks, British Gas had overtaken EDF as associated Nectar partner.
- Registrations surpassed the target by 139 per cent after week 21.
- Enrolments hit 2.7 million by week 25 – significantly ahead of target.
- Registrations over-indexed amongst the highest value segments. This was linked to British Gas' wider commercial strategy of increasing customer numbers and share of wallet by increasing retention amongst Nectar members, who accounted for 60 per cent of the British Gas customer base through offering great value.

Customer commitment increased in the first six weeks of the promotional campaign by 13 per cent and non-customers were more available to British Gas post-campaign (5 per cent Nectar users and 7 per cent non-Nectar users). Leakage was significantly reduced by 35 per cent, contributing to lower churn levels. The share of customers' wallets was increased through implementing Nectar reward-based communications.

An additional 362,000 customers were now contactable by British Gas. There were 300,000 new energy accounts directly attributable to Nectar, which exceeded targets by over 40 per cent. (For a discussion on how to make effective cold calls, see Guru in a Bottle®, *Art of Influencing and Selling*.)

Repeat purchase promotions often overlap with volume promotions and existing customers are most likely to be prepared to bring forward their regular purchases and buy in bulk. Repeat purchase promotions are also an effective way of achieving other marketing objectives, such as running a 'spoiler campaign' or an 'ambush marketing' campaign that deprives the oxygen of publicity to the competitor's planned sales promotion.

This technique is effective where customers are enticed to continue to buy a particular brand as the preferred choice because it's attached to some redemption that delivers a reward for loyalty. Tried and tested techniques that are effective in driving repeat purchases include:

- coupons on the product that provide a discount off the next purchase;
- specific incentives for multiple purchases, for example, 'buy three, get one free'; and
- collector promotions, such as collecting 10 tokens and sending for free merchandise or a cash refund.

Competing on price can drive prices into a downward spiral that could result in being forced to sell products or services at an uneconomical price point simply to keep sales volumes buoyant. Eventually the unprofitable business will cause irreparable damage to the enterprise – something often witnessed in the competitive private car insurance sector.

Promotions can offer an antidote to this downward spiral by helping to maintain a higher price differential compared to a competitor's product or service. There is a variety of tried and trusted sales promotion techniques that can help defend a higher price differential:

- variations on price cuts including cash backs and money off next purchase;
- extra-fill packs , short term multi-packs, joint packs or part of the product or service free; and
- collector or points promotions (see the British Gas example above).

Ultimately, the objective of any sales promotion comes down to one thing – driving more sales!

Use of creativity in sales promotions

MOBO and Sony Ericsson (2010)

The MOBO show is the biggest music awards event of its kind in Europe – and is constantly seeking ways of increasing sponsorship income to defray some of the costs for staging the show in some of the biggest venues in the UK.

Through discussions with the product development team at Sony Ericsson it became obvious that the sales of its mobile phones had taken a dent in the face of fierce competition from rivals Samsung, Motorola and Nokia.

MOBO entered into negotiations with Sony Ericsson to explore how it could reconnect with young people through the excitement of the MOBO event and MOBO music. As a result, MOBO was able to get Sony Ericsson on board as a sponsor and manufacture a special limited edition MOBO mobile phone with exclusive pre-loaded music content and videos.

The promotion for the limited edition phone was highly successful in shifting over 50,000 units as a result of above-the-line (ABT) and bus shelter campaigns by retail partner Carphone Warehouse in the UK.

The key to using imagination and creative thinking in sales promotions is to consider what motivates the desired customer or client segment; what's important for them and how can the sales promotion deliver something that has high emotional value and appeal that doesn't feel strained or unnatural.

An excellent example is the sales promotion run by Jaguar cars in the UK, which was a finalist in the prestigious UK National Business Awards for the Excellence in Marketing Category 2011.

Jaguar (2010)

Luxury car manufacturer Jaguar was actively looking to rejuvenate its brand and break free from the perception it was an 'old man's car'; it wanted to appeal to a younger customer segment of professionals who may be tempted to purchase a BMW, Mercedes, Porsche or Audi instead. As a pilot for Jaguar in Manchester, the sales promotion had several business and creative objectives:

- increase awareness of the new Jaguar nameplates;
- reappraise the Jaguar brand;
- drive sales leads and test drives; and
- take over the city of Manchester for the month of May 2010 with a series of different events.

'The sales promotion was a pilot and had never been attempted anywhere else in the UK. It had to be innovative and "blitz" the city yet not leave Manchester's community feeling saturated and fatigued,' explains David Wolfe, managing director of Journey 9, Jaguar's marketing and experiential agency.

Experiential marketing was key to the entire sales promotion campaign and the Spinningfields development – a premium financial and professional services complex with a footfall of 20,000 – was turned into 'Jaguarfields', providing a dedicated Jaguar rig and 'Ride and Drive' activity.

Targeted events included a launch VIP event at Manchester's new Rosso Bar, owned by soccer star Rio Ferdinand, which hosted a party for more than 200 key influencers; three invitation-only showroom events for current and prospective clients hosted by Jaguar designers; and several sponsored events allowing targeted and sustained product placement and data capture. This included events involving key influential customer segments such as the Federation of Jewish Services at its golf day. In addition, a series of VIP dealership events hosted an intimate group of just 50 prospects to hear Jaguar designers speak first-hand about the marque.

Hollywood film director Derrick Borte was hired to direct a unique campaign film that was shown at each event and played daily on the screens at the Spinningfields development. The buzz was assisted by a fully integrated PR and social media campaign that carefully created just the right amount of 'noise' using traditional media alongside Twitter, Facebook, blogger outreach and YouTube.

Social media were used to amplify the experiential and live activity in Manchester and to directly target individuals and groups known to be social web users and likely to be interested in Jaguar cars. Advertisements were placed in all key regional media and 30 Manchester taxis were branded with Jaguar imagery.

As part of the campaign finale, Jaguar wanted to say 'Thank you' to the city while connecting with current and prospective customer segments, irrespective of their age profile. David Wolfe explains:

> *Understanding that the family unit is a major influence in the decision to purchase a new car, we conceived and delivered a 'Jaguar Family Fun Day'. The positivity of the day would create a connection with the brand and the cars that would remain with the child for years to come and act as an influence over parents. We wanted to represent the luxury and 'Britishness' of Jaguar so a central part of the day was the opportunity for people to take a test drive. This was done on pre-qualifying and booking test drives to ensure the highest quality data for Jaguar. A variety of kids' and family activities was organized to cement the 'fun' element of the day – it was something that Jaguar had never undertaken before and was a unique way of getting additional prospective clients into their cars and capturing more than 2,000 data records.*

The result of the sales promotion was that Jaguar was able to measure a 63 per cent increase in dealer enquiries directly attributable to the sales promotion that also resulted in a 70 per cent increase in new and used car sales compared with the period prior to the promotion and is now rolling this out nationally in the UK.

It's worth remembering that the most successful marketing and promotional activity is one that doesn't simply alter perceptions about a product, brand or service but influences the behaviour of the desired customer segment.

Off-the-shelf promotions

Groupon and OFT investigation (2011)

In 2011, the Office of Fair Trading (OFT) in the UK investigated discount promoter Groupon over complaints it had received about Groupon's daily off-the-shelf promotions and trading practices. In addition to receiving complaints directly, the OFT was passed complaints by the Advertising Standards Authority (ASA) for nearly 50 breaches of its CAP Code.

Groupon offers daily deals ranging from beauty treatments to restaurant discounts, which only go ahead if enough people commit to buy them. It advertises these deals on its website and via e-mail. One complaint concerned a promotion for restaurant discounts and an ad for a safari experience – both of which misled consumers.

However, it's possible to run an off-the-shelf promotion without getting into deep water. A good example is holiday vouchers, which have become much more popular to providers in the face of the decline in international airline travel due to the current economic climate, and to consumers as they tighten their belts. Holiday vouchers can provide savings of around 8 per cent but can be as high as 20 per cent in order to entice consumers to book holidays in certain 'trouble spots' such as Turkey and Egypt where pockets of civil unrest have almost totally destroyed them as holiday destinations.

From a sales promotion perspective, the savings can be given in a variety of ways – as a cash discount, traveller's cheques, a duty-free shopping voucher or a high added-value item. The most popular mechanics are foreign currency and cash discounts.

The size of the discount could be related to the price of the holiday or a minimum stay at a hotel or resort. It can be a flat sum with certain conditions, for example, a holiday needs to be booked for two adults for a minimum of two weeks. With the increase in online bookings, more operators are trying to entice people with less disposable income in real terms to want to go on holiday.

Other off-the-shelf mechanics include discount coupons, two-for-one flights, free hotel accommodation, and high street vouchers that entitle the holder to special discounts on particular shopping nights where all goods for store card holders are marked down by 20 per cent for that evening only.

Joint promotions

These can be extremely effective, as the British Gas sales promotion demonstrates.

British Gas and Nectar

As discussed above, the financial benefits of the joint promotion were to be found in overall customer retention, increased customer value through multiple product holdings, and in Nectar-incentivized acquisition. Chris Allin, director of loyalty and customer communications, explains:

Our Nectar rewards scheme was designed with the aim of incentivizing more sustainable customer behaviour and some of our more targeted, secondary layer, communications focused on this aspect. One of our objectives was to encourage less meter reads, helping reduce our carbon footprint as a business. To this end, part of our campaign targeted certain customer groups, providing Nectar incentives to switch to EnergySmart – our online service which enables customers to input their own meter readings and receive accurate monthly billing.

As a result of the joint promotion, one-third of the enrolled base now read their own meters, significantly more than the unenrolled base, and British Gas now utilizes a strand of communications to encourage more customers to switch to a more sustainable practice of paperless billing. This has resulted in 5 per cent of British Gas customers switching to paperless direct debit payments, attributable to the joint promotion with Nectar.

Price promotions

With the Christmas trade in 2011 predicted to be the worst on record, it was no surprise that the retailers pulled out all the stops to beat their rivals for a dwindling share of wallet as hard-pressed shoppers went on the search for a bargain ahead of the Christmas holidays.

John Lewis (2011)

In the UK, high street store John Lewis reacted to Debenhams' Big Gift Event sale with press ads highlighting its 'Never knowingly undersold' commitment to price-match its high-street competitors. In a reflection of the lengths that retailers were prepared to go to, John Lewis ran full page national newspaper ads stating: 'If our competitors have a sale, we have a sale' and promising to price match every item. In addition to the depressed state of family finances, the major retailers were trying to shift a large amount of winter clothing that had remained unsold as a result of the unseasonably warm winter weather in 2011.

Price promotions can come in a variety of forms, as shown in Table 8.1.

Some marketers have an allergic reaction to price promotions – they spend the vast part of their working lives building brands and points of value differentiation that are capable of sustaining a price premium and higher profits. A price promotion can tear up all those carefully laid plans and market positioning in an instant if the focus is on price alone.

Research tends to show that customers don't only not buy because the price is unattractive – there are often many other factors such as quality, customer service, logistics and distribution that can have an adverse impact on sales.

Premium promotions (gift with purchase)

This is one of the dark arts of marketing: we've all been swayed by the 'gift with purchase' (GWP). A highly successful sales promotion back in the

Table 8.1   Different types of price promotions

Type of price promotion	How it works
Seasonal discounts	As in the John Lewis example, retail sales have become highly formalized, particularly at Christmas and other holiday periods.
Multi-buys	One of the most popular is 'buy one, get one free' (BOGOF). Since 1990, leading detergent brands had increased the proportion of their consumer promotional spending on multi-buys from 20 to 65 per cent.
Banded packs	Two or more of the same product are banded together or placed in an additional outer wrap so that the customer buys them together. This is often applied to clothing accessories or garments such as underwear.
Reduced shelf price	This is the most common form of price promotion where a standard product is on sale with a shelf sticker or poster showing a reduced price.
Reduced price offers	These are similar to reduced shelf price except that the price reduction is flashed on the pack, such as '10 pence off'.
Extra fill packs	These are flashed '25% extra free' or '550ml for the price of 440ml'. They differ from reduced price offers in that the price remains the same but the quantity is greater.
Delayed discounts	This applies to those mechanics where a money saving coupon needs to be redeemed; where there's a cash rebate of money back; where there's a guaranteed trade-in price offered – 'old for new'.
Coupons	These are becoming increasingly popular although consumers are becoming wary of what may look like a price promotion but actually has strings attached. Coupons have existed in newspapers and magazines but now tend to be online as well as offered by SMS text on a mobile.
Finance deals	Zero interest or 'nothing to pay for three years' offers have tended to keep furniture retailers turning over sales until some have realized they have a mountain of bad debts and have run out of cash, even gone into liquidation. These types of price promotions have a whiff of desperation about them.
Trade promotions	These can take a number of forms and include overriders – an overriding discount is agreed at the beginning of a year between a supplier and a purchaser and is payable if the purchaser achieves certain targets.

1990s by premium ice-cream brand Häagen-Dazs worked a treat and lifted sales.

Häagen-Dazs (1995)

To support the ATL campaign for its ice cream aimed at the adult market, Häagen-Dazs hit upon the idea of 'guilty pleasures' as its brand platform and working with EMI to produce under licence a superb double CD, 'Dedicated to Pleasure', which included 'She Makes My Day' (Robert Palmer), 'Make Yourself Comfortable' (Sarah Vaughan), 'Sexual Healing' (Marvin Gaye), 'I Want Your Sex' (George Michael) and many others.

The Sarah Vaughan track was used in its cinema and TV advertising spots. The album was made available free for a large number of proofs of purchase and also was available at 3,500 music stores, generating over 60,000 sales, and even entered the British Top 20 for compilation albums – not bad for a premium promotion!

Other premium promotions involve the free gift being physically attached to the product, such as a DVD or CD that's attached to the front of a newspaper supplement or consumer magazine, known as 'cover mounts'. These mechanics are very popular with marketers given the instant gratification they deliver at the point of sale and have become a key strategy in some segments of the leisure publishing market, such as music magazines.

GWP can be one of the quickest ways to rescue a disastrous quarter for sales. Never mind that you've had to take the brand advertising budget for the whole year and place it into the hands of Shanghai plastics factory!

The challenge is striking the right balance and not damaging the brand in the process. The starting point should be determining what premium is suitable as part of the sales promotion and how this links back to the brand so that product sales aren't dependent on the presence of GWP in perpetuity.

Given that consumers are highly cynical about GWP, ideally the gift should have a high perceived value, but this shouldn't outweigh the intrinsic value of the product to which it's attached. So understanding the behaviour and emotional drivers for the desired customer segments is critical in the success of a premium promotion. (Refer to Chapter 1 for a detailed discussion on market and customer segmentation.)

Apart from avoiding overuse of premium sales promotions that run the risk of cheapening the brand, British marketers need to be wary of falling foul of the Bribery Act 2010 with respect to business gifts. (For further discussion on the legal framework on providing hospitality and gifts to customers and clients, refer to Guru in a Bottle®, *Essential Law for Marketers*, 2nd edition.)

Prize promotions

Among the most engaging and powerful aspects of business to consumer (B2C) and business to business (B2B) customer marketing and communications are prize promotions and incentives. They are also some of the most difficult things to get right, requiring an understanding of a web of complex competition, data protection and media laws and regulations. But just because they are complex tactics shouldn't mean you can't employ them to achieve powerful results.

Part of the reason why prize promotions and incentives have gained in popularity over the decade is that marketers have been adjusting to a new era of deep customer engagement. They've tacked on new functions, such as social media management, altered processes to better integrate advertising campaigns online, on TV and in print, and added staff with web expertise to manage the explosion of digital customer data – yet this still isn't sufficient to keep pace with changing consumer behaviour.

As discussed in Chapter 1, to truly engage customers for whom 'push' advertising is increasingly irrelevant, brand owners and organizations must do much more outside of the confines of traditional marketing. At the end of the day, customers and clients no longer separate marketing from the product – it *is* the product! They don't separate marketing from their in-store or online experience – it *is* the experience! And in the era of engagement, marketing *is* the company or enterprise.

According to Jeremy Stern, who runs Promoveritas, one of the UK's leading promotions specialists, many marketing agencies are also lagging behind changes in consumer behaviour that have helped to make prize promotions and incentives so popular not just in the UK but all over the world:

> *As a communications company, you get involved with consumer and trade interactions – often they involve a reward. These are 'promotions' and need to be run correctly and compliantly. Business to business, social media, online or offline, text or post, it makes no difference. Getting it right requires an understanding of statutory and regulatory frameworks, self-regulation policies, and best practice as defined by certain trade bodies, as well as embedding a company's ethics and policies in the running of such promotions.*

(For a full discussion of the UK law that impacts this area of sales promotion, refer to Guru in a Bottle®, *Essential Law for Marketers*, 2nd edition.)

There are several key characteristics that distinguish prize promotions and incentives from a price promotion. In essence, a price promotion can be limited to a number of entrants who qualify by purchasing a product, whereas a prize promotion can't be contained in the same way. There are offers where the maximum cost can be predicted in advance and doesn't vary with the numbers of participants.

'A far bigger benefit can be given in a prize promotion than in a promotion where the benefit is available to everyone who participates,' observes Roddy Mullin, a British marketing expert in this area. He explains:

There's a difficult balance to be struck in writing about prize promotions. On one hand, they are staggeringly successful. The chance to win a car, a holiday, or a substantial sum of money at little or no cost is permanently attractive to consumers. Reader's Digest has built its business on this basis, giving away nearly £3 million a year. On the other hand, they are a legal minefield. Too much stress on legal niceties can lead promoters to regard it as a no-go area. Too much stress on promotional effectiveness can lead promoters to forget the need for caution. Provided there's no change to the purchase price then a prize promotion is likely to be ok.

The most common types of prize promotions and their mechanisms are listed in Table 8.2. Each type is distinct in legal terms and subject to different legal and code of practice restrictions.

Table 8.2 Different types of prize promotions

Type of prize promotion	How it works
Competitions	Offer prizes for the successful exercise of a significant degree of mental or physical skill or judgement. Participants may be required to pay or to make a purchase to enter.
Free draws	Make available prizes by distribution of random chances. The selection of the winning ticket is separate and later, not instantaneous with its distribution. No skill or judgement is involved and participants can't be asked to pay or make a purchase to enter.
Instant wins	Offer prizes by distributing a predetermined number of winning tickets. Consumers know instantly whether or not they they've won. No skill or judgement is involved and consumers can't be asked to pay or make a purchase to enter.
Games	These are a form of free draw or instant win that have the appearance of requiring skill but in fact rely on probability. They can be based on brand names, such as Monopoly or Trivial Pursuit, or on generic games like bingo or snakes and ladders. Because there's no significant degree of skill or judgement involved, no purchase or payment can be required to enter.
Lotteries	These work in the same way as free draws or instant wins but participants pay to enter.

International sales promotions

Cross-border and multiple-country promotions can be very challenging for the marketer who must navigate through different legal jurisdictions that have their own rules and regulations; but they're not impossible.

One of the most successful international sales promotions is part of Shell's sponsorship of the Ferrari F1 team, which has supported its petrol and lubricants global business for over a decade.

Shell and Ferrari Formula 1 Team (2006)

In 1996, Shell became the world's largest distributor of die-cast model cars, selling over 26 million via its worldwide 'Collezione' promotion.

The international objective was to reinforce Shell's sponsorship of the Ferrari F1 Team, and model Ferrari cars were offered by local Shell companies in any way they felt was appropriate within their market. Some gave away these replica F1 cars with oil purchases and some redeemed them free on petrol sales, while others offered only a discount on the model in return for a smaller purchase of petrol. The promotional objectives were selected locally, subject to market interest.

In this type of international promotion, the global platform provides a more powerful mechanic than any of the individual strategic business units (SBUs) could afford to provide for themselves, given the economies of scale that such a promotion can provide to the marketer. Multiple-country promotions run on a regional basis are becoming increasingly popular as brand owners set up a single structure to market their products and services across a group of countries and territories. This has long been the pattern in Northern Europe and is growing as a result of the widening of the European Union. The practice is also common in South East Asia where emerging brands are increasingly international in outlook.

International Chamber of Commerce Code (2011)

A set of principles has been developed by the International Chamber of Commerce (ICC) to govern international sales promotion activities.

The ICC Code is designed primarily as an instrument of self-regulation but is also intended for use by legal or administrative bodies as a reference document within the framework of applicable laws (in the UK it has influenced the Advertising Standards Authority's approach to regulation in this area). The ICC believes that the 2011 Code will promote adherence to high standards of sales promotion practice globally.

Scope of the ICC Code

The ICC Code applies to marketing devices and techniques that are used to make goods and services more attractive by providing some additional benefit whether in cash or in kind, or the expectation of such a benefit, and covers sales and trade incentive promotions, editorial promotional offers and to those made on audio-visual media channels.

For the purposes of the ICC Code, promotions are treated as temporary marketing activities, but the Code also applies to long-term and permanent use of promotional techniques:

- premium offers of all types;
- reduced price and free offers;
- the distribution of stamps, coupons, vouchers and samples;
- charity-linked promotions; and
- prize promotions of all types including incentive programmes.

ICC Code of Principles of Sales Promotions (2011)

The ICC Code (2011) has a number of principles that both the promoter and its partners and intermediaries should adhere to and include:

- All sales promotions should deal fairly and honourably with consumers.
- All sales promotions should be so designed and conducted as to meet reasonable consumer expectation associated with the advertising or promotion thereof.
- The administration of sales promotions and the fulfilment of any obligation arising from them should be prompt and efficient.
- The terms and conduct of all sales promotions should be transparent to all participants.
- All sales promotions should be framed in a way that is fair to competitors and other traders in the market.
- No promoters, intermediaries or others involved should do anything likely to bring sales promotions into disrepute.

Terms of the sales promotion offer

Sales promotions should be so devised as to enable the consumer to identify the terms of the offer easily and clearly, including any limitations. Care should be taken not to exaggerate the value of the promotional item or to obscure or conceal the price of the main product.

Presentation

A sales promotion should not be presented in a way likely to mislead those to whom it is addressed about its value, nature or the means of participation. Any marketing communication regarding the sales promotion, including activities at the point of sale, should be in strict accordance with the general provisions of the ICC Code (2011).

Administration of sales promotions

Sales promotions should be administered with adequate resources and supervision anticipated to be required, including appropriate precautions to ensure that the administration of the offer meets the consumers' reasonable expectations. In particular:

- The availability of promotional items should be sufficient to meet anticipated demand consistent with the express terms of the offer. If delay is unavoidable, consumers should be advised promptly and necessary steps taken to adjust the promotion of the offer.
- Promoters should be able to demonstrate that they have made, before the event, a reasonable estimate of the likely response. Where a purchase or a series of purchases are a precondition for obtaining the promotional item, promoters should ensure promotional items are sufficiently available to match the number of purchases being made.
- Defective goods or inadequate services should be replaced, or appropriate financial compensation given. Any costs reasonably incurred by consumers as a direct result of any such shortcoming should be reimbursed immediately on request.
- Complaints should be efficiently and properly handled.

Safety and suitability

Care should be taken to ensure that promotional items, provided they are properly used, don't expose consumers, intermediaries, or any other persons or their property to any harm or danger.

Promoters should ensure that their promotional activities are consistent with the principles of social responsibility contained in the ICC Code (2011) and in particular take reasonable steps to prevent unsuitable or inappropriate materials from reaching children.

Presentation to consumers

Complex rules should be avoided. Rules should be drawn up in language that consumers can easily understand. The chances of winning prizes should not be overstated.

Information requirements

Sales promotions should be presented in such a way as to ensure that consumers are made aware, before making a purchase, of conditions likely to affect their decision to purchase. Information should include, where relevant:

- Clear instructions on the method of obtaining or participating in the promotional offer, for example conditions for obtaining promotional items, including any liability for costs, or taking part in prize promotions.
- The main characteristics of the promotional items offered.
- Any time limit on taking advantage of the promotional offer.
- Any restrictions on participation (for example, geographical or age-related), availability of promotional items, or any other limitations on stocks. In the case of limited availability, consumers should be properly informed of any arrangements for substituting alternative items or refunding money.
- The value of any voucher or stamp offered where a monetary alternative is available.
- Any expenditure involved, including costs of shipping and handling and terms of payment.
- The full name and address of the promoter and an address to which complaints can be directed (if different).

Promotions claiming to support a charitable cause should not exaggerate the contribution derived from the campaign. Before purchasing the promoted product consumers should be informed how much of the price will be set aside for the cause.

Information in prize promotions

Where a sales promotion includes a prize promotion, the following information should be given to consumers, or at least made available on request, prior to participation and not conditional on purchasing the main product:

- any rules governing eligibility to participate in the prize promotion;
- any costs associated with participation, other than for communication at or below standard rate (mail or phone);
- any restriction on the number of entries;
- the number, value and nature of prizes to be awarded and whether a cash alternative may be substituted for a prize;
- in the case of a skill contest, the nature of the contest and the criteria for judging the entries;
- the selection procedure for the award of prizes;
- the closing date of the competition;
- when and how the results will be made available;
- whether the consumer may be liable to pay tax as a result of winning a prize;
- the time period during which prizes may be collected;

- where a jury is involved, the composition of the jury; and
- any intention to use winners or winning contributions in post-event activities and the terms on which these contributions may be used.

Information for intermediaries

Sales promotions should be so presented to intermediaries that they are able to evaluate the services and commitments required of them. In particular, there should be adequate details as to:

- the organization and scope of the promotion, including the timing and any time limit;
- the ways in which the promotion will be presented to the trade and to the public;
- the conditions for participation;
- the financial implications for intermediaries; and
- any special administrative task required of intermediaries.

Information on outer packing

Where appropriate, relevant information for intermediaries, such as any closing date or time limit, should appear on the outer packing of products bearing promotional offers, so that the intermediary is able to carry out the necessary stock control.

Interests of intermediaries

Sales promotions should be devised and administered with due regard to the legitimate interests of intermediaries and should respect their freedom of decision (where they are involved in the selection of winning entrants, for example).

Interests of employees, employers and consumer relations

The terms of sales promotions should be so designed as to respect the bond of loyalty between employees and their employers. Promotion and incentive schemes should be designed and implemented to take account of the interests of everyone involved and should not conflict with the duty of employees to their employer or their obligation to give honest advice to consumers.

Rights of intermediaries' employees

The prior agreement of the intermediary or their responsible manager should always be sought if the proposed promotion involves inviting the employees of the intermediary to assist in any promotional activity and offering any inducement or reward, financial or otherwise, to such employees for their assistance or for any sales achievements in connection with any sales promotion.

In the case of an offer addressed openly through public media for which such prior permission cannot be obtained, it should be made clear that employees must obtain their employer's permission before participating.

Timely delivery of goods and materials to intermediaries

All goods, including promotional items and other relevant material, should be delivered to the intermediary within a period which is reasonable in terms of any time limitation on the promotional offer.

Contractual relationships between intermediaries and consumers

Sales promotions involving active cooperation by the intermediary or their employees should be so devised as not to prejudice any contractual relationship which may exist between the intermediary and the consumer.

Particular obligations of intermediaries

Honesty

Sales promotions which have been accepted by the intermediary should be fairly and honestly handled, and properly administered by their employees.

Misrepresentation

Sales promotions involving any specific responsibility on the part of the intermediary should be so handled by them that no misinterpretation is likely to arise as to the terms, value, limitations or availability of the offer. In particular, the intermediary should adhere to the plan and conditions of the promotion as laid down by the promoter. No changes to the agreed arrangements, for example, alteration of the time limit, should be made by the intermediary without the prior agreement of the promoter.

Responsibility

The onus for observing the Code falls on the promoter, who has the ultimate responsibility for all aspects of sales promotions, whatever their kind or content. Anyone taking part in the planning, creation or execution of any sales promotion has responsibility for ensuring the observance of the Code towards intermediaries, consumers and other parties affected or likely to be affected by the promotion.

(For further discussion on the legal framework as it relates to sales promotions in the UK, refer to Guru in a Bottle®, *Essential Law for Marketers*, 2nd edition.)

References

Books

Kolah, A (2013) *Essential Law for Marketers*, 2nd edn, Kogan Page
Mullin, R (2010) *Sales Promotion*, 5th edn, Kogan Page

Websites

International Chamber of Commerce: http://www.iccwbo.org (accessed 21 January 2012)
The UK Code of Non-broadcast Advertising, Sales Promotion and Direct Marketing (CAP Code): http://www.cap.org.uk/The-Codes/CAP-Code.aspx (accessed 21 January 2012)
MOBO website: http://www.mobo.com (accessed 21 January 2012)

"One last check before I dive in!"

Top 10 common marketing mistakes to avoid

In this chapter:

1 No vision or purpose to the marketing effort
2 Assuming you know who your customers or clients are
3 Linear thinking rather than creative thinking
4 Looking at the world from your point of view
5 Failing to understand the link between marketing and selling more stuff
6 Being in 'transmit mode' rather than in 'receive mode'
7 Living in the past
8 Not thinking in terms of outcomes but outputs
9 Not learning from your customers and clients
10 Not learning from your mistakes

Introduction

By the time you've reached this section of the book, you should have gleaned sufficient insight to avoid all of the above traps and pitfalls. But to make mistakes isn't automatically a bad thing – so long as they aren't whoppers!

It shows you are trying to achieve a result, an improvement in what may have taken place in the past. You take a calculated risk with a particular marketing programme but there's no guarantee it will always succeed. Not trying is a greater sin.

1. No vision or purpose to the marketing effort

One of the most important foundations of any marketing programme is the vision and purpose behind it. This is the DNA of the organization or company that you work for or the client organization for which you undertake marketing. If the vision and purpose are blurred, indistinct, unclear or simply confused, how on earth can the organization's employees understand what they're expected to do, let alone those involved in marketing and communications?

2. Assuming you know who your customers or clients are

When was the last time the perspectives of customers or clients got discussed at board level? Who on the board of the organization or company that you work for is the champion of the customer or the client? Stunned silence? You bet.

And yet it's the customer or client that ultimately is responsible for the financial success of the enterprise. It's simply breath-taking that the voice of the customer or client isn't heard amongst the galaxy of other points of view that make it to the boardroom. Sadly, this is very common, particularly amongst those organizations with traditional, monolithic cultures and structures. The world has changed and is constantly changing. And so too are the behaviours of customers and clients. Assuming what worked 12 months ago will work again now is wishful thinking.

3. Linear thinking rather than creative thinking

Logic in business is important. But critical thinking isn't the only mode of approaching a problem, challenge or issue.

Dr Edward de Bono was famous for pioneering a methodology called 'Six Thinking Hats', one of the most successful ways to rewire our approach to problem solving as we can train ourselves to think more creatively, which can produce some surprising results.

4. Looking at the world from your point of view

You may firmly believe that your brand, product or service is the best on the market, offers the best possible performance that meets the needs and requirements of your desired customers or clients and is at a price point that your competitors can't match. In fact you're so convinced about this that all your marketing, advertising and news releases broadcast this very loudly.

Spot anything missing? Nowhere did you talk about the customer or the client! This is a classic marketing mistake to avoid. How on earth can this be great marketing if it isn't packaged from the point of view of the recipients? And how will what you say motivate their behaviour? Marketing has got to be about much more than this.

5. Failing to understand the link between marketing and selling more stuff

It doesn't matter whether you're a charity, voluntary organization or NGO – you are in the business of selling a message, right?

From a commercial perspective, whether B2B, B2C or B2B2C, marketing can't just be about brand awareness and precious little else. Why bother? If it doesn't create an environment where a sale is more likely to take place, then how is it to be justified and signed off by the board?

In a world where there's a higher degree of transparency and accountability, the safest place for a marketer to be is sitting next to the sales professional and working out how he or she can influence behaviour that will translate into more sales of stuff.

6. Being in 'transmit mode' rather than 'receive mode'

Marketers feel that they've been blessed with the 'gift of the gab' – the ability to speak, present, create powerful communications, wonderful advertising, fabulous websites, incredible blogs. Trouble is, as good as all of this stuff is, we still can't escape the fact that we need to make a sale or get someone to buy into our message. The only way we are going to be able to achieve this is through trust. And trust can only be built if, as marketers, we are prepared to listen.

Given that the legal and regulatory regime around marketing has changed so dramatically that the balance of bargaining power has shifted in favour of the customer or client and away from the brand owner, marketing is now an increasingly driven permission-based exercise. And this necessitates being in 'receive' rather than in 'transmit' mode.

7. Living in the past

Many organizations have a number of senior executives who have served there a long time and who may have become comfortable with the way they preferred to deal with analysts' briefings and shareholder meetings, for example. But as the complexity of managing these relationships grows, so too should the need to change and adapt. This isn't something that very large companies or multinational organizations are particularly good at.

In some cases, the senior management team could be sleepwalking into oblivion if they're not prepared to change the way they think and see things from a different point of view – usually that of their customer or client.

Professional marketers have a duty to diplomatically navigate their organizations away from perpetuating mistakes of the past and try to see things in a different way. It's not easy or that comfortable, but it is essential. It must be done on a business case basis, as senior managers have an in-built suspicion that anything put forward by marketers is likely to incur costs rather than save or make money.

8. Not thinking in terms of outcomes but outputs

Marketing professionals enjoy recognition, both internally and from their peers. Let's face it, marketing is a cool job.

It requires an in-depth understanding of business, of the brand, its products and services, the use of the marketing channels, particularly e-marketing and m-marketing. This tends to set apart those who work in marketing from the rest of the organization. But this is extremely dangerous.

Without a connection to all the other departments, including human resources and finance, the activities of those involved in marketing can be consigned to simply 'doing stuff'. And this is likely to be output-driven activity rather than trying to focus on creating outcomes that are valuable for the organization or company.

9. Not learning from your customers and clients

It's staggering how many marketers will try to guess why something may work or not work as a campaign, a promotion, a competition, a news story or a newsletter. The experts who can answer these and other questions don't turn up for work every morning at your premises: they are your customers and clients. The simple act of 'ask and you shall receive' appears to have disappeared from the textbooks most marketers read in the past.

Removing the guesswork by asking customer and clients through social network forums about concepts, new product or service ideas, even a new T-shirt design, is a powerful way of collaborating with them profitably. And it also removes a large part of the commercial risk factors in new marketing activities.

Learning from customers and clients is the safest way to conduct virtually any aspect of marketing practice in any market.

10. Not learning from your mistakes

Customer and clients are on a journey; so are you. And the organization you work for is also on a journey and, as a result, not everything goes according to plan. Actually, it never will. But successful organizations embrace the opportunity to understand what didn't work in the past in order to put this right for the future.

In the bestselling book, *Failure is Not an Option*, former flight director of NASA, Gene Kranz, observes that successful missions such as Apollo 11 could only have been achieved as a result of all the previous missions to space as well as the disasters and setbacks that befell the Gemini and other NASA space programmes, the hundreds of thousands of hours spent flight testing and simulation ready for the biggest mission ever undertaken. And it was still touch and go as to whether the Apollo 11 mission would be successful and land on the surface of the moon.

It's a remarkable story with the clearest message: learning from your mistakes can ensure that you're successful in the future. And anything is possible.

References

De Bono, E (2000) *Six Thinking Hats*, Penguin Books

Kolah, A (2013) Guru in a Bottle, *Essential Law for Marketers*, 2nd edition, Kogan Page

Kranz, G (2000) *Failure is Not an Option*, Berkley

"Every little helps!"

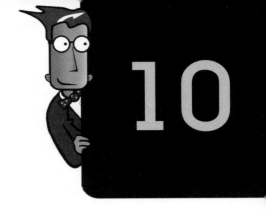

Top 10 ways to save money in marketing

In this chapter:

1. Seek an opportunity in adversity
2. Do more with less
3. Think and act flexibly
4. Keep it simple
5. Use the web
6. Avoid dependency relationships with external agencies
7. Spend less than others say you should on marketing
8. Don't just market to people you know – network
9. Collaborate with your customers and clients for profit
10. Know your ends from your means

Introduction

The philosophy of Guru in a Bottle® is that with the right tools and know-how, you've the ability to be successful. Very successful.

We believe that anyone with enough enthusiasm and determination can make millions out of nothing more than a simple idea. Marketing will help get that idea to market. And then you need to sell it – profitably.

A secret to saving money in marketing is obviously not making cock-ups that are costly in terms of the amount of capital invested or indeed in missed sales. And that means being prepared to learn from others. It also means being prepared to experiment with leadership and innovation where your competitors fear to walk. Far from being risky, it could be brilliant. And save you money, too.

1. Seek an opportunity in adversity

Reading the writing on the wall is a great place to start to save money. You avoid wasting it.

Inertia, complacency and over-confidence are your inner demons. Get rid of them. They'll cost you money.

Too many marketers pay insufficient attention to the early warning signs of big shifts in demographics, technology and regulation. As a result they miss out on a great opportunity to proactively innovate their business and their marketing to take advantage of these shifts.

Successful marketers know how to turn adversity on its head and get it to work in their favour. The key is to translate challenges into opportunities and use constraints to spur innovation. It's about seeing the glass as half full, not half empty.

2. Do more with less

Being resourceful in a resource-scarce world should become second nature to most marketers. But it isn't.

Successful marketers don't necessarily have multi-million dollar marketing budgets. In fact some of the most successful marketers on the planet are able to get more from less by applying frugality to every activity they perform at every step of the value chain.

They're frugal in how they design products, how they produce them, how they deliver them and how they perform after-sales or after-care. Their frugality shows up not only in their parsimonious use of capital and natural resources but also in how they maximize their limited time and energy. Rather than driving everything themselves, which can be very costly, they rely extensively on partners to perform various operations, saving resources, time and money.

Try to reuse and combine rather than create something new from scratch.

3. Think and act flexibly

Try walking across a road in Mumbai, India. You'll only make it to the other side if you're prepared to think and act flexibly! And there's no point thinking the Highway Code is going to be your saviour when you're behind the wheel. It won't. Linear thinking won't always help.

The same is true in marketing. Western brand owners and their leaders often operate in a black-and-white world that confers a sense of predictability on the order of things. For example, competitors are 'bad' and partners are 'good'. Regulations are typically 'bad' for business whereas protectionist policies are 'good'. And although some brand owners may like 'doing good' as part of their corporate social responsibility initiatives, they worry primarily about 'doing well' financially. Yet such binary thinking that's anchored in deep-seated assumptions prevents brand owners from reconciling priorities, a process that could yield creative, innovative and highly cost-effective marketing solutions.

The sheer diversity, volatility and unpredictability of global markets demand that marketers are flexible. Inflexibility will result in failure and a waste of resources. Marketers must think laterally, out of the box. They should experiment. They should improvise.

There are really just two stark choices: adapt or die. In many respects, this diversity, volatility and unpredictability empowers flexible thinking and action.

4. Keep it simple

In the Western hemisphere we seem obsessed with the bigger and the brighter approach to marketing.

Marketers often get seduced by the power of technology, yet the vast majority of consumers in the developing world are put off by complexity. Complicated and elaborate marketing that is costly and employs gimmicks isn't what's required. Equally, Western consumers are 'down-shifting' and opting for simpler, more meaningful lives.

Brand owners that respond to these attitudes, values, beliefs and behaviours will benefit in the long run. All that glistens isn't gold.

5. Use the web

Marketing methods that attract new customers and clients need not cost anything. Being part of the community, being yourself, being transparent, being a great listener and a genuine problem solver builds trust, and the fastest way to do this with the biggest community of like-minded people is on the web.

6. Avoid dependency relationships with external agencies

Fact: agencies exist to make money. *Fact*: no matter how good they are, they'll never have your best interests at heart. *Fact*: it's in their interests to do everything on the clock. It's chargeable time. It's a great way of ensuring that each agency person's utilization rate is maximized profitably.

From the client perspective, it's not the only way to procure powerful marketing support. The answer to your challenges could be much closer than you think. It could be you.

7. Spend less than others say you should on marketing

Anyone who's ever been into a car showroom to buy a new or used car will know that having an idea of what you want to spend can evaporate in the presence of a convincing salesperson who knows how to pull the emotional levers and customize the product 'just for you'.

It's not just alloy wheels or a nicer in-car entertainment system, but it's the extended warranty, freedom of not worrying about the gap in resale value when you go to sell the car at the end of the payments period and other 'extras' that all come at a price. One that's invariably not the same figure as the one you started with.

The same is true in marketing, particularly when it comes to designing and building a website. Beware of buying extra bells and whistles. Chances are, you don't need them.

8. Don't just market to people you know – network

Marketing to people you have a connection with is how pyramid selling works. Yes, it can be profitable. But what happens when you run out of people you know and who you think may want to buy the product or service you're peddling to them?

Networking is by far more effective in the long run. For one thing, building a new relationship with a customer or client could unlock marketing and sales opportunities well beyond the spending constraints of those who you already know.

Effective marketing increasingly depends on word of mouth. And the best way to stimulate effective word of mouth is to network. And the best bit is that it doesn't have to cost you anything if you join a relevant social networking group where you are free to exchange thoughts and ideas.

9. Collaborate with your customers and clients for profit

Why use expensive market research to come up with insights and answers to some of the most challenging marketing issues when you can collaborate with your customers and clients and get them to help you design your products and services?

After all, if they like them, they'll want to buy them. Isn't that the point of marketing?

10. Know your ends from your means

Winston Churchill, one of the greatest statesmen that ever lived, once said: 'However beautiful the strategy, you should occasionally look at the results.'

The best marketing plans and investment in a range of marketing activities will all turn to dust if they don't deliver the outcomes you're looking for. Being outcome-focused rather than output-driven means that you know your ends from your means. And that's by far the most profitable place to be.

References

Harris, M (2008) *Find Your Lightbulb*, Capstone

Prabhu, J, Radjou, N and Ahuja, S (2012) *Jugaad Innovation*, Jossey-Bass

Index

(*italics* indicate a figure or table in the text)

Endorsements

Strategy, tactics and guidelines for improving marketing effectiveness are brought to life in this excellent book. I can warmly recommend it to any student or practitioner who wants an up-to-date view on how to engage with key market and customer segments. Written in an authoritative but accessible way, the Guru in a Bottle® Series is an excellent contribution to the understanding of marketing practice. **Sir Paul Judge, President, Chartered Institute of Marketing (Global)**

High Impact Marketing that Gets Results is a must-read for any marketer. This book will certainly show you how to get the marketing results you'd require for any campaign. I highly recommend it! **Patrick Singh, former Head of Marketing, Microsoft (Global)**

This comprehensive and insightful book has numerous real life anecdotes any serious marketing practitioner will enjoy reading. **Steve Madincea, Founder & Group Managing Director PRISM (WPP)**

Ardi Kolah is not only an expert on marketing but he also knows how to make everything even clearer with the use of pictures. What more could one ask for? **Quentin Blake CBE, one of the world's foremost 20th century illustrators (Global)**

Serving and responding to the customer is the key driver of economic activity. It seems obvious. But doing it – day in, day out – is a relentless activity that requires structure, and learning from others. This book is a bible of marketing. It gives both academic and practical tips. It helps to make marketing happen. Use it to ensure the prosperity of your enterprise. **Raoul Pinnell, former Chairman, Shell Brands International (Global)**

As a management discipline, marketing is changing faster than ever, with both the web and mobile opening up new possibilities almost on a daily basis. This book provides an invaluable insight for the student or practitioner of marketing who is looking for guidance on how best to deploy these channels in order to create high impact marketing. Essential reading. **Dusan Hamlin, Joint CEO, M&C Saatchi Mobile (Global)**

This book comprehensively covers the essential issues, topics and subjects that every marketer needs to know about in practical, plain English. **Justin Cooke, Chair, British Interactive Media Association (UK)**

Yet another incredible addition to the Guru in a Bottle® Series. This forms a comprehensive guide to high-impact, high-value campaign strategy. If you need marketing which will give you a competitive advantage then this is the only place to start. Learn from a guru to become one yourself. **Richard Teideman, CEO, London Creative (UK)**

Ardi Kolah conveys his expert knowledge in this comprehensive, up-beat guide, taking complex themes and breaking them down into clear, coherent segments, each providing relevant examples and practical advice on every aspect of high-impact marketing. This book really 'lets the guru out of the bottle' and is an invaluable resource and essential reading for marketers, business managers or anybody active in the field. **Frank Saez, MD, SMG Insight/YouGov (Global)**

This book provides a practical and enjoyable way for non-marketing people to get to grips with marketing. Readers will increase their knowledge and understanding of the subject but, more importantly, learn how to make a difference in day-to-day decisions. **Professor Harris Beider, Coventry University (UK)**

High Impact Marketing that Gets Results *from the Guru in a Bottle® series is an impressive piece of work. It should be required reading for all those studying marketing in its widest sense. There is plenty of theoretical under-pinning and interesting case studies which back up the claims to best practice. A must for any marketing practitioner or academic studying this discipline.* **Di Burton, Managing Director, Cicada Communications (UK)**

I heartily recommend this new book on marketing as a first class introduction to the topic. **Martin P. Lee, Associate Lecturer, Open University (UK)**

A comprehensive, indispensable, incisive guide to legal touch points for the 21st century marketing professional. Another exceptional 'plain English' offering from the Guru in a Bottle® series! **Simon Clothier, General Manager, Aggreko (EMEA)**

Attention all professional and future marketers. If you're serious about maximizing your business outcomes, this book is a must-read! **Dr Denis Cauvier, International Best Selling Author, North America's top Expert on Attracting & Retaining Great People. (Canada)**

For those who had the pleasure to work together with Ardi Kolah, we can tell 'Guru in a Bottle' is his perfect mirror; it is as rigorous, direct and close as he is. Ardi Kolah is a highly recognized professional who has the ability to see what is relevant based on his wide perspective of the communications world. He always goes straight to the point and explains complex concepts in an easy way. High Impact Marketing that Gets Results® *is an excellent reference book in the marketing field for its approach to all the changeable and controversial aspects of marketing, communications and obviously its effect to sales. As in soccer, you are not valued by the amount of effort you put in but by the goals you score. This book provides a game plan to beat the competition and go straight to the goal.* **Roberto Abad, CEO, Ulled PR (Spain)**

This book has a way of explaining complex marketing theory in an easy-to-follow and engaging manner. The author has enormous and varied experience himself on which to draw... and he does this with the skill you're accustomed to from his previous work. A must-read for aspiring marketers! **Peter Gandolfi, former Head of Brand Strategy, Nationwide (UK)**

Filled with step-by-step chapters to walk you through the essence of marketing, this book is packed with best-practice guidelines and diagrams from industry leaders and trusted advisors, punctuated with topical case studies and cheerful illustrations – all fabulous ingredients to make this a complete yet compact and accessible book. I wish I had had this when I was studying marketing and as I developed my own career – very useful then, very insightful now and in the future for all those who believe in the power of marketing in driving business success. **Sandra Macleod, FIPR, CCMI, Group Chief Executive, Echo Research (Global)**

High Impact Marketing *is one of the most comprehensive guides to marketing available today. The Guru in a Bottle style makes it an enjoyable as well as an informative read, cutting through the usual waffle that normally accompanies these types of books. For anyone looking for an enlightening and enjoyable introduction to marketing, this is the place to start.* **Andrew Levy, MD, Licensing Pages (Global)**

High Impact Marketing That Gets Results *is an excellent book that delivers transformational insights for managers who want to get up to speed with current marketing thinking and practice in how to engage with desired audience and customer segments both online and offline. Written by one of the most accomplished marketing practitioners in the industry, this book shows you how to create, win and dominate global market segments profitably.* **Phil Jones, internet pioneer and inducted in the British Interactive Media Association Hall of Fame 2012 (Global)**

A must-read for every non-marketer. Well written and very insightful, it will help drive high impact marketing results. **Zubin Saklatwalla, Regional Manager (Global MNC), DHL Express (Global)**

The vast majority of business books are boring. High Impact Marketing That Gets Results *is a wind tunnel of fresh air, filled with practical and no-nonsense advice. It should be a must-read for business people of all kinds including first-time entrepreneurs. I also commend it to teachers, lecturers and students.* **Michael Murphy, Global CEO, Grayling (Global)**